Praise for *The Raw and the Cooked*:

"Harrison is the American Rabelais, and he is at his irreverent and excessive best in this collection."
—John Skowles, *San Diego Union-Tribune*

"There's nothing false in *The Raw and the Cooked*. It's straight to the heart . . . and leaves you content and full but wanting more."
—Robert Baldwin, *Bloomsbury Review*

"What we're reading about is a life voraciously lived . . . engrossment with the natural world, engorgement at its harvest plentiful, and engagement with just about any topic (principles of Zen, the merits of writers as varied as Kierkegaard and Gary Snyder, the restorative powers of walking). . . . Alternately breezy and dense, sometimes serious as a crusade and the next second seriously funny."
—Steve Byrne, *Detroit Free Press*

"For [Harrison], a great meal is a mindful act, a call to attend the sensual, while bad food is the least digestible aspect of a puritanical business culture that puts money, progress and other abstractions before life's simple pleasures. . . . Such views have a long history in American letters—read Thoreau and Henry Miller. . . . His vivid language and comic sense earn him a place near the head of the literary table."   —Chris Waddington, *Minneapolis Star-Tribune*

"Like a fine meal, this book satisfies."
—Anne Stephenson, *Arizona Republic*

"Harrison's passion for food—and sex—are matched by his muscular writing." —Janet K. Keeler, *St. Petersburg Times*

"Calling *The Raw and the Cooked* a book about food is like calling *The Old Man and the Sea* a book about fishing. . . . Harrison's writing is full of power and passion." —Jim Carvalho, *Tucson Weekly*

"Sophisticated and earthy . . . impossible to pigeonhole . . . Most of us will never be lucky enough to share a meal with this 'roving gourmand,' but this volume provides a satisfying alternative."
—Wendy Miller, *Library Journal*

"By turns hysterically funny, heartbreaking, meditative, irreverent, mystical, and more fun than a double portion of *ris de veau rotis* with a slab of headcheese, a brace of game birds, and a coney dog."
—*Hour Detroit*

"A man of appetites . . . a trencherman of the soul . . . [Harrison] wears his erudition lightly. Whether musing about the poetry of Verlaine or the joys of Breton oysters, he never beats you over the head with his knowledge. . . . Harrison is a raconteur of the first order."
—William Porter, *Denver Post*

"To read this book is to come away convinced that Harrison is a flat-out genius—one who devours life with intensity, living it roughly and full-scale, then distills his experiences into passionate, opinionated prose. Food, in this context, is more than food: It is a metaphor for life." —Wolf Schneider, *Santa Fe New Mexican*

"A rumination on the unholy trinity of sex, death, and food, this long-awaited collection of gastronomic essays reads like the love child of M. F. K. Fisher and James Thorne—on acid."
—*Publishers Weekly*

"*The Raw and the Cooked* provides a tantalizing, scrumptious read, a smorgasbord of the finest food writing, one that's entertaining, engaging, witty, and full of savoir-faire; all in a voice that reveals a man fully given over to the pursuit of the art of writing (and eating). Bon appetit!" —Beef Torrey, *Lincoln Journal-Star* (Nebraska)

"One of the most important authors to emerge from this country in the last fifty years . . . *The Raw and the Cooked* . . . is about more than food; it is about being human in a difficult time. . . . You will not read a book more genuine than this one."
—Barry Graham, *Chattanooga Times Free Press*

"You'll never find a person who savors every kind of foreign food-stuff with more orgasmic glee than Harrison. In his mind, good food, good sex, and good literature . . . are the only things that keep a sensible person going in this world."

—Craig D. Lindsey, *Houston Chronicle*

"A man of firm opinions and titanic appetites . . . Harrison is in search of the transcendent, whether in nature (trekking is the only pastime he seems to feel as passionate about as food) or on the plate. He finds it in intense flavors, the American landscape, his past, and his family: the subjects of most of his essays. . . . Delightful."

—*Kirkus Reviews*

"To call this a book about only food would be to narrow its scope. Although Harrison is knowledgeable about all kinds of fare, has read thousands of cookbooks and eaten in the world's finest restaurants, he comes across as a man who simply likes to eat and enjoys his life and the company around him."   —*Parsippany Daily Record* (NJ)

THE
RAW AND
THE COOKED

Fiction

Wolf

A Good Day to Die

Farmer

Legends of the Fall

Warlock

Sundog

Dalva

The Woman Lit by Fireflies

Julip

The Road Home

The Beast God Forgot to Invent

Poetry

Plain Song

Locations

Outlyer

Letters to Yesenin

Returning to Earth

Selected & New Poems

The Theory and Practice of Rivers & New Poems

After Ikkyu & Other Poems

The Shape of the Journey: Collected Poems

Nonfiction

Just Before Dark

Off to the Side: A Memoir

Children's Literature

The Boy Who Ran to the Woods

THE RAW AND THE COOKED

Adventures of a Roving Gourmand

Jim Harrison

Grove Press
New York

These pieces have previously appeared, sometimes in slightly different form, in the following magazines, to which grateful acknowledgment is made:
Smart (New York): "Eat or Die" (published as "Sporting Food"), "Meals of Peace and Restoration," "Hunger, Real and Unreal," "Then and Now," "Consciousness Dining," "The Tugboats of Costa Rica," "Midrange Road Kill," "The Panic Hole," "Piggies Come to Market," "The Fast"
Esquire (New York): "What Have We Done with the Thighs?," "The Days of Wine and Pig Hocks," "One Foot in the Grave," "Just Before Dark," "Cooking Your Life," "Ignoring Columbus," "Eating Close to the Ground," "Return of the Native, or Lighten Up," "Let's Get Lost," "Principles," "The Last Best Place?," "The Morality of Food," "Contact," "Coming to Our Senses," "The 10,000-Calorie Diet," "Walking the San Pedro," "Back Home," "Repulsion and Grace," "Outlaw Cook," "Unmentionable Cuisine," "Heart Food in L.A.," "Fresh Southern Air," "Borderlands," "A Huge Hunger in Paris"
Men's Journal (New York): "Thirty-three Angles on Eating French" (published as "Eating French"), "American Food Journal"
Revue des Deux Mondes (Paris) and *Kermit Lynch Wine Merchant Newsletter*: "Wine"
Beaux Arts (Paris): "Wild Creatures" (published as "Jim Harrison & Gérard Oberlé Food Correspondence")
Brick (Toronto): "Meatballs"
Gérard Oberlé's letters to Jim Harrison in "Wild Creatures" were translated by Diana Odasso.

Published simultaneously in Canada
Printed in the United States of America

FIRST PAPERBACK EDITION

Library of Congress Cataloging-in-Publication Data

Harrison, Jim, 1937–
The raw and the cooked : adventures of a roving gourmand / Jim Harrison.
        p. cm.
ISBN 0-8021-3937-X (pbk.)
1. Harrison, Jim, 1937–   2. Gastronomy.   3. Food writers—United States—
Biography. I. Title.
TX649.H35 A3 2001
641.3—dc21   2001033464

Grove Press
841 Broadway
New York, NY 10003

02 03 04 05 06   10 9 8 7 6 5 4 3 2 1

To Terry McDonell and Gérard Oberlé

CONTENTS

INTRODUCTION

I would like to avoid here the merest suggestion that there is anything wrong with my food and wine obsession. How easily we forget that the life overexamined is also not worth living. Rather than descend into the sump of neuroticisms that makes many of us what we are I'd like to think that my eating and drinking comprise a strenuous search for the genuine, that I am a voyager, an explorer, an adventurer in the ordinary activity of what we do every day: eat and drink. Once I jokingly suggested in a column that my sole motif was "eat or die," falsely ascribing it to the Russian author Lermontov to give it greater sonority and authority, but "eat or die" is also a veiled koan suggesting that eating well, however simply, is part of a life fully lived.

Eating in America is a grand puzzle of thousands of pieces, many of them lost, with the final picture a diorama of our history led by economic considerations and ethnic influences. This diorama can be as confusing and surreal as sex in our nontraditional society, the dimensions of which daily boggle the mind, forcing the food-writing community to try to simplify matters, to separate the practice of eating from the lives of the people who are doing the eating, as if eating were a detachable activity or object like the Ouija board, a bridge, or an artificial limb.

There is so much that is deeply comic in the arena of American food. Health authorities are less than pleased but we have surged well ahead in the world obesity sweepstakes. We're Big and getting Bigger, despite thousands of hours and column inches devoted to our faux fitness revolution. Last November, on a plane trip between Memphis and New York City, I talked to a heart surgeon from the Utica area of New York State who was thinking of moving, but there was an overwhelming and rewarding demand for his services in that locale, where the most popular exercise was the trek between the couch, kitchen, and television. In the three modest places my wife and I live, I am frequently asked why I'm seen walking or hunting a couple of hours a day the year around, and I like to say, "So I can eat without it directly killing me." From the Pleistocene up until recently our exercise and ensuing fitness were an essential part of our survival. Jeffrey Steingarten in a brilliant essay on our food fears in the *New York Times* pointed out, "We are the first society in human history in which gluttony is economically an option for probably half the population." I would guess that the number is closer to three-quarters. Even so, this isn't true eating, this is taking in too much fuel.

My search for the genuine in the food in my life came about slowly and certainly wasn't a product of how I grew up in the upper Midwest, a region notorious for its bad food. Perhaps the only thing that saved our senses was the two months a year our gardens were operable in this sour climate. My own obsession with food began in my late teens with reading and budget travel. In the Midwest the common diet draws most heavily from the worst aspects of the Scandinavian and the German, coupled with an attitude summed up as "we eat to live not live to eat," as if this were an assigned moral choice. Added to this is the historical move from the agrarian to the city, which comprises the demographic revolution of the twentieth century—a move from growing and gathering your own food to jumping in a car for the trip to the supermarket.

We largely became lost and we got a great deal larger. It is startling to study older cookbooks and see how much more inventive the mass of people once were. Visit the Ajax Diner in Oxford, Mississippi, for instance, and experience a mode of eating where such traditions are not lost. Every day there is an offering of at least six well-cooked vegetables. I'm not pretending that Mississippi is a version of the delights of Provence, the apex of the vegetable, only that the food there reminds me of the way my grandmothers once cooked so providently in their rural bailiwicks. Such cooking has been widely banished because it takes time away from whatever.

I love to cook, hunt, fish, read good books, and not incidentally try to write them. Even the occasional glories of our sexual lives can be drawn into this picture. Not that much is finer than a morning spent at the Metropolitan Museum of Art in New York or the Musée d'Orsay in Paris followed by a good lunch. All of our senses and passions merge because we are one person and it's best not to neglect any of these passions if we wish to fully live our lives. As my friend the novelist Barry Hannah writes, "When you eat well you are eating memory."

This little collection includes the good and a measure of the bad and ugly. I have also hoped to be democratic amid my extravagancies. Much food writing seems to assume that readers quite naturally make several hundred thousand dollars a year and can easily join the fun. I have tried for a more encompassing attitude toward what's possible when we sit down at the table. Occasionally I fantasize that I have saved a million dollars by learning how to cook and being married to someone who does an even better job, but if this were true what did I do with the money? Good wine looms, as does travel.

I append the following fable as a metaphor for so much of *The Raw and the Cooked*.

The Man Who Ate Books

It started very early, as do most bad, perhaps fatal, habits. The first incident became one of those silly family stories that bore anyone else. He was a mere baby of seven months when he crawled up on a chair and pulled the huge leather-bound family Bible off the table. The book fell to the floor and he lay next to it chewing on the salty leather, which, if not delicious, had a slightly beefy flavor, the salt coming from the hands of generations of poor farmers. In the back of the Bible were several pages of family genealogy but the baby did not chew on these suspicious documents, the filigree of our existence so beloved by those of supposedly noble birth, showing the thin string of semen and egg that we have in common with dogs, apes, and suchlike.

Naturally the baby was punished, if only with screams, when he was discovered with the corner of the Holy Bible in his mouth, chewing quite happily, the pleasure equal to his mother's teat. The baby was not overdisturbed by the screams of the aunt who towered above him. He merely looked up her sturdy brown legs, the thighs disappearing into darkness, his twelve billion neurons recording a mystery that would later compete with chewing on books.

Unfortunately the Holy Bible was the only leather-bound book the family owned. Another story was added to the family collection when at the age of two he accompanied his mother to the public library. She was doubtless reading a ladies' magazine that gave recipes on how to make tasteless food. She looked up from her reading and screamed, of course. Her two-year-old had climbed the library shelves like a primate and was up near the ceiling sniffing and licking old leather-bound volumes that were histories of Michigan describing how courageous settlers murdered the Indians, bears, and wolves, and replaced them with cows, chickens, and pigs. The library staff needed a ladder to retrieve the child. He was spanked and shit his pants in protest.

The years passed slowly as they always do when we are young, the torpor increased by teachers who openly wept with boredom and disgust at their miserable lot of being teachers instead of businessmen. In truth, they were paid so poorly that they were at the bottom of the social ladder in any village they taught. But luckily there were books in the schools, where our young hero had taken to reading one every day, sometimes two, while totally neglecting his other studies. There were also many books at home but at home he was forbidden to tear out the endpapers and chew on them, which he sneakily did at school. Endpapers were his gum and candy.

All he cared to do was read, run, hunt, and fish. He even read when he fished from their small rowboat, and he took a book along to read while resting from hunting. When he ran through the fields and forest he thought about what he would read next. He would be thinking about a book when he ran and collided with a tree or bush, and once into the side of a barn, where he hurt his shoulder.

When first picking up a fresh book he would smell it and give a random page a slight lick, then check out the page for the secrets of life. He had looked up "life" and "sex" in the encyclopedia but the encyclopedia was old and musty and words were inadequate. The words were not causally related to the life he knew. The information on sex bore no relation to looking up his aunt's skirt or fondling the girl next door, or the beauty of dogs, cats, and farm animals coupling.

He was about eleven when he snuck away with his father's copies of Erskine Caldwell's *Tobacco Road* and *God's Little Acre*, which finally revealed sex in its rather fundamental glory and struck him as similar to eating roast chicken or frying fish or deer meat, a pleasure equal to reading a good book!

From that day onward he would read only fiction and poetry, which meant he would do poorly in chemistry, mathematics, biology, and history, all of which dealt with abstractions that were meaningless to him.

The dice were now cast. He flunked high school and college, repeated and barely made it through because he imitated in writing the grace of what he read, which pleased the teachers because other students wrote so poorly. The teachers passed him even though they knew this young man was ignorant of anything concrete other than the contents of his own galantine brain.

He bummed around the country checking if writers from dozens of states knew what they were talking about. He chewed endpapers from books borrowed, bought, and stolen in every region of the United States. He was fired from every job for trying to read while working. Once in San Francisco he was reading a William Saroyan book in the public library and one of the pages smelled like lavender. He was not satisfied until he found a girl who smelled like lavender. He had a brief affair with a very tall thin girl because she was reading Stendhal on the library steps in New York City, another because she was reading Faulkner while eating chocolate ice cream, a red-haired girl (he didn't like red hair) because she was reading Valéry and soaking her pink feet in the fountain in Washington Square. In those days not many girls read books so you had to make do. His sexual possibilities were also limited because the girls had to be reading good books not trash. He figured out that good literature had serious side effects.

In his early twenties his life became hopeless. He had to do manual labor, carpentry, cement, and farm work, which required his hands so he couldn't read. He met a lovely girl who also read a lot and was pleased to see her smell a new book when she opened it. She didn't chew the endpapers but then you can't have everything. The day he impregnated her they had been talking about Dostoyevsky's *Notes from the Underground,* not a sexy book but one that made you turn to your body for solace. They had a baby who began reading books in the cradle, which illustrates that the disease may be genetic, then another baby who was equally obsessed with literature.

He was fired from two good office jobs because he neglected his work in order to read fiction and poetry. He couldn't help himself and did so openly. The young couple were in despair from eating only macaroni while reading. (Even forty years later he can remember what he was eating back then from food stains in old books. Grouse and wine stains on Mishima and Cioran.) Finally the young couple accepted their grim fate of this bloody voyage of life. They took vows of voluntary poverty for a decade so he could continue to eat books and, finally, write them. There was nothing else for him to do.

The moral of this story is to keep leather-bound Bibles well out of reach of your babies, but if it's too late and they've already begun to chew try to teach them that sex, food, and books aren't in the same category (though they probably are).

Jim Harrison
Patagonia, Arizona
February 1, 2001

PROLOGUE:
THE 10,000-CALORIE DIET

It is easy to remember the cheekbones that once emerged, not sur-prisingly, above my cheeks. In my unpublished manuscript *Zen Sex*, I counseled men to pad their boney protuberances to avoid bruising women. If I recall, this was in a chapter titled "Sensual Compassion: Dos and Don'ts for the Eighties," which included rather compendi-ous notations on the flip side of the void that is sex, including the advice that it is unseemly to bray and hoot during orgasm. The main thrust of the chapter, however, was a ten-thousand-calorie-a-day diet so that boney lovers might not injure one another.

Not so sad to say, this manuscript was lost to a computer virus called Spritzer in 1981. But I took my own well-considered advice and presently have what women call a "safe" body, though I rather miss the way they would whisper "sinew" through moistened lips when I shed my war-surplus jumpsuit. It is not for me to point out that their own sexual behavior is shot through with irony, frivolity, and an icy captiousness that recalls Lola Delmonte at her most dis-couraging. For instance, a friend in Beverly Hills told me how a very famous (international) actress had aimed her bare bottom at him at poolside as if taking a photo, then rushed into her palatial villa with a trilling laugh, my friend in pursuit. Alas, he was delayed by pain when he bumped his wagging member against the usual mauve wainscoting. He both crooned and bellowed her name as he padded through twenty-nine rooms not including the bathrooms and clos-ets, without success. He later discovered through her previous lover that there was a secret, cryptlike room in the villa where she would hide, lying on a cold, white marble slab, and where she could achieve orgasm only by hearing a frustrated man call out her name, over and over. That would take the cake, should one be offered.

Before being sidetracked, I mentioned the ten-thousand-calorie compassion diet, assuming the one you love deserves it, and this includes any of the three gender combinations. Despite their efforts, it is best not to leave definitions of sexuality up to members of Congress, the governments of the nation and states, and their multifoliate police bureaus. The diet itself is a cross-cultural barrage of feast dishes including cassoulet, *feijoada* from Brazil—the black-bean stew that contains a dozen smoked meats—a *daub* made of hindquarters of Charolais and a case of good Burgundy, a Michigan doe for six, a Thracian lamb for four, a Georgia piglet for three, a wild turkey stuffed with fruit and sausage for two, the ten-pound rice-and-fish Sumo stew for one. I forgot the *choucroute garnie* made of pig hocks, seven varieties of sausage, potatoes, and sauerkraut for seven, and the *bollito misto* for six or nine, whatever.

The cassoulet is the last dish on this thirty-day wonder, as you must start on the first day with three fat geese to make the confit, then wait at least twenty-nine days for the confit to cure. It is no fun to butcher your own geese, but the supermarket birds are far too lean, and then neither is it fun to live a life where all the dirty work, the realities, are left to someone else by virtue of our purchasing power. Country wisdom says to buy fat geese from a fat farmwife, as a lean woman tends to feed them on potato skins rather than troughs laden with grain and corn, which a fat woman readily imagines to be in order. I'll spare you the gory details, including the fact that geese do not want to die, and that it is better to lock up your bird dogs in the house because they are overeager to help out in the process.

The rest of the ingredients, including lamb and sausage and a couple of heads of garlic, plus instructions on the processes of cooking, are readily available in sophisticated cookbooks (I'd recommend Paula Wolfert's). I beg you, though, not to make one of the dreadful shortcut versions one sees featured in the media, especially newspaper cooking pages or in ladies' magazines slipped between articles on estrogen, cellulite, and flaccid-weenie problems (be shameless!).

Now the new you is on your kindly way after thirty days, having gained at least fifteen pounds because you have also eaten all the leftovers. You will immediately notice that women are now likely to tweak at your ears, tug at your wattles, back up to you like a sleepy truck to a loading platform. You have become the teddy bear their moms tossed out when they left for college. If they are also burly, they'll give you sheepish grins during long pauses at the protein counter at the super-market. In short, everyone is more amenable, gentler, if not actually happier.

Of course, there are specific drawbacks. Last year I attended the funeral of a southern writer of no consequence who had weighed more than four hundred pounds previous to death, his final go at the diet business and one in which he was to be an odds-on favorite. He passed away a scant week after winning a soft-shell-crab-and-corn-on-the-cob-eating contest, and the resultant impaction, plus a real bad crab, had taken him from us. At graveside his preco-cious nine- year-old son, who reminded me of Kolya in *The Brothers Karamazov*, had whispered to me, "Death is not the less unique for being so widespread an activity." A true southern writer in the making, already having adapted the coloration of intelligent lassi-tude—unlike the North, where writers assume a bogus heartiness and wear lumberjack shirts in classrooms and on their drunken for-ays into nature of whose actual processes they are utterly ignorant, somewhat like the famous blimp *New Yorker* poet on Nantucket, who raised his face from his desk for the tenth time of the summer and asked his wife the name of the bird, a gull, that perched on the porch railing. For reasons of her own, she rammed a well-bred little finger deep into his ear, perhaps the better for him to hear, and left for good without packing.

So there are downsides to becoming a gentle beast. Compassion can be an impure virtue, a mixed bag containing, among other things, a puff adder. Even now, at this very moment, I am splayed out on a mat on a cold stone floor aiming down my gunsights through the opened door at a Mexican blue mockingbird (*Melanotis caerulescens*). This bird has never appeared in this country before, and dragging behind him are hundreds of dweeb bird-watchers hanging on my fence with huge camera lenses and spotting scopes. I cannot get up at dawn and bow to the six directions in my birth skin. I am under a scrutiny that far exceeds the nastiness of book publication.

It was severe pain that drove me to the floor, somewhat like Robert Jordan on that bed of pine needles so long ago, a pain so severe that I had to crawl to the closet to get the shotgun. I lift my head above the sights and watch the gabbling row of birders adding this unique creature to what is known as their "life list" in the sport. They can't see me and thus are ignorant that this bird can soon disappear into a halo of blue feathers, an unnatural mood indigo. I pause thinking of my pain and how it came to be: *Maybe it is the wolf in my body growing not like those chickypoo hyenas in Kenya living off lions' spoils. I can see the enemy coming, but it happened I think in the mountains on surveillance with Peacock when we ran out of the Bordeaux, five bottles, which was very good with the thick, juicy rib steaks we put between tortillas because we had no plates and forks, also the Italian sausages, which were very good rolled in hot tortillas. Then it was dawn and the time of coyotes was gone; also the Bordeaux bottles lay bleak and empty as a politician's head. We woke and drove hard and well on the rutted red-dirt roads of Indian country to a store without Bordeaux and bought whiskey, which around the campfire that night after hard walks through canyons we pretended was good wine. Not. So I slept on cold ground with frost thick in hair and eyebrows, my body twisted like a pretzel from false amber wine, and when I awoke I could not untwist myself. I was frozen in a bad shape and the javelinas passed upwind without seeing me and I could see two ravens coming up the dry riverbed.*

Now it is an hour before twilight and the birders are coming again, as they do at dawn, relentless nature zombies. Mexico's only a few miles south of here, but the bird wouldn't "count" in Sonora. I take aim again at this lovely creature, the grayish blue of wet slate, its eyes turning to my movement through the door. He peeks out from behind my Weber barbecue, and my finger gently touches the trigger, the pain blurring my vision. Beyond the Weber, the bamboo thicket, the turbulent creek and cottonwoods and green willows, the watchers are still coming and I can't pull the trigger that would send them away. I shot in the air last week, but they came back. In the face of an old woman raising her binoculars I see my widowed mother, who, not incidentally, has 582 birds on her life list. What if she found out? And startlingly enough, against all racial stereotypes, there is a young black couple joining the rest. The blue mockingbird flits up into the bamboo thicket, and I turn on my side, suddenly letting the shotgun fall with a sharp clatter to the stone floor. In a seizure of compassion I think I'll settle for sending someone across the border for a case of Zebras, setting off the firecrackers, string after string, until everyone is gone.

Out in the wilderness with Peacock it occurred to me again that the natural world is made up of nouns and verbs on which we have heaped millions of largely inappropriate and self-serving adjectives. I wondered how we may shape ourselves, body and mind, to fully inhabit this earth.

1992

SPORTING FOOD

EAT OR DIE

In no department of life, in no place, should indifference be allowed to creep;
into none less than the domain of cookery.
—Yuan Mei

It is a few degrees above zero and I'm far out on the ice of Bay de Noc near Escanaba in the Upper Peninsula of Michigan, beyond the last of the fish shanties. It doesn't matter how far it is but how long it takes to get there—an hour out, and an hour back to my hotel, the House of Ludington. Unfortunately, I've been caught in a whiteout, a sudden snow squall out of the northwest, and I can't see anything but my hands and cross-country skis, a short, broad type called Bush-whackers, which allow you to avoid the banality of trails. I turn myself around and try to retrace my path but it has quickly become covered with the fresh snow. Now I have to stand here and wait it out because, last evening, a tanker and Coast Guard icebreaker came into the harbor, which means there is a long path of open water or some very thin ice out there in the utter whiteness. I would most certainly die if I fell in and that would mean, among other things, that I would miss a good dinner, and that's what I'm doing out here in the first place—earning, or deserving, dinner.

I become very cold in the half hour or so it takes for the air to clear. I think about food and listen to the plane high above, which has been circling and presumably looking for the airport. With the first brief glimpse of shore in the swirling snow I creak into action, and each shoosh of ski speaks to me: Oysters, snails, maybe a lobster or the *Kassler Rippchen*, the braised lamb shanks, a simple porterhouse or Delmonico, with a bottle or two of the Firestone Merlot, or the Freemark Abbey Cabernet I had for lunch . . .

The idea is to eat well and not die from it—for the simple reason that that would be the end of your eating. At age fifty that means I have to keep a cholesterol count down around 170. There is abundant dreariness in even the smallest health detail. Skip butter and desserts and toss all the obvious fat to your bird dogs.

Small portions are for smallish and inactive people. When it was all the rage, I was soundly criticized for saying that *cuisine minceur* was the moral equivalent of the fox-trot. Life is too short for me to approach a meal with the mincing steps of a Japanese prostitute. The craving is for the genuine rather than the esoteric. It is far better to avoid expense-account restaurants than to carp about them; who wants to be a John Simon of the credit-card feedbag? I'm afraid that eating in restaurants reflects one's experiences with movies, art galleries, novels, music—that is, characterized by mild amusement but with an overall feeling of stupidity and shame. Better to cook for yourself.

As for the dinner that was earned by the brush with death, it was honest rather than great. As with Chinese food, any Teutonic food, in this case smoked pork loin, seems to prevent the drinking of good wine. In general I don't care for German wines for the same reason I don't like the smell down at the Speedy Car Wash, but both perhaps are acquired tastes. The fact is, the meal demanded a couple of Heileman's Exports, even Budweisers, but that occurred to me only later.

Until recently my home base in Leelanau County, in northern Michigan, was more than sixty miles from the nearest first-rate restaurant, twice the range of the despised and outmoded atomic cannon. This calls for resourcefulness in the kitchen, or what the *tenzo* in a Zen monastery would call "skillful means." I keep an inventory taped to the refrigerator of my current frozen possibilities: local barnyard capons; the latest shipment of prime veal from Summerfield Farms, which includes sweetbreads, shanks for osso bucco, liver, chops, kidneys; and a little seafood from Charles Morgan in Destin, Florida—triggerfish, a few small red snapper, conch for chowder and fritters. There are also two shelves of favorites—rabbit, grouse, woodcock, snipe, venison, dove, chukar, duck, and quail—and containers of fish fumet, various glacés and stocks, including one made from sixteen woodcock that deserves its own armed guard. I also traded my alfalfa crop for a whole steer, which is stored at my secretary's home due to lack of space.

In other words, it is important not to be caught short. It is my private opinion that many of our failures in politics, art, and domestic life come from our failure to eat vividly, though for the time being I will lighten up on this pet theory. It is also one of a writer's neuroses not to want to repeat himself—I recently combed a five-hundred-page galley proof of a novel in terror that I may have used a specific adjective twice—and this urge toward variety in food can be enervating. If you want to be loved by your family and friends it is important not to drive them crazy; thus the true outer limits of this compulsion are tested only in the month of eating during the fall bird season when we are visited by artist Russell Chatham and the writer and Frenchman Guy de la Valdene, as well as during a few other brief spates throughout the year.

The flip side of the Health Bore is, after all, the Food Bully. Several years ago, when my oldest daughter visited from New York City, I overplanned and finally drove her to tears and illness by Christmas morning (grilled woodcock and truffled eggs). At the time she was working at Dean & DeLuca, so a seven-day feast was scarcely necessary. (New Yorkers, who are anyway a thankless lot, have no idea of the tummy thrills and quaking knees an outlander feels walking into Dean & DeLuca, Balducci's, Zabar's, Manganaro's, Lobel's, Schaller & Weber, etc.) I respected my daughter's tears, albeit tardily, having been brought to a similar condition by Orson Welles over a number of successive meals at Ma Maison, the last of which he "designed" and called me at dawn with the tentative menu as if he had just written the Ninth Symphony. We ate a half-pound of beluga with a bottle of Stolichnaya, a salmon in sorrel sauce, sweetbreads *en croûte*, a miniature leg of lamb (the whole thing) with five wines, desserts, cheeses, ports. I stumbled to the toilet for a bit of nose powder, a vice I've abandoned, and rested my head in a greasy faint against the tiled walls. Welles told me to avoid hatcheck girls as they always prefer musicians. That piece of wisdom was all that Warner Brothers got for picking up the tab. Later John Huston told me that he and Welles were always trying to stick each other with the tab and once faked simultaneous heart attacks at a restaurant in Paris. In many respects, Orson Welles was the successor to the Great Curnonsky, Prince of Gourmands. This thought occurred to me as I braced my boots against the rocker panel to haul the great director from his limousine.

Last week when my oldest daughter, who has since moved to Montana (where the only sauce is a good appetite), came home to plan her May wedding, her mother cautioned the Food Bully, threatening the usual fire extinguisher full of lithium kept in the kitchen for such purposes. While dozing, I heard my daughter go downstairs to check out the diminishing wine cellar. (I can't hear an alarm clock but I can hear this.) Certain bottles have been preserved for a few guests the evening before the wedding: a '49 Latour, a '61 Lafite, a '47 Meursault (probably turned, but the disappointment will be festive), a '69 Yquem, and a couple of '68 Heitz Martha's Vineyards for a kicker. It is a little bizarre to consider that these bottles are worth more than I made during the year she was born.

The first late evening, after a nasty January flight, we fed her a winter vegetable soup with plenty of beef shanks and bone marrow. By the next evening she was soothed enough for quail stuffed with lightly braised sweetbreads, followed by some gorgeous roasted wood ducks. I had shot the quail and wood ducks earlier in the month down south, and we especially enjoyed the latter because I will never shoot another in my life. Wood duck are the most beautiful (and tasty) of all ducks, and are very simpleminded in the way they flutter down through the trees. I felt I deserved to be bitten by the six-foot water moccasin sleeping off the cold under a nearby log. I don't feel this preventive remorse over hunting other birds, just ducks and geese.

This meal was a tad heavy so we spent the next afternoon making some not-exactly-airy cannelloni from scratch. Late that evening, I pieced up two rabbits and put them in a marinade of an ample amount of Tabasco and a quart of buttermilk, using the rabbit scraps to make half a cup of stock. The recipe is an altered version of a James Villas recipe for chicken (attribution is important in cooking).

The next evening, we floured and fried the rabbit, serving it with a sauce of the marinade, stock, and the copious brown bits from the skillet. I like the dish best with simple mashed potatoes and succotash made from frozen tiny limas and corn from the garden. The rabbit gave one a thickish feeling so the next evening I broiled two small red snappers with a biting Thai hot-and-sour sauce, which left one refreshingly hungry by midnight. My wife had preserved some lemon, so I went to the cellar for a capon as she planned a Paula Wolfert North African dish. Wolfert and Villas are food people whom you tend to "believe" rather than simply admire. In this same noble lineage is Patience Gray, a wandering Bruce Chatwin of food.

Naturally, I had been floundering through the deep snow an hour or two a day with my bird dogs to deserve such meals. My system had begun to long for a purging meal of a mixed-grain concoction called Kashi, plus a pot of mustard and collard greens with a lump of locally made salt pork. This meal can be stretched into something bigger by adding barbecued chicken laved in a tonic sauce, which I call the sauce of Lust and Violence. The name refers to what it does to the palate rather than a motivation of behavior.

We weren't exactly saving up for the big one when the few guests begin to arrive the following evening. The cautionary note was something Jack Nicholson had said to me more than a decade ago after I had overfed a group in his home: "Only in the Midwest is over-eating still considered an act of heroism." Still, the winter weather was violent, and lacking the capacity to hibernate it was important to go on with the eating, not forgetting the great Lermontov's dictum: "Eat or die."

We made a simple, nonauthentic "scampi" as an appetizer. Garlic is a vegetable and should be used in quantity, and must never be burned. To avoid this I broil the shrimp for two minutes in the shells, then add the garlic, oil, butter, and lemon juice. Infantile but good with sourdough bread. Next came the innovation of the evening, an idea that came after talking to my neighbor and hunting friend

Nick. We breasted eighteen doves and my wife made a clear stock of
the carcasses. Each whole breast was cut in four pieces. We added
finely julienned red pepper, mostly for color, and a little shredded
endive to the clear stock. We poached the pieces of dove breast briefly
so they would be soft and pinkish in the center. It was a delicious
soup and we looked forward to making it with surplus woodcock in
the fall. The final course, rare venison steaks with a sauce made of
venison marrow bones and a little of my prized woodcock stock, was
almost an afterthought. Enough is enough.

The final evening we went to a restaurant called Hattie's in the
small nearby town of Suttons Bay. I wondered if we had actually
planned a wedding but didn't want to ask. My wife and two daughters were in good humor and ate lightly. I couldn't resist the cassoulet
with an enormous preserved goose thigh smack dab in the middle—
true homemade confit here in northern Michigan when it is hard to
find even in New York! I would resume running at night, all night
long across frozen lakes, were it not for the dangerous holes left by
the ice fisherman.

1988

MEALS OF PEACE
AND RESTORATION

I believe it was the late John Wayne who said, "It pushes a man to the wall if he stands there in the buff and looks straight down and can't even see his own weenie." I *think* it was John Wayne who said that. However, I'm a poet and novelist, not a John Wayne authority.

The import of the statement is pretty tough stuff. You can make light of the problem as I did years ago in my Emily Dickinson Diet Poems (which were a response to Tom McGuane, who said that according to our correspondence I had lost twelve hundred pounds in the last three years, so I must be "getting right down there"). Here are two samples in the manner of that melancholy warbler of yore:

At dawn I saw a breast bone,
'Twas mine own I thought, rising
as boney Horeb from the plain:
what, long desuetized? Now come forth
as turkey's, Phoebe's bright crow's song?

Or more *au point:*

I saw my dink today whilst
standing up, O Halcyon nubbin!
But bending over it fled again
'neath a fuchsia billow.
Yet in Vanity's cold mirror
it winked as May's pink morel,
winked its age old, Hello, Goodbye.

Verse in itself moves us away from the personal toward the eternal verities. So what if I'm a tad burly? A victim of being weaned too early, an essentially climatological neurosis got from living too far north—less light and more cold, ergo more food is needed. In my childhood we prayed every evening for the starving children in Europe, causing a primitive fear of hunger, not to speak of being genetically implanted by generations of rural kitchen hogs. There are also the scars from my youthful New York City art wars, when I thought I was Arthur Rimbaud and the average Dumpster ate better than I did. Is all this true, or is it merely the notion of the French surrealist poet Alfred Jarry: "I eat, or someone will eat in my place"? Isn't it time to escape the sodden mysteries of personality and try to help other folks? Not that I really wish to become the Baba Ram Jimmy of food advice, but something calls me to offer a handful of garlic along the way.

Times have changed. We have witnessed the passing of the blackjack and the accordion. Few of us sing alone on our porches on summer evenings, watching the sexual dance of fireflies in the burdocks beside the barn. The buzz of the airport metal detector is more familiar than the sound of the whippoorwill or coyote. The world gets to you with its big, heavy, sharp-toed boot. We are either "getting ready" or "getting over." Our essential and hereditary wildness slips, crippled, into the past. The jackhammer poised daily at our temples is not fictive, nor is the fact that all the ceilings have lowered, and the cold ozone that leaks under the door is merely a signal that the old life is over. There is a Native American prophecy that the end is near when trees die from their tops down (acid rain).

To be frank, this is not the time for the "less is more" school when it comes to eating. The world as we know it has always been ending, every day of our lives, though sometimes faster. Good food and good cooking are a struggle for the appropriate and, as such, a response to the total environment. Anyone who has spent an afternoon in New York has seen the sullen and distraught faces of those who have eaten a julienne of jicama with raspberry vinaigrette and a glass of European water for lunch.

Let's not dwell on the negative, the wine of illusion. You begin with simple truths in food: for instance, peeling sweetbreads is not really exercise. When you're trimming a two-pound porterhouse, don't make those false, hyperkinetic motions favored by countermen in delicatessens. Either trim it or skip trimming. Eat the delicious fat and take a ten-mile walk. Reach into your memory and come up with what restored you, what helped you recover from the sheer hellishness of life, what food actually regenerated your system, not so you can leap tall buildings but so you can turn off the alarm clock with vigor.

Chances are you will come up with something Latin. It is the Third World, perhaps the Fourth, that offers genuine solace. For the reasonably well traveled the tip-off is always the music and food. (Notice how the whey-faced designer-drug types prefer heavy metal.) Their music and food are quite different from our own in areas of fruit growth, where garlic and flowers abound, where there is blue water and hot sun. At the bottom of dampish arroyos are giant butterflies and moths, extravagantly plumed birds who feed on the remains of lightning and sunbeams, the unique maggots that feed only on the spleens of road kill. Farther up the cliffs, where the cacti is sparser, rattlers sun themselves. At first you are uncomfortable, then disarmed by the way they contract over hot coals. They are particularly good with the salsa that goes by the brand name Pace.

Last March I was hiking out of the Seri Indian country, south of Caborca along the Sea of Cortés, with Douglas Peacock, the fabled grizzly bear expert. We were both out of sorts: he, because he can't seem to make a living; I, because my sinal pain was so extreme that I had to bash my head against the car door and specific boulders we passed. Luckily, we were able to dig a full bushel of clams at a secret estuary and make a hearty chowder with a pound of chiles and garlic, which started me on the road to recovery. Giant Guaymas shrimp helped, as did broiled tripe from an unborn calf. (Don't falter; most everything we eat is technically dead.) After this infusion of health I was able to dance five hours with a maiden who resembled a beige bowling ball. She was, in fact, shaped rather like myself.

In the morning my clothes were crisp from exertion, my head bell clear, and the world was new again, like a warm rain after a movie. No matter that a few months later they had to jerk a tooth and vacuum my skull with an instrument devised by NASA to suck cosmic dust from the space capsule. People are enamored with the drama of their own personal survival, which is always a succession of temporary measures.

One late November night on the Navajo reservation in Arizona, I was camped out with two old men who I was reasonably sure were witches, although kind witches. I was researching a film on the life of Edward Curtis and that morning had received word that the studio had fired me again. But that night there was a big moon through the intermittent snow, and above the fire a *posole* was cooking, with its dark freight of several different chiles, a head of garlic, sun-dried hominy, and the neck, ribs, and shanks of a young goat. After eating the *posole* we hiked for several hours in the moonlight, and one of the old men showed me his raven and coyote imitations, jumping in bounds the length of which would have shamed Carl Lewis.

Posole is a generic dish, and I've eaten dozens of versions and made an equal number of my own. The best are to be found in Mexico. *Menudo* is a similar dish and a fabulous restorative, the main ingredient being tripe. If you are in Chicago, you can eat your fill at Rick and Deann Bayless's splendid Mexican restaurant, Frontera Grill. I've made a good start on the project.

Curiously, though, *menudo* has specific effects around which you can design a day. Picture yourself waking on Sunday morning with a terminal hangover and perhaps a nosebleed, though the latter has fallen from favor. You have a late-afternoon assignation with a fashion model you don't want to disappoint with shakes and vomiting rather than love. Just eat a couple bowls of *menudo* sprinkled with chopped cilantro and scallions, wild Sonoran chiltepins, and a squeeze of lemon. The results are guaranteed by the tripe cartel, which has not yet been a victim of arbitrage.

Last fall I felt intense sympathy for a friend, Guy de la Valdene, who was arriving in Michigan for bird season after a circuitous road trip through Missouri, Iowa, and Minnesota. You doubtless know that these are not food states. On the phone I could tell Valdene's spirit was utterly broken, so three days before his arrival I began making Paula Wolfert's *salmis de cuisses de canard,* from her *Cooking of South-West France*. Since there were to be two of us, I increased the recipe, using nineteen duck legs and thighs, a couple of heads of garlic, two pounds of lean salt pork (homemade by my butcher), a half-cup of Armagnac, a bottle of Échezeaux, and so on. (Wolfert's new effort, *World of Food,* can also be read as an edible novel.) During the three days of preparation, it occurred to me how Reagan was outsmarted by Mitterrand a few years back. Reagan purportedly concentrates on a diet of lean fish, turkey breast, raw zucchini, and jelly beans, while Mitterrand snacks on caviar, truffles, foie gras, and jellied calves' feet and drinks fine Bordeaux and Burgundy (rather than Reagan's habitual Riunite on the rocks with seltzer). At least George Bush eats pork rinds—a step in the right direction. Anyway, I helped my friend from his vehicle directly to the table, and within twenty-four hours after we had finished the dish, his health completely restored.

Not to belabor the peasant motif, a week later Valdene ordered two pounds of beluga from Caviareria in New York, which we ate in a single sitting with my wife and daughter. I reminded myself not to do this too often since the next morning my goutish left big toe tingled, making bird hunting awkward.

It's interesting to see, in the manner of a pharmacist, how particularized the food nostrum can be: for clinical depression you must go to Rio to a *churrascaria* and eat a roast slice from the hump of a Zebu bull; also try the *feijoada,* a stew of black beans with a dozen different smoked meats, including ears, tails, and snouts. For late-night misty boredom go to an Italian restaurant and demand the violent pasta dish known as *puttanesca,* favored by the whores of Rome. After voting, eat collard greens to purge you of free-floating disgust. When trapped by a March blizzard make venison carbonnade, using a stock of shin bones and the last of the doves. If it is May and I wish to feel light and spiritual I make a simple sauté of nuggets of sweetbreads, fresh morels, and wild leeks, the only dish, so far as I know, that I have created.

I recently went down to Chicago to see the Gauguin retrospective at the Art Institute. The show was so overwhelming I actually wept, jolted into the notion that art does a better job for the soul than food for the body. I remembered reading, though, that the great Gauguin, when a little low and cranky in the Islands, liked to have a goblet of rum followed by breadfruit, a fresh steamed fish with ginger, and perhaps a roast piglet. No mention was made of dessert. During my art-dazed walk back to the hotel I slipped into the Convito Italiano for a bite—a simple carpaccio, then a bowl of excellent pastae fagioli with shellfish and an endive salad, together with five Tuscan wines and a hit of grappa. Following a long nap with South Seas dreams I went up to Café Provençal for a grand feast. So it goes.

1989

HUNGER, REAL AND UNREAL

"Did you ever notice how we never allow ourselves to be actually hungry?" said Russell Chatham, a burly painter of some note.

We were eating a prehunt breakfast, parked beside Oleson's buffalo paddock outside Traverse City, Michigan. All of the little boy buffalo, ignorant of gender, were chasing one another around, hell-bent on sex, their red wangers bobbing in the chill October air. "Those guys are a tad confused," Russell added, eyeing the corked bottle of wine, at which we both coughed, thinking that ten in the morning isn't too early for a sip of red wine with a sandwich. Way up here in the northland there's a fine Italian delicatessen, Folgarelli's, and Russell was having a hot Italian sausage with marinara sauce and melted mozzarella while mine was a simple prosciutto, mortadella, Genoa salami, and provolone on an Italian roll.

Throughout the hunting day we mulled over the original and not exactly metaphysical question of why we never, for more than a moment, allowed ourselves to be hungry. Could this be why we were both seriously overweight? But only a fool jumps to negative conclusions about food, especially before dinner. *Cuisine minceur* notwithstanding, the quality of food diminishes sharply in proportion to negative thinking about ingredients and, simply put, the amount to be prepared. There is no substitute for Badia a Coltibuono olive oil. Period. Or the use of salt pork in the cooking of southwest France. Three ounces of Chablis are far less interesting and beneficial than a magnum of Bordeaux.

I have mentioned before that we are in the middle of yet another of the recurrent sweeps across our nation of the "less is more" bullies. When any of these people arrive in my yard I toss a head of iceberg lettuce and some dog biscuits off the porch. I heard recently

that a New York society botanist has been attempting to crossbreed
kiwi and jicama trees, which, if successful, will keep these bliss-ninnies
happy for years. Lucky for the rest of us these folks aren't visible side-
ways. From the front, you can see through their hands as if they were
raw shrimp.

Despite these apparent truths, almost biblical in veracity, and
bearing some of the grandeur of our Constitution, I recently learned
that hunger is the actual sensation of the body burning its own fat.
This is not a very appetizing idea but is, nonetheless, a positive
experience when the body wears too much fat. I learned this just
recently when I spent two weeks at the Rancho La Puerta health
spa in Tecate, Mexico, in order to quit smoking, a project at which
I failed, but an obnoxious vice I'm still battling on a moment-
to-moment basis.

Almost incidentally I lost seventeen pounds in two weeks. This
appears impossible, but some of it was "easy" weight from a feast
(the usual wonderful squid, chicken, tuna, carpaccio, lamb, etc.)
at Rondo's in Los Angeles the evening before my incarceration. I
also worked out six to eight hours a day, including a solo four-hour
mountain hike each morning to look for birds and follow the tracks
of coyote, bobcat, and puma, plus up to three hours of floor exer-
cises and gym work.

Now this was an unconscionable and pathetic amount of exertion, but necessary to avoid cigarettes. I plummeted into a depression where the first of my ideals to fly away into the mountains was
literature. The menu was total vegetarian with fish twice a week.
Chef Ramon Flores took this limited cuisine as far as it can be taken,
but not quite far enough for the grief of a man who had temporarily
lost his calling. One late morning after an exhausting hike, I began
to tremble uncontrollably, a state I recognized as protein starvation.
A tumbler of Herradura tequila was a temporary measure until I
gathered the strength to call a cab and head into town for a slab of
swordfish with garlic sauce and a full order of *carne asada*.

Quite naturally, as Americans we all loathe decadence though
our notions of decadence change from time to time. Around the

turn of the century, a man's girth was a fair estimate of one's prosperity and moral worth, and the thin sallow look, so much the rage at present, was considered fair evidence of low birth and probable criminal intent. (Curiously enough, of the countless times I've been swindled in Hollywood, the guilty parties were always thin.) Men nowadays will not settle for a Paul Newman washboard stomach but want an entire washboard body, even though none of them remembers an actual washboard in his past.

Let's all stop a moment in our busy day and return to some eternal verities. It's quite a mystery, albeit largely unacknowledged, to be alive, and, quite simply, in order to remain alive you must keep eating. My notion, scarcely original, is that if you eat badly you are very probably living badly. You tend to eat badly when you become inattentive to all but the immediate economic necessities, real or imagined, and food becomes an abstraction; you merely "fill up" in the manner that you fill a car with gasoline, no matter that some fey grease slinger has put raspberry purée on your pen-raised venison. You are still a nitwit bent over a trough.

At the Rancho one day at lunch I told some plumpish but kindly ladies what I thought was a charming story of simple food. One August, years ago, I was wandering around the spacious property of a château up in Normandy, trying to work up a proper appetite for lunch. The land, owned by a friend, doubled as a horse farm and a vicious brood mare had tried to bite me, an act I rewarded with a stone sharply thrown against her ass. Two old men I hadn't seen laughed beneath a tree. I walked over and sat with them around a small fire. They were gardeners and it was their lunch hour, and on a flat stone they had made a small circle of hot coals. They had cored a half dozen big red tomatoes, stuffed them with softened cloves of garlic, and added a sprig of thyme, a basil leaf, and a couple of tablespoons of soft cheese. They roasted the tomatoes until they softened and the cheese melted. I ate one with a chunk of bread and healthy-sized swigs of a jug of red wine. When we finished eating, and since this was Normandy, we had a sip or two of Calvados from a flask. A simple snack but indescribably delicious.

I waited only a moment for the ladies' reaction. *Cheese,* two of them hissed, *Cheese,* as if I had puked on their sprouts, and *Wine!* The upshot was that cheese is loaded with cholesterol and wine has an adverse effect on blood sugar. I allowed myself to fog over as one does while reading bad reviews of one's own work.

That evening, Gail Greene, also a Rancho guest, spoke of the travails of being a food critic, which made me ache for the usual foie gras and truffles. Later I told her that I used to carry a notebook and dictaphone into restaurants, assuring myself a good meal as a bogus food critic. I never actually said I was a critic, only that I couldn't talk about it. I reflected, too, on the idea of food snobbism: some friends in Paris are cynical about the idea of a good meal in New York, and in New York the idea of eating in Chicago is somewhat laughable, and so on through Los Angeles and San Francisco in every direction. I enjoy telling them that in recent years my best meal was at the Ali-Oli in San Juan, Puerto Rico. True.

At dawn the next morning I decided to skip human life and spend the day in the mountains. I figured that Aldous Huxley, one of my boyhood heroes, who used to hang out at the Rancho, would have done the same thing. I took my binoculars, an orange, a hard-boiled egg, and a one-ounce bottle of Tabasco for the egg.

Four hours into the mountains I ate the egg and the orange with relish. I was seated downwind from a bobcat cave, hoping for a sighting but knowing it was doubtful until just before dark. The cave had a dark, overpowering feline odor similar, I imagined, to the basement of a thousand-year-old Chinese whorehouse (the visionary propensities of hunger!). Then out of the chaparral appeared a tough, ragged-looking Mexican who asked me if I had anything to eat. I said no, wishing I had saved the orange. He smiled, bowed, and continued scampering up Mount Cuchama, presumably toward the United States and the pursuit of happiness, including something to eat. He had chosen the most difficult route imaginable, and I followed his progress with the binoculars, deciding that not one of the Rancho's fitness buffs, including the instructors, could have managed the mountain at that speed.

I didn't feel the couch liberal's guilt over not having saved the orange for him, just plain old midwestern Christian guilt. In my deranged state I thought that maybe the guy was Jesus, and I had denied him the orange! Then I lapsed into memories of things I had eaten when I was actually hungry, such as the fried trout I used to eat at streamside with bread and salt. I remembered, in my wandering starving-artist years in the late 1950s, spending subway fare for a thirty-five-cent Italian-sausage sandwich and walking seventy blocks to work the next morning, eating free leftovers given to me by Babe and Louis at the Kettle of Fish bar, buying twenty-five-cent onion sandwiches on rye bread at McSorley's. I had wonderful meals working as a poetic busboy at the Prince Brothers Spaghetti House in Boston; I often devoured two fried eggs at a diner after Storyville, the best jazz club ever, closed at dawn. In the San Francisco area there were two-for-a-nickel oranges, the oddly delicious macaroni salad at the Coexistence Bagel Shop for a quarter, the splurge of an enormous fifty-cent bowl of pork and noodles in Chinatown. And let's not forget the desperation of eating ten-cent cafeteria bread and ketchup in Salt Lake City or the grapefruit given me by an old woman in the roadside dust near Fallon, Nevada.

When I arrived home from one of these trips, mostly brown skin and bones, my father said, "If you had stayed away longer you wouldn't weigh nothing at all. It's plain to see it will be some time, if ever, before you know what you are doing, James." Then he fired up the grill and we went into his enormous garden and picked all manner of fresh vegetables. He broiled some chickens with lemon, garlic, and butter. That's what I remembered on the way down the mountain.

1989

THEN AND NOW

I have a good memory, though *good* is somewhat questionable as there is a tendency to overremember life rather than to look for new life to be lived. "Late in the Great Depression, on the first day of spring in 1938, in fact, I gazed from the cradle as my parents ate smoked pork chops and the last of the home-cured sauerkraut, which was particularly redolent from six months in the crock, whose stone surface I often licked for salt while crawling around the floor looking up at the underside of the world, the small strawberry birthmark on the back of my lovely aunt's thigh just below the apparent bird's nest wrapped in white cotton. I rejected baby food with sobs and howls, preferring whole venison hearts, herring, pike, perch eggs, the 'souse' Grandmother boiled down from an enormous pig's head on the woodstove."

That sort of thing. "I still remember the mosquito-bite scab on the dirty left knee of the little girl who put out my eye with a broken bottle on a cinder heap at the edge of the woods in 1945. We were playing doctor. The Tigers were in third place and Hal Newhouser was going to pitch that day. On the way to the doctor, our car smelled because I had left a bluegill in the trunk behind the tire but was afraid to admit it. In the hospital my parents brought me herring, the odor of which repelled the nurse. I thought I'd look like the little pig who lost his eye to a rusty nail protruding from a pen board. The second board from the bottom on the north side. For several painful months, the blind eye shone like a red sun in my head."

Again, that sort of thing. Luckily we eat in the present tense, else we might travel further into madness. That goes for fishing, too. When you combine fishing, eating, and a little drinking, you are riding the cusp of sanity as you did, quite happily, the school-yard swing or that rope at the swimming hole that arced you out over a deep hole of cold, clear water, where you dropped down on startled brown trout whose fingerlings were speared by the kingfisher perched on the elm's bald branch. Jerry Round jumped from the bridge top and died, driving his head into his body. Naturally, I thought of turtles, which Vince Towne purged in a washtub before he ate them. He told us that fried turtle would make our peckers grow big, a comment about which we had mixed feelings.

Fishing and eating, not without a few drinks at day's end. Hundreds of years ago, a *roshi* admonished his students not to prate about Zen to fishermen, farmers, and woodchoppers, since they likely already knew the story. Because I live up in Michigan and don't much like ice fishing, I've been going to the lower Florida Keys for a little winter fishing since 1968. With ice fishing, you dress up bulky like an astronaut and stare through a round black hole you've spudded in the ice. The "spud" is the tip-off that you're in the wrong place—it is an enormous forty-pound chisel. The sandwiches we brought along used to freeze in our pockets, and one day the wine froze at twenty below zero.

The question at hand is, "Are the Keys the same or as good as in the old days?" This is an especially stupid question that I have been asked countless times by dozens of people. My answer, "yes and no," is usually unsatisfactory except to the timid, so I add a little gingerbread, to wit, isn't the past the silliest of tautologies? Have you forgotten Mircea Eliade's blessed "concrete plane of immediate reality"? Didn't René Char tell us not to live on regret like a wounded finch?

Where have any of us ever been that some nitwit doesn't tell us that we should have been there before? They are only pissing on a fireplug to establish territory in the face of recent arrivals. In Aspen, at the Hotel Jerome, you will always meet a stockbroker with an overbite much envied in London who is eager to establish he was there first. I've developed a good tactic: wherever you are, say that you were born and raised there, but infinitely prefer living in Detroit.

The fishing in the Keys is about the same, but the food is better. There are more fishing guides, but the water is scarcely cluttered. I wouldn't return again in March, when college students on spring break flood the town. They invariably march around in groups, puking drunk, reminding one of the Nazi youth that cursed the world. They are all apparently the soul children of Ronald Reagan and should be packed off to Daytona Beach before they further destroy the nature of the community. If you like this sort of thing you can save a lot of money by hanging out in a college community after a football game.

Far from this caveat is the notion that much of the food used to be quite awful except for Rene's, down on Duval, or in the better Cuban restaurants such as El Cacique. Now you can eat better in Key West than in any town I can think of in America fifteen or twenty times its size. Of course, there was a period in the early seventies when one might fly-fish for tarpon on three hits of windowpane acid backed up by a megaphone bomber of Colombian buds that required nine papers and an hour to roll. You weren't exactly ready for fine food when you got off the boat. What you had in mind has still not been determined. Certain early songs by Neil Young, or by Jimmy Buffett, will still put me in a cold anguished sweat. Now when I hunt or fish with Buffett we talk about what we're going to cook for dinner. He doesn't even sing "The Way We Were," the reality of which no one can accurately remember. It has also become convenient to blame all of our bad behavior on Tom McGuane, who, as Capt. Berserko, was the leader of our social organization, Club Mandible. He can also absorb the blame as his character has now attained a Tolstoyan grandeur.

There is something in the character of flats-fishing in the tropics that somewhat diminishes the appetite: a mixture of sun, heat, fatigue. You are fly-fishing in the shallow water of a river that is fifty miles wide, and casting only to visible fish. The energy expended in the relentless staring into water is exhausting. You are utterly immersed in the act and dare not let a single extraneous thought enter or you'll miss the fish. It was upsetting this year to find that I have become much better at fly-fishing now that my drinking has vastly moderated. A hangover, simply enough, internalizes the quality of attentiveness, and you're looking inside at your myriad fuck-ups rather than outside at fish.

Not that I couldn't eat adequately, only that I'm usually a multiple-entrée type of guy, and I came to know the certain sadness of watching my wife, two daughters, and son-in-law eat more than I did. This passes the gauntlet of piggery, I thought.

Chef Norman Van Aken's Mira is a grand place, with a first-rate wine list devised by Proal Perry. For day-to-day excellence we chose Antonia's, eating rather elaborate meals there three times in two weeks, though you can order simply from the appetizers and list of pastas (including stone-crab claws and mussels in a cream sauce on homemade linguine). Frankly, I find no fault with Antonia's. In a dozen visits I've never met the chef, Phillip Smith, or the owner, and not a single visit was an expense-account meal. There were no disappointments and the serving staff is deft and unobtrusive.

We also frequented Louie's Backyard, whose upstairs café is informal and beautifully decorated. One day, chef Bill Prahl will become as inventive as Van Aken. The menu could be called "nouvelle Cuban," and Prahl's squid rings with citrus aioli are exquisite, as are the Havana pork roast and the shellfish *zarzuela*. Downstairs the atmosphere is more formal but the food, prepared by Doug Shook under the direction of co-owner Phil Tenney, fine indeed. I prefer it for lunch when the fried-chicken salad is available, also onion rings made from marinated Spanish red onions. One day a shellfish gumbo beat senseless anything Louisiana ever offered me. A short drive up the Keys to Cudjoe to Rick Lutz's Cousin Joe's will give you a taste of what the area used to be like, only the food is much better.

Back in Key West I can also recommend Café des Artistes (unbelievable desserts), Dim Sum, the Crêperie, and Kyushu. For a relief from the pricey and somewhat formal, we returned frequently to the Full Moon Saloon for the hottest chicken wings imaginable, grouper and conch sandwiches, conch chowder, and conch fritters, as well as more elaborate meals, all turned out by chef Tom Sawyer.

(I keep mentioning chefs for the same reason you tell folks who wrote the book.) I eat breakfast at Dennis Pharmacy on Simonton because it doesn't limit you to the nutritional vacuum of bacon and eggs, offering a number of Spanish soups, including red bean, and pigs' feet. For sandwiches for the boat, go to Uncle Garlins Food Store out on Flagler, where the meat loaf is better than Mom's.

Curiously, I didn't gain an ounce in two weeks. At least I don't think I did. I defy the mechanistic world of scales, banks, lawyers, dentists, and I wouldn't balance a checking account or touch a computer at gunpoint. My aide-de-camp handles all of this except the dentist. A scale is meaningless when some days you feel light and some days you feel heavy. I have chosen the weight of 135 pounds as appropriate and have stuck to it. You might ask the local farmers who see me running in the dawn mists well ahead of my panting bird dogs. Once, at the Denver airport, a bald girl in an orange dress told me I could be what I wanted, so it's 135, period.

Back to the old days, the late sixties and early seventies. I don't miss all of the stuff that made me feel bad, and gentrification, wherever it takes place, tends to wipe out all but a charade of the indigenous culture. It can still be there, but you have to look for it. I miss the fighting roosters crowing at dawn, but not the cocaine jag that enabled me to hear them. I miss feeling the thrill of the possible future so adumbrated by despair and empty pockets, the night thick with the scent of garbage and flowers, the fecund, low-tide odor of our beginning.

Now I go there just for the fishing and, secondarily, the eating. My family likes it, and it's doubtful I'd chance a trip without them. There are the ghosts of those I cared for who did not survive the behavior the rest of us survived. But it is the water, the life we can only visit and barely comprehend, the thousand life-forms of the flats, imperceptible unless you care to learn, a saline *mysterium*. This year there were two beached, rotting sperm whales on the flats facing Snipe Key, their skins too tough for the seabirds to feed on. I wondered where those whales were born, where they traveled on this bloody journey, what they felt when they died together far from their natural home, all of it quite beyond the range of my speculation or imaginings, the vast, brownish, sun-blasted hulks resting on the lovely flats. Some locals had cut out their valuable teeth with chain saws, but this fact seemed singularly puny, however coarse, compared to the inviolable beauty of the seascape, the whales resting not in peace but, as all of us will, in inevitable resignation.

1989

CONSCIOUSNESS DINING

An artist (a generic term covering poet, composer, painter, sculptor, perhaps novelist) consciously or unconsciously takes a vow of obedience to awareness. In order not to be lost in the whirl of time, either past or present, the artist must look at all things with the energy and clarity of a hyperthyroid Buddha.

Frankly, this awareness is not always a lot of fun, a fact that explains certain consciousness-reducing vices. In certain locales it is even less fun than in others. Just recently I drove south from my wilderness cabin in Michigan's Upper Peninsula to my farm, where I packed for a trip to Los Angeles. We all know that air travel is currently a big step down from what Greyhound travel was in days of yore. And in the past year or so, the food has further degenerated in the first-class cabin of my favorite airline, American. Now a bottle of Tabasco lasts only three trips, whereas in the old days it lasted a dozen. I have filed an application to be towed by future planes in a gunnysack full of fish guts, which will improve the trip.

I am mindful that what takes a novelist initially to L.A. is greed and, often enough to be worth mentioning, a fascination with movies. My arrival is always buffered by getting naked into bed in a darkened hotel room, no matter the time of day, and listening to Mexican music on the radio. This is a little trick you all might try. I stay either at the Westwood Marquis, because you can walk in the UCLA Botanical Gardens and also because it is a fine hotel, or at the Shangri-La out in Santa Monica, which offers, right out the window, the nonclaustrophobic feature of the Pacific Ocean, or the "Big P.," as it is known locally.

Hollywood is not a kind and gentle place, but it's where my work takes me. On the first day of a recent meeting we worked fourteen hours, another reminder that the place doesn't necessarily dollar up on the side of frivolity. This schedule continued for several days, until I felt like one of the well-known, three peeled throats of Cerberus, exhausted, fluttery, my imagination a mud puddle rather than a mighty river. To put it simply, I wasn't getting enough to eat. My partners (Harrison Ford and Douglas Wick) own the sharpish features of the underfed, features that any phrenologist will tell you reflect an interest in money and power rather than the fruits of the imagination.

Anyway, in the middle of a serious point, I slipped into an out-of-body experience and was swept away to New York City, tracking myself as I left the therapist's office where I am treated for the usual obsessive-compulsive disorders. My first stop was the Ideal Lunch & Bar on Eighty-sixth Street for a quick boiled pig hock, then on to the Papaya King hot-dog stand on the corner of Eighty-sixth and Third for a quick frank with sauerkraut and mustard, down Third to Ray's for a slice of pizza with eggplant, then over to JG Melon for a simple rare burger and a double V.O. When I came to, I discovered that I had been talking with incisive brilliance and the meeting was over, which proves that even ghost food is better than none. Unfortunately, I don't have any of the notes.

The point is that there's no snack food in L.A. on the order of New York. I ate very good dinners at Dan Tana's, vastly improved since my last visit, and at Osteria Orsini, where my table was presided over by the best waiter on the West Coast, the fabled Igor. The last night I agreed hesitantly to Chaya's, doubtful that a restaurant that "hot" could also be good. The meal was splendid, again highlighting the fact that I have never had an accurate intuition (raw-tuna salad, a pasta with peerless squid and slivered jalapeños, a small grilled chicken with a side of garlic the equal of any I've ever had, *pommes frites*, and a whole bottle of Château Montelena just for me).

Despite this grand send-off, I arrived home in a palsied state—tremors of exhaustion, near tears, that sort of thing. My wife noted a burnt-rubber scent coming out of my ears, firm evidence of my brain's drag racing with itself in film country. To set the brakes I wandered for hours in the woods looking for morels, but it had been a dry, bitterly cold spring and the mushrooms were scarce. At one point I walked three hours to find four morels. I did, however, gather enough to cook our annual spring rite, a simple sauté of the mushrooms, wild leeks, and sweetbreads. Regardless of this tonic for the body, I fired off inconsolably angry letters to no one in particular and lightly spanked the bird dogs for minor infractions, until I gave up on domestic life and packed north to the cabin, with three cartons of books on Native Americans and John Thorne's *Simple Cooking*. Native Americans are an obsession of mine, totally unshared by New York and Los Angeles for the average reason of moral vacuum. Native Americans are like good poetry, and it is particularly banal that we are dying from the lack of what both tell us.

A number of years ago I had the notion that I wished to write a poem as immediately fascinating as a recipe or a dirty picture. Fat chance. Art is in no position to duke it out with our baser appetites, appetites that are the cornerstones of our individual pyramids; art is only the pointed, three-corner capstone, signaling finally what we had in mind. Meanwhile, down at the bottom, it is clear that instincts toward sex and food must be aesthetically satisfied, or the pyramid is the usual garbage heap. It is also clear, in a historical perspective, that our current, most active generation—those between twenty and forty— is laying a giant fiber-laden, aerobic turd of greed on the history of the republic.

John Thorne is not to be confused with Nicholas Thorne, the dark genius of contemporary classical music. John Thorne's unqualified genius is for food, and I suspect he will justly inherit the mantle from M. F. K. Fisher as our best food writer. Others, Paula Wolfert, for instance, have a much more startling flare, and I suspect that since I am an outright pig I'd choose her table over Thorne's. But for day-in, day-out innovative brilliance and lucid prose Thorne is my favorite. For years he has been writing a newsletter called *Simple Cooking,* and he's published a cookbook of the same name. Perhaps living at the northeasternmost tip of America keeps Thorne unencumbered with the faddish, those tiny points of dullish light that signal some new craze like homemade tomato soup. In both the newsletter and the book, he writes of food as varied as red beans and rice, versions of corn bread, roasted red pepper and mushroom *tian*, bread and olives, focaccia, varieties of chowder, olive oils, nun's farts (*pets-de-nonne*—a type of fritter), *boeuf à la ficelle*, collards, pork, and apple pie.

Thorne's Yankee modesty shields innovation from pretension. He simply doesn't show off, and all of his energies go toward food that resonates, that is genuine and memorable. His ego is quite barren and the attributions generous—it is an oddity of the genre that most cookbooks pretend they are the only ones in existence. Thorne even writes a convincing essay on why he isn't a good cook. He admits he loves fried-chicken-skin sandwiches—a truly nasty idea, but to admit you would eat them is admirable. On a long, warm flight up from New Orleans, he imagined that the two pounds of *boudin* in his suitcase were spoiling so he ate them all on arrival, the sort of timeless wisdom to which I can respond.

So I was rereading all of Thorne and experimenting with his recipes rather than beginning the revision of the screenplay (*revision* being a euphemism for doing the whole thing over without saving a word of the first draft). Simply enough, hunger had overly cleansed our doors of perception, and we had come up with a better idea. After a few days at my cabin, I found that the food reading and long hikes had restored my appetite for life the way Henry Miller used to do when I was a young bohemian.

Curiously, in both writing and cooking you're a dead duck if you don't love the process. When you short-circuit or jump-start the process in either, you end up with an imitation of your own or someone else's best effects. You will get away with it a few times but the germs of shame will be there, and inevitably you will end up serving your dinner guests or your reading public mere filigree, plywood gingerbread, M.F.A. musings, housebroken honeycomb, in short, the thief of fire as a college cheerleader.

Back to the obedience to awareness: still within the aftereffects of L.A. burnout, I nearly stepped on a nest of grouse chicks and forgot that Buddha's birthday was falling on the same day as the full moon. When will this happen again? I forgot to leach the eggplant and the parmigiana was mushy! So were the cannellini beans I cooked too hard, neglecting to add the pancetta rind! Son of a bitch, but I was delaminating!

I decided to start over as a regular guy, an ordinary fellow. For dinner I'd cook a Thorne version of fish chowder. Dad used to say that fish was brain food. Since I was busy with the screenplay, I put out an illegal setline in the river next to the cabin, already cheating on the process. I tended to ignore the writing, rechecking my setline every fifteen minutes or so, the first I had used since my youth. In fact I became childish, imagining that the salt pork, potatoes, onion, and cream were lying in wait for the fish.

Finally, late in the afternoon, the line was headed upstream rather than downstream where I had tossed it. I began to draw it in, then discovered that, though indeed I had a fish on, the fish had wrapped the line around some sunken alder branches. I scrambled back up the bank and put on my waders. Unfortunately, when I stepped in the river, the water came a full foot above my waders and the current swept my feet out from under me. I howled in shock— there was still some snow in the woods, and the water was very cold— and hauled myself out on a log. Now I was, frankly, pissed off. I grabbed the line and jerked mightily, launching both broken branch and fish into the air, where the fish parted from the hook. I lunged back into the river, grabbing at the stunned fish. She glanced at me a moment, recovered her senses, and sped off. For some reason I'm sure it was a female.

I changed clothes and headed to town for some beverages, re-membering a line from Stephen Mitchell's fine translation of the *Tao Te Ching*:

I am different from ordinary people.
I drink from the Great Mother's breasts.

1989

THE TUGBOATS
OF COSTA RICA

Many of us like to think we own some unappreciated talent, modestly concealed and perhaps lacking the urgency to rise toward the light. Youngsters playing catch on the lawn make elaborate movements, hoping that the passing green '49 De Soto contains a pro scout who might take notice, even at this early age. It is said that Henry Kravis, the fabled Wall Street predator, can pick up a coin without bending over.

While I have the gravest doubts about the durability of any of my writing, few can beat me at the graceful dance of knife, fork, and spoon across the plate or the capacity to make a pickle last as long as a sandwich. I have thought of rigging tiny lights to my eating utensils and getting myself filmed while eating in the near dark: imagine, if you will, the dancelike swirl of these points of light. Stills of this film will be published in *Life*, a White House invite in the offing. Just last evening in my cabin the performance took place over a humble, reduced-calorie Tuscan stew (very lean Muscovy duck, pancetta, white beans, copious garlic, fresh sage, and thyme). Since I was alone in the twilight, the applause rang a bit hollow.

To be sure, our limitations strangle us, letting us know who we are. On a semireligious level, normally we have a secret animal we favor but this is dangerous territory. Never tell a government official your secret animal, for it will one day be used against you. On a more mundane plateau, if you were a boat, what kind of boat would you be? You must be honest as I can't interrogate you, what with each of us being alone. No dream boats, grand sloops, ghostly galleons, if you please. As for me, and I'm doing the writing here, I have long confessed to being a tugboat: slow, rather stubby, persistent, functional, an estuarine creature that avoids open water. It would be immodest

to mention the vast engines and power of these boats, their oversized
fuel needs, their ability to shove around immense ocean liners and
freighters.

This is all prefatory to my irritation lately on being asked if I
was a good fly-fisherman. I had just returned from a trip to Costa Rica
with the painter Russell Chatham and the sportsman Guy de la
Valdene, where we were fly-fishing for billfish up in Guanacaste Prov-
ince on the Pacific. A little of my testiness might have been caused
by coming home with garden-variety dysentery and a skin rash that
turned my entire torso into a pizza. The consolation is that dysentery is a grand leap forward on a brand-new diet, though Chatham
noted that the connection between his dysentery and diet was like
pitching a shuffleboard puck off a cruise ship. I shall never forget his
pathetic yelp in the night as he pooped his bed during a feverish dream
about trying to eat a giant Mindanao clam that wouldn't stop moving. This artist is a walking field day for a psychotherapist's conven-
tion. My skin rash, incidentally, left doctors helpless, but I cured it
myself with a slush devised out of baking soda and Epsom salts, patent
pending.

Russell and I questioned why Guy remained disease-free, but
then it occurred to us that he no longer eats his way through a menu
merely out of curiosity. He also has an incipient hiatal hernia, which
excludes gluttony as a profession. We wished him an attractive middle
age at La Cascada outside of San José, a fabulous place with good wine
and an array of fresh seafood and beef. For some reason (I drew a blank
on repeated inquiries), Costa Rican beef is exquisitely flavorful,
though very lean. It tastes like the best beef of your childhood, before the advent of short-cut packing, feed lots, chemicals, and no
aging.

But to address my irritation about whether I'm good at fly-
fishing: why bother if you haven't taken the time to learn to make
the throw? Beyond that point, any spirit of competition in hunting
or fishing dishonors the prey. It means that you are either unaware
of or have no feeling toward the nature of your fellow creatures. Fishing tournaments seem a little like playing tennis with living balls,

say, neatly bound bluebirds. Competition also engenders anger, and there's little point in being out in the forest, in a river, or on the ocean if you're going to be pissed off. A number of years ago a friend was angry and shot a raven, and his life hasn't been the same since. Of course religious beliefs vary deeply but even Kravis doesn't have enough money to get me to shoot a raven.

It just occurs to me that I shouldn't tell you where we went fishing in Costa Rica. There's no travel writer's obligation here. Find your own place. The location isn't lacking in business, and I'd hate to return and find the place mobbed. Anyhow, there are certain disadvantages: the charter plane from San José had no workable gauges, and the land beneath the plane, a lovely green hell, lacked landing strips. Just hills and gorges. There were scorpions on the path from the marina and restaurant to the hotel, shaking their malevolent asses at seaweary drunks. We did miss the bandied-about march of tarantulas. Our presiding captain had a softball-size, pitch-black sore on his arm from a "little spider" he'd rolled over on in his sleep. Our wonderful captain of the last day, a surgeon who took early retirement from the frenzy of the States, said that the occasional missing arms and feet in surrounding villages were the work of the fer-de-lance, an aggressive viper. To me this added to the fabulous beauty of the place, the green mountains meeting the blue sea, the deserted beaches, the hundred-acre schools of spotted dolphin, the 333 green parrots sitting in a shoreline tree above an immense green marine iguana sunning on a rock. The location is doubtless safer than crossing Lexington on Seventy-second, or turning left on Laurel Canyon off Sunset Boulevard.

Modest dangers make one attentive, while extreme danger can explode the equilibrium, sometimes permanently, as we see in certain Vietnam veterans. When your engines quit far out at sea, you become a great deal more conscious of the immensity of the ocean. But then you have a ship-to-shore radio, though this is scarcely foolproof. One afternoon we monitored a Mayday from another charter boat. It had broken a shaft, lost a propeller, and couldn't offer a navigational fix for rescue craft! Moreover, the current was drifting the boat toward Nicaraguan waters. Our Spanish captain assured us that the latter wasn't significant, because the two countries aren't hostile. Looking north across the expanse of water, I found it difficult to feel the threat of this country, which, as William Greider pointed out, owns only two workable elevators. Perhaps the Russian atomic subs cruising the Jersey waters are more important. Perhaps the Nicaraguan threat was a red herring to cover up the massive savings-and-loan swindle, the HUD pillaging, the Pentagon procurement scandal, the eight solid years of ignoring the environment. Locally, the Japanese long liners and drift netters, surely the pigs of the ocean, are a graver threat than Nicaraguans. For some reason our country tends to ignore the needs of Costa Rica, the only viable democracy between Texas and Antarctica.

I'm feeling a little squirrely of late, so I just went outside my cabin and had my daily squawking confab with a raven. I asked him (or her) why ladies tend to ignore me as if I were wearing a janitor's uniform with "Fred" on the pocket. In Costa Rica the ladies are un-rivaled except for those in Brazil. The three of us looked at them from afar, like Dan Quayle, having discovered that adding vowels to the ends of English words did not constitute passable Spanish. It all served to draw me back to the humiliation of college French when the pro-fessor told me I would have to learn English first.

The purpose of my trip, however, was to fly-fish for billfish, which might be called stunt fishing. I had done it a decade before in Ecuador, where the current run of striped marlin had proved unman-ageable. In Costa Rica we hooked some Pacific sailfish, and for an hour I fought one that was more than 150 pounds. The excitement is intense when fish are rising to the baits, which are large rubber squid. You tease the fish with the squid, and when the fish are prop-erly turned on you stop the boat and fly cast. It sounds quite ordinary but several times the fish in question were blue and black marlin weighing in excess of five hundred pounds, bigger around than an oil barrel and more than ten feet long. The blue marlin in particular seems to live in a state of perpetual anger. I watched from the flying bridge as an enormous blue slashed at the baits, half out of the water, then took de la Valdene's streamer fly, thrashing his head and breaking the line. Marlin flash iridescent blue and green when they attack a bait, startlingly beautiful against the darker water. Our surgeon-captain told me he has seen spotted dolphin bump marlin away from baited hooks, which is something to think over.

Curiously, our most pathetic meal on the coast was also our best. Hubert and Agnes, the proprietors of the Amberes Restaurant, had prepared on our request a bourride, a fish stew made up of a variety of the fresh local catch and shellfish. It was pathetic because Agnes was doctoring Chatham's dysentery and allowed him only plain rice with a ginger ale on the side. He glowered, beet red from the sun and fever and in pain from boating a fish while aching with a bad back, fighting the sailfish hunched over like a nautical Quasimodo. I expressed my sympathy by losing a lot of money at the casino.

Tonight I'm dealing with the raven's advice or my interpretation, which was "learn to fly." To give strength to my primaries and pinions I'm steaming a smallish chicken (a noble flier) on a bed of mushrooms, eggplant, green and red peppers, scallions, a few sprigs of tarragon, a pinch of lemon zest, and a couple of heads of garlic. Peasants somewhere surely eat this simple dish. I don't know, as I've recently banned cookbooks at my cabin as a diet measure. The dish proved to be quite delicious. If you're serving two, add another chicken. The only off note is that I found myself brooding about what could be called the Challenge of the Fava. Tomorrow, for the first time, I would be cooking dried fava beans. The adventure in the air was tempered by the notion that there were no cookbooks at hand.

Addendum

I've retitled the event Fava Nightmare. When I precooked the husky beans there was a decidedly barnyard odor pervading the cabin, yet there are no barns within thirty miles. A sign outside the tiny village five miles down the road announces NATURE IN ABUNDANCE as if the natural world were a successful civic project, along with raging garbage fires at the dump. Frankly, I checked my shoes to see if I had stepped in something, but it was becoming clear the odor had emerged

from the boiling favas. I concocted a casserole using fresh pork
sausage made by the Mennonites down in Seney, onions, shredded
cabbage, a jalapeño, two tomatoes, garlic, two eggs, some Sicilian
cheese.

Jeezo-peezo, but it was awful. There was no way to pick out the
wonderful Mennonite sausage from the general decrepitude. I had the
hunger of a lumberjack but not the bravery. I thought long and hard
about who I could wish it on. It was the kind of casserole favored by
married college graduate students, those who prefer any kind of ethnic nastiness over the heartland's bounty. They would eat it with pink
zinfandel, a contemptible wine. After dinner they'd go to a French
movie at an art theatre, and after the movie they'd chat about their
dreams of going to Paris and learning mime at the feet of a mime
master. Their first public performance would be in front of the Hotel
Lotti, from which a dark brown one-eyed stranger would emerge, flail-
ing at them with a Hermès riding crop.

1989

MIDRANGE ROAD KILL

For a reason that must be specific, albeit untraceable, there is no phrase in the language that causes me more mental discomfort than "sudden weight loss." This condition, of course, presages dozens of fatal diseases that will pluck us off the earth as if there had never been any gravity, or gravy, for that matter. A psychoanalyst has helped me locate the nexus of this terror but not the particularities of the childhood trauma hidden in the mists of stateside World War II. The central images, doubtless from *Life* magazine, are the great vegetarians, Hitler and Tojo, who wished to chop off our country's head. From Buchenwald to Bataan, these two managed to make upwards of seventy million souls permanently thin and to nominally rape the consciousness of a round, brown country child. Closing my eyes all these years later, my mind can still reel off the photos of the carnage of starvation, as if my brain were a slide show manned by a speed freak. In those years we were advised daily at dinner to finish our plates because the children in Europe had nothing to eat—a warp of logic typical in parent-child control.

The child is father to the man, as Wordsworth would have it, so the time and energy I've spent avoiding sudden weight loss come as no surprise. At no time is this effort more energetic and heroic than when my system is verging on depression. Now, I've had five identifiable whoppers in my life (none in eight years), and once you get past the early stages you should turn yourself in for whatever professional help you can find or afford, because you can't truncate the process by yourself, and simply living through it makes you vulnerable to suicide. (The most elegant and intense record of an encounter with the disease was written by William Styron, in a book called *Darkness Visible*.) Beyond the early phase, the pathology of the disease establishes itself as icy, sodden, and remote, and Inertia herself becomes queen of the endless days and nights. The anguish is so palpable that an actual fractured skull would be a sweet relief, and there is a relentless temptation to kiss the Back Wall.

However, an attention to early-warning signs, and a great deal of resourcefulness, can put you in what fighter pilots call an "avoidance posture," though sometimes the causes of depression are so directly connected to the roots of life that any precaution resembles the taffy psychobabble of self-improvement schemes. As an instance, in 1956, in the winter of my eighteenth year, I lost my first love and spent my life savings—twelve hundred dollars earned at a dollar or two an hour—on a totally unsuccessful eye operation. This was money I had saved with which to run away to Paris and become a clone of Modigliani and paint, not incidentally, some naked girls. Things would certainly come to pass. Unfortunately, I chose the eye operation and got for my pain the same red-hot, rolling, sightless ball in my head that I had earned through an injury at age seven.

After the operation I lost thirty pounds and could no longer do one hundred one-arm chin-ups. Joyce, Faulkner, and Dostoyevsky further helped to make me mentally ill. In the late spring I threw the contact lens, which looked like it had been lifted out of a welder's goggles, out into a swamp and drove north in my 1947 Plymouth, with a .22 Remington and a fishing pole. The Remington was a bit ambivalent, as hunting was months away, but instead of myself I shot a grouse after sitting in a swamp for an hour or two. I roasted it clumsily, ate the parts that were cooked, then roasted what remained. Next day I caught a bunch of illegal bass and ate them with bread and salt and a six-pack of beer. The next day I drove over to the Pine River, my father's stomping grounds, and caught a limit of trout, frying them at streamside. I was thinking about shooting a deer and eating it when a call came through from a nearby farm I hadn't visited in years, saying I had a job digging footings for a construction crew. I emerged from the forest and found a pretty girl who claimed to have read an entire book. She liked to rub her bare body with flowers. We'd be the only whites eating chicken and ribs at a black barbecue. I dug holes with vigor and looked at the full moon through the crack of her butt, framing it just so. I regained those thirty vital pounds lost to the sucking chest wound that is depression.

Thinking about the experience more than thirty years later it occurred to me that I had inadvertently surprised myself. I had run off to the woods as I had done after the initial injury, and I've more or less stayed all my life. In Gerald Vizenor's terms, the woods are my "panic hole," a Chippewa Trickster term. Later in life my own primal cause of depression became atrophication of the senses by dint of routine. Routine and habits are essential and productive to a writer, comforting as long as they work as mimetic devices, but then one day the elevator cable begins to fray, or the shaft is totally empty, and on the bottom lie piles of the white bones of writers who didn't know that they had to destroy the routine or die.

When entering a depression you become a consensus human, a herd creature going through the motions that the wolves, the interior predators, can spot a mile away. You go through the motions of consensus: eating food from consensus cookbooks and restaurants; imbibing consensus beliefs, and knowledge from consensus newspapers and magazines; feeling consensus feelings offered by consensus television, music, and drama, and reading poetry, fiction, and nonfiction from consensus publishers. You have become the perfect midrange road kill. You are suffocating in lint. The nervous laughter that was occasioned by Divine's eating dog shit in *Pink Flamingos* was caused by the shock of recognition.

You shouldn't read another word if you think you're going to get some free advice. Over the years my advice has been a contributing factor in at least a half-dozen suicides. Seriously. Now I am limiting my wisdom to food and, occasionally, the connection between food, sex, and depression, in hopes of saving millions of lives.

There is a poignant anecdote here under the category of the wisdom of the weird. In the late seventies I visited a friend on a movie set in a canyon near Trancas, in western Malibu. The movie being shot was a soft-core porn / nature feature called *The Legend of the Myna Bird*, which eventually did well in Ireland and Western Australia.

My friend the director was coked up and kept sending the naked star-
let up a steep arroyo on a dead run, through eleven takes, until a break
was called because she had developed exertion blotches. Her boy-
friend had been on a rice rampage, his eyes crusty in the corners from
vitamin A deprivation. He was selling Humboldt County weed and
a homemade Kama Sutra lotion that smelled like fish oil and badly
burned onions. He pointed at his girlfriend, whose blotches I was
watching disappear, and said, "For every top there is a bottom. She
must eat. She must make love." It occurred to me later that he was
also hustling the lady, but the wide blue Pacific to the west beckoned.
In short, I had to get out of there, and I filed the information under
the wisdom of California.

Despite our cultural snobbism, we are all not unlike our lady of
the disappearing blotches, though she was far more attractive than
most of us. Eat and love, to be sure, but you better eat first. And if
you are verging on depression and you wish your loins to stir mightily, be careful about what you eat. Don't, for instance, head into a
big platter of *choucroute garnie*, a heap of wurst, bacon, pig hocks, and
sauerkraut, since this meal will make you feel bumpy and murderous.
You are suited only for a fistfight or a Big Ten pep rally, or maybe for
driving your car into a fire hydrant or an abortion center, but not for
a lifting of spirits and the sacred act of love. I'm not talking about
the garden-variety smut machinations pushed on us by the media,
but the collision of Heathcliff and Catherine on the moors, Zhivago
and Lara in the frozen attic, or even Ava Gardner and a bullfighter.

The initial suggestions are obvious: tripe in any form; oysters raw
or roasted with shallots, butter, and cayenne; clams raw or *alle vongole*;
sweetbreads in any form; the New Iberian rendition of "dirty rice" with
an adequate amount of gizzard; squid in any form except the Japanese,
which is too self-conscious and can cause performance difficulties.
An ample mixed grill is a mistake unless you are Sean Connery or
Winston Churchill, though grilled kidneys or *rognons de veau à la
moutarde* are fine.

Far be it from me to say that women are the more glandular sex,
but for some reason the cookbooks written by women are a better di-

rection for those in this condition: Paula Wolfert, Diana Kennedy, Patience Gray, Mireille Johnston, Elizabeth David, Alice Waters, and Marcella Hazan come to mind. For instance, Hazan's *bollito misto* with picante sauce will enrage your privates, while the fabled *feijoada* of Brazil will put you to sleep unless you dance until dawn. Don't roast a whole lamb punctured with a hundred cloves of garlic, rubbed with olive oil, and stuffed with a thatch of fresh thyme over a wood fire, because it is too dramatic. A simple marinated rabbit grilled over the same fire with veal sausage, however, will destroy sexual torpor. The fat lady in the rum ads will stir your weenie after this meal.

Less than a decade ago, in the middle of January, I was in bad shape. Professional help had been rejected, but my wife had alerted a country friend. When he arrived I was standing out in our pasture; a white hat of snow had gathered on my head. He waved an enormous bird in front of my face, and, though I had tunnel vision, it was clearly recognizable as a wild turkey, the finest table bird on earth. We walked gravely toward the house, plucking the bird as we made our way through the snowdrifts. He said he had hit the bird accidentally with his car, but when we finished plucking I saw the neat dark hole of a .22 bullet. He had broken the law for his friend! (These birds are ineffably better in the North, where they feed on acorns.) We roasted the beauty, and by the time it was done I could see the entire kitchen and my beloved family and friends. We drank my last two magnums of Margaux, remnants of the vile but prosperous times that had sent me into the pasture. I am not sure I awoke the next morning as a bearded gobbler, but I was on the road back.

1990

THE PANIC HOLE

I am on the road for reasons unshared by Kerouac and Kuralt, Charlie Starkweather and William Least Heat Moon. A movie, *Revenge*, that I had had a modest part in by writing the novella and a few drafts of the script, was on the eve of coming out, and I felt raw, exhausted, and, worst of all, vulnerable. What is thought of as success meant only that absolute strangers bothered you in restaurants or on the street in resort towns. Success tends to make you think backward, where you rehearse the steps that brought you the check, an event that caused good feelings at the time. People use cocaine to feel successful, which means there are dubious aspects to the emotion. Anyway, I was feeling put-upon, a close second to self-pity as a destructive state. On the way home from the bar I suddenly wanted to drive a Butternut Bread truck and eat a hasty meal of fish sticks and coleslaw before going bowling.

So I got out of town. One of my favorite authors, Gerald Vizenor, said that "the present is a wild season, not a ruse." As you get older it occurs to you that "the present" is in increasingly short supply. The virtue of spending a couple of weeks stuck in a dentist's chair is less apparent than it used to be. The notion of "taking your medicine" like a sick dog poised before the phone is morose and Calvinistic when all you have to do is disappear. "Vamoose. Sayonara, motherfucker," as we used to say in high school. Man is not an answering machine.

Vizenor developed a saving idea called a panic hole in his novel *The Trickster of Liberty*. *Panic hole* is self-defined as a place where you go, physically or mentally or both, when the life is being squeezed out of you or when you think it is, which is the same thing. A panic hole is where you flee to get back the present as a wild season rather than a ruse. For the time being, my panic hole is an enormous red

Toyota Land Cruiser. A mile from my house, which has a bull's-eye painted on its roof, I felt a whole lot better, the oppressiveness slipping out the window and discoloring the 185 inches of snow we had received thus far.

For reasons that are obtuse, perhaps genetic, I headed even farther north than my own frozen landscape. White snow and black trees are soothing and more anguish-absorbent than the obvious tropics, where the foreign heat bubbles your skin and brain. The tropics tend to distract you rather than empty you out. In the north it can be a really big day when you see three crows. And there are times when three crows more than equal a girl in a bikini, the Gulf Stream, and conch fritters.

Curiously, my first stop was Escanaba, at the House of Ludington, where I began my food column two years ago. I succeeded in not thinking about the time in between by using a few mail-order secrets on how to give up your name. After twelve hours of sleep I took a long dawn walk far out on the ice, where I glassed three ravens feeding on a fish. What luck! I lay on the ice to make myself less obtrusive and listened to the vast nothingness of Lake Michigan beneath two feet of ice. The landscape was empty except for the lump of me and three ravens watching one another across a hundred yards of blinding white.

This sort of epiphany goads an appetite savaged by sixteen months of work. Other than during bird season I had become so picky that I had lost a few pounds. At the hotel's Sunday brunch, I got a "tsk-tsk" from the waitress when I failed to polish off the plate of fruit and basket of breads, the platter of eggs, bacon, ham, roast beef hash, and chicken livers, accompanied by another platter of roast beef, fish, chicken, and vegetables followed by an assortment of desserts, including a whipped-cream-stuffed pastry swan. My error was in reading during the meal—Bernd Heinrich's *Ravens in Winter*, from which I learned that in the late forties in Illinois a hundred million crows were destroyed in a single night by hand grenades. This was the American version of Cortés burning the aviaries of Montezuma, and it put me off my feed.

My spirits were revived at the Chippewa midwinter powwow that afternoon. On entering, I watched a very old man dancing in a full bearskin cape, his skull encased in the bear's head. He gracefully shook his war club at the gymnasium ceiling. A little later, fifty young girls in Native costume did the crow dance so convincingly that I shivered, then, not surprisingly, wept. One day out and I was getting a long way from show business.

The next morning before I left I called the Swedish Pantry to check on its soups. "We always have the same soups," I was advised, the phone voice informed with what passes for mystery among the Swedes. It was, however, the best pea soup I had ever eaten, and, accompanied by *limpa* bread and a side of herring, it was a fine load of fuel for the drive to Appleton, Wisconsin, where I visited my daughter at her college. That evening a peculiar thing happened at a restaurant with the equally peculiar name of Hobnobbin'. The gizmo used to clamp an escargot backfired and shot the snail directly into my chest, spraying its freight of garlic-laden butter all over my expensive suede sport coat. For some reason I thought this was very funny. Normally I wouldn't think this was very funny. I had a fine chat with my daughter and went on to eat an enormous slab of heart-smart rare roast beef, something I rarely order but found utterly delicious in this fine restaurant.

There were moments of backsliding in the Midway Motor Lodge in La Crosse, Wisconsin, quarters I shared with a group called the Young Farmers and another named the Tri-County Breeders (presumably cattle). A phone call, naturally, told me that the fish-wrap technocrats of the movie arts didn't care for *Revenge*. Sad that they'll never realize their fond dreams of being slammed in the butt by Don Johnson's speedboat, I thought, and went for a long walk during which I saw three bald eagles feeding on dead shad in the partially frozen Mississippi River. This was not a "sign" of anything except that the bald eagles were hungry.

That evening I dined on pork and beef ribs at Piggy's in downtown La Crosse on the river, a restaurant that had recently won the National Pork Producers Restaurant of the Year Award, no mean feat.

The ribs were well cooked and the locally brewed Heileman's Export was delicious, though I am not a beer drinker. Piggy's should add a hot sauce as an alternative to its regular offering. My dinner was disturbed by the gradual evolution of an idea, the pinpointing of a grave threat to America. I slept on the idea under the notion that it was not yet ready for the man on the street.

The next morning, at the beginning of my long drive to Lincoln, Nebraska, I could not contain myself and delivered a speech through the windshield to the subzero landscape: "Who *are* these WASP eco-yuppies? They are afraid of blacks and ignore them. They think Native Americans are hopelessly messy. They scorn all cowboys, hate ranchers, loathe hunters, fishermen, and trappers (I agree on this one), won't eat beef or pork or drink hard liquor. These folks are thinking about their lifestyles and missing the point: the bitterest of struggles against business, industry, and government, which are using the environment, as always, as a cheap toilet. The struggle is against a nation that will always spit in its grandchildren's faces for immediate profit. As Vizenor would say, "Their Mother Earth is a blonde."

In Lincoln I checked into the Cornhusker Hotel, another of my panic holes. They know what they're doing at the Cornhusker and they mean to be normal, with food and service nearly the equivalent of those in a deluxe hotel in New York for less than one-third the price. But then one of the main reasons I like Lincoln is that it is not Manhattan. On your first visit you will sense a haunting boredom that, on following trips, you will recognize as Life herself without rabid hype. In Lincoln I eat relentlessly at the Bistro, where there is a surcharge of thirty-five cents if you want a Caesar salad rather than a tossed salad. At lunch I have red beans and rice the equal of any of the dozen versions I've had in New Orleans. At dinner I enjoy the spinach gnocchi and Italian sausage. One night for dinner, John Carter, a folklorist and historian, took me to the Steakhouse, where we had a delicate appetizer of several pounds of fried chicken gizzards followed by wonderful porterhouses and Geyser Peak Cabernet. During the day I looked at nineteenth-century photographs at the Nebraska State Historical Society.

After four days at the Cornhusker I've become prelapsarian Adam and am ready for a slow drive home by the identical route. I want to see the same landscape from the opposite direction. At dawn I do the same thing I've done for years, a not so banal trick I learned from the Navajo. You bow deeply to the six directions. That way you know where you are on earth—at least for the time being. Much earlier in this century an Austrian journalist, Karl Kraus, pointed out that if you actually perceived the true reality behind the news you would run, screaming, into the streets. I have run screaming into the streets dozens of times but have always managed to return home in time for dinner—and usually an hour early so that I can help in the preparation.

A few weeks ago, while preparing roast quail stuffed with leeks and sweetbreads (served on a polenta pancake with a heavily truffled woodcock sauce), I realized that it was far too late for me to cooperate politically or artistically with a modern sensibility that so apparently demands the cutest forms of science fiction for its soul food. After dinner I floundered in the drifts, looking at the full moon up through the blizzard. The moon had somehow ignored the destruction of the middle class, the most recent fall of Europe, the Trump split, and the release of dozens of movies and books. It was the same moon I had rowed toward in a wooden boat as a child, my dog and a pet crow on the backseat facing me. This winter moon was a cold but splendid comfort.

1990

PIGGIES COME
TO MARKET

Betimes, when I awake at dawn or a few hours thereafter, I must remind myself that I am not a coal miner or even the farm laborer I was in my youth. I no longer work twelve hours a day to take home fifteen bucks. What happened to my battered tin lunch bucket, where I stored my dreams of New York City and the beautiful girls who looked as if they changed their underwear every single day? What does it mean that this year I will make forty times what my dad did his best year? He doesn't mind up in heaven, but for some reason I do. In such somber moods I glance in the mirror and I don't see Mother Teresa. In such moods I am infected by the disease of social conscience brought about by my youthful forays into civil rights and the reading of Eugene Debs, Thorstein Veblen, Frantz Fanon, and others. Nowadays a social conscience is a disease you can purportedly cure by sending off a check for the rain forest.

Don't for an instant believe that I'm going to chug along on this banal train of thought, certainly a nexus of regret many of us are familiar with, particularly those who never expected to be successful in financial terms. There is also a specific danger in manufacturing, like William Buckley, a social and philosophical system to justify your prosperity. Life gets used up damned fast by the exhaustion of peripheries. Besides, I have proved repeatedly that I have no gifts for rational discourse, no gifts outside the immediate confines of the imagination. A number of years ago, at a rancorous public meeting, I said, "In the wrong hands even a container of yogurt can be a fatal weapon." Perhaps it was an acid flashback.

It was only last evening, while I was working on a screenplay with, of all things, the Academy Awards on the tube in the background, that I identified the malaise. It was the painful rejuvenes-

cence of March, the brutality of a northern spring, when the song-
bird that was celebrating sixty degrees one day flops in its death throes
at ten below under a cedar tree the next morning. This year a group
of mallards had their feet frozen to a pond's surface, and now a bald
eagle busies himself swooping in and tearing off their heads. Rages
and pleasures mix themselves in this spring stew. Last week, a dear
friend in a tequila rage shot himself in the parking lot of a bar. My
beloved and saintly glutton of a Labrador must have her ulcerated
left eye removed. Now we will be blind on the same side. Perhaps
while we are hunting next fall, if she makes it, we will run into the
same tree in the woods. When I was a boy my left side was always
bruised.

Of course, an older fool should be able to counter the emotional
claymores brought about by the change of seasons and the pummel-
ing of fortune's spiky wheel. The first move is to question whether
certain of my grand assumptions about life have turned cheesey. Perhaps it is time to take down the motto from Deshimaru pinned to
the wall above my desk: "You must concentrate upon and consecrate
yourself wholly to each day, as though a fire were raging in your hair."
Perhaps this coda I so devoutly try to follow is allowing insufficient
oxygen? This Oriental ruthlessness may be inappropriate unless you
work for Sony, which in fact I do, via Columbia Pictures, come to
think of it.

Naturally, this foment has had a negative effect on my cooking.
A few weeks ago, passing through my grocer's, I bought a packet of
dehydrated French's pork gravy. The label noted that this gravy was
award-winning. Since I have never won an award, who am I to question this gravy? Tom Wolfe probably won an award for *Campfire of
the Banalities,* so he doesn't have to try this gravy. I can't recommend
it, even with the addition of garlic. My wife, Linda, watched quizzi-
cally from the far side of the kitchen.

No lessons were learned. Two days later I felt another rage for
normalcy and bought two cans of Hormel chili (one with beans, one
pure "meat") and a copy of *People* magazine. After this luncheon mud

bath I actually burst into tears, then walked exactly eleven miles to purge the whole experience. That evening, after a classic French-roasted capon, I trashed my notes (seriously) for a somewhat scholarly essay I had intended to write, to be called "Brain Vomiters: The Twilight of the American Novel."

Things were plainly getting out of hand. One warm morning, before it snowed again, I yelled at the birds in the barnyard because they were too noisy. I stopped cooking altogether. Linda tempted me with fine new dishes made according to the recently published *Monet's Table*. They were splendid, but I could not eat the accustomed quantity, and I began to shed ounces. Then pounds dropped off. Contrary to most folks I have to eat *real* big to stay big. The most destructive force in my life tends to be the unwritten poem, but despite my best efforts I was stropheless, except for my first epitaph: All Piggies Must, Finally, Come to Market.

There was the possibility that I had been sucker punched by a dangerous fad last year. In an effort to shape up for bird season, I had begun to eat a nasty, fibrous cereal for breakfast. It was something to be endured, like a theater line. Not that I wanted bacon and eggs, another nasty fad that had its inception in the dizzy thinking that followed shortly after World War I. But in my heart I knew I'd rather eat the cow than the oats the cow eats.

This notion prompted a rage at the nitwits on the National Beef Council and their sniveling ads. Why don't they say you can have your beef if you give up all that fat-laden junk food, tasteless domestic cheeses, and ersatz French desserts. A T-bone has to be better for you than the $28 sea-urchin custard that is all the current rage in Gotham. Mind you, I have eaten versions of this dish in Paris and its alter ego, Los Angeles, and wouldn't feed it to Donald Trump, Tom Wolfe, or Hitler's daughter, Gretchen, who may also work for Sony.

Naturally, I rushed out and bought a largish Delmonico for brunch, but a watery pink fluid came out at first cut. What the fuck! I ate it anyway and dreamt of the fine steaks I used to eat in New York at Bruno's, Pen & Pencil, the Palm, and Gallagher's, or the sirloin at

Elaine's before which you eat mussels and then spinach as a side to the meat. Florentine wines are better with steak than those of Bordeaux or Burgundy.

Beef is pleasure food, and we deserve pleasure because we live nasty, brutish lives. In ten days I'll be in Valentine, Nebraska, where I'll eat a thirty-two-ounce aged porterhouse with two bottles of Cabernet because there's no Barolo in Valentine. The following morning I will take a four-hour walk in the unfathomably beautiful Sand Hills and count meadowlarks. I predict my cholesterol count will not rise above its current 147, the same number of meadowlarks I'll see.

My disease of consciousness was somewhat alleviated by a week's trip with my wife and youngest daughter to Boca Grande, on the west coast of Florida. Boca Grande is lovely, safe, and sedate, and no one there is likely to slip you a manuscript or borrow money. I went sailing and bird watching with my old friend Tom McGuane, who is a part-time resident (so much for our shared reputation as rounders). Oddly, we saw only three birds on the wilderness island of Cayo Costa. How could this be, we wondered, the unused binoculars flapping on our chests. Then we noticed there were a lot of birds walking around on the ground just like us. We presumed they were feeding. On close inspection some of the birds were brown, and so were others. They were clearly, we decided, critic birds.

On the way home there was another pratfall after a pleasantly lavish night in Chicago at a hotel called 21 East, recently changed to Le Meridien. The dining room is among the three or four great restaurants in that city. Unfortunately, the next morning, after riding to O'Hare in one of the hotel's fleet of 750 BMWs, I watched a family of six poor folk there to pick up Grandma (I was listening). I was eating an expensive breakfast hot dog, which they decided against for financial reasons. I computed that hot dogs and soft drinks for this family of six would come to just over twenty-seven bucks. Anytime a hot dog approaches an hour at minimum-wage work, the state is in peril. My scalp prickled in shame for my sad country, its veins swollen with the pus of greed and dark scorn for the poor.

I also wondered about the eight hundred bucks I had spent in the last twenty-four hours. I could barely finish my hot dog but did, because I was thinking how in the past nine years the Republicans, with the dithering cooperation of the shamelessly class-conscious media, had isolated the bottom one-third of our population as social mutants. Frankly, this is unchristian and these assholes better pay for it in hell, since they are doing quite comfortably on earth.

Back to the Academy Awards and the shrill evidence of an extreme black phobia in Beverly Hills. Spike Lee and Ed Zwick don't drive Miss Daisy. Afterward, I watched an intriguing video, rented at a convenience store, called *Cheerleader Camp,* starring Lucinda Dickey. These gals looked real good until they started killing one another. Blood is antierotic except in a steak. I was reminded of Eric von Stroheim's description of his life as "a symphony of disappointments." I was also reminded of hot dogs and the questions, How can a modestly prosperous writer cast his spiritual lot with the social mutants?

In a few days I am beginning an utterly irrational ten-thousand-mile car trip. I am going to look at a secret half-man and half-wolf petroglyph in Utah. After all, Thoreau said it is in "wildness" (not wilderness) that we find our preservation.

1990

THE FAST

Throughout the long night I ate nothing. The fast had begun early the evening before, after a bowl of Brazilian salt-cod chowder with a wedge of corn bread and a large glass of cold water. The meal was a bit simpleminded for so auspicious an event—auspicious at least to me—and I was the one going without food, not you, gentle reader, with your vibrant nightmares of self-indulgence.

But why was I fasting alone in my cabin, thirty-seven degrees in early July with a fifty-knot gale blowing north-northwest off Lake Superior? What's the point of fasting when no one is there to admire you—the same problem, in fact, in being a spy when you can't tell anyone you're a spy? Many years ago in Key West, when I was a private detective, I'd have a few drinks in a saloon and admit to strangers that I was a private detective, which somewhat decreased my effectiveness. Word gets around via the coconut telegraph in that city of sucking head and chest wounds.

Frankly, I was fasting for wisdom. A career change was imminent and I was in transition. (In case you don't know, and you probably don't, in traditional cultures one fasts for wisdom at such junctures.) During the past week I had walked seven miles a day in the undistinguished, slovenly wilderness of the Upper Peninsula. It was only wilderness by default, because no one could make another buck out of the depleted land, the enormous white-pine stumps forming their own ghost forest.

That morning I had mentally taken myself out of contention for the presidency of Harvard. There were no sandhill cranes in Cambridge, and they were my current obsession, along with other birds, bears, coyotes, and wolves, all quite scarce in the Boston area. Harvard would have to get along without my leadership as it entered the next millennium maintaining its casual, aristocratic pout. My obvious sacrifice was the stewed tripe at Locke-Ober's, the flavors married dizzily to a bottle or two of La Tache, certainly a power lunch, especially if taken solo.

The hungry night found me caught in the lateral career change from writer to amateur naturalist. Life is short and money buys so little. I felt depleted beyond reason, burned out to the point that I could actually hear the unearthly screams of the butchered piglet within me, and no animal's cries were more anguished in my forty-year-old barnyard memories. I could not balance the idea that, while the exposed heart is richest in feeling, there is a point at which it never recovers. The merest news item of another child beaten to death would occasion tears. And the princelings of the evil empire in Washington had burned five hundred billion flags in the savings-and-loan swindle, leaving not a sou to help the so-called social mutants, the poor and homeless, the Chicanos, blacks, and Native Americans. These princelings were the same shitbirds of greed cutting down six-hundred-year-old trees on public land while reassuring us they were replanting; now if we could hang in there six hundred years the forest would again have grand trees. The only soothing fantasy was that a million-strong lynch mob would invade Washington to terminate a political life that had become a paradigm of child pornography.

Of course this sort of maudlin bullshit, the furious introspection we are prey to when society runs amok, covered a deeper unrest that I had revealed to myself in a naive sentence in a novel, to the effect that we are all, in totality, what we wish to be, barring unfortunate circumstances. And I no longer wanted to be a writer; I wanted to become an amateur naturalist.

The dominant question on the eve of this rebirthing was: "What does an amateur naturalist eat?" For starters, nothing; hence the fast. Writing is such a sedentary profession that I had become a tad burly, and to whirl through the forest with my single eye cocked on the flora and fauna, I needed to be light of foot. But then there were the contrasting styles of two friends who are naturalists, Peter Matthiessen and Doug Peacock. Matthiessen is rail lean from such small numbers as walking across East Africa or hauling fifty-pound bags of rice over nineteen-thousand-foot passes on the Tibetan Plateau of Nepal. In *The Snow Leopard*, he unfortunately neglects to mention what spices and condiments were used to prepare this rice. Peacock is decidedly chunky but owns a pair of legs somewhere between Arnold Schwarzenegger's and Herschel Walker's, the result of twenty years of tracking grizzlies and neurotic twelve-day forced marches through the desert, the working theory being, When you are out of sorts walk a hundred miles.

On a recent trek into Utah to look for petroglyphs, Peacook and I had, I thought, eaten rather poorly, concentrating on a big bag of *tsampa* that Yvon Chouinard, the famed mountaineer, had prepared for us. *Tsampa*, Tibetan in origin, is a mixture of grains, tasting something like the mixed sweepings off a granary floor, despite the addition of hot peppers. *Tsampa* swells up in your gut and displaces any interest in women, whiskey, cigarettes, or foie gras, and it quickly turned us into rambling eco-dopes in the vast canyon lands of Utah.

It was barely dark at eleven outside my cabin in the Upper Peninsula when I went out to the pump house and turned off the generator. I remembered that a sage had said, "There must be freedom before there can be freedom," and I scooted back to the cabin, hearing a pack of coyotes in chase under the howling wind. The meaning of the sage was clear enough: I had been wandering around the woods ever since my left eye was severely injured at age seven. All I had been doing recently was taking it to its proper limits, becoming more technically attentive to what I saw. I had already discovered that if you're not in a sex or food trance when you walk you can see the cranes before their enraged flush and note the change of pace in the bear tracks after it has caught your scent. You see that birds squeeze their eyes shut when they lay eggs and that the raven who answered you fifty-seven times was saying nothing in particular.

It was a very long night without my usual trip to the Dunes Saloon for a few nightcaps or the assortment of snacks that aid sleep. Might I offer myself a sprig of parsley in my cheek? No, the parsley, like marijuana, could lead to further crime. How about a large glass of red wine, which, after all, was technically fruit juice? Nope. The coyotes passed within a few feet of the window, closing in on their midnight snack, a snowshoe hare. The beasts were eating but not me; but then, raw rabbit lacked appeal.

Total sobriety and an empty stomach made for a restless, dream-filled sleep. I tended the votive fire relentlessly so that the flames would acquire the correct shape. In a weak moment I allowed myself to relive a great meal I had had recently at Lutèce (*soupe de poisson, poussin en croûte*), after which I had the privilege of shaking hands with the great chef André Soltner himself, an event that beat any experience in showbiz except for dinner years ago with Fellini, Marcello Mastroianni, Alberto Sordi, Giulietta Masina, and Anouk Aimée and her stunning daughter. You know, those folks.

At about 4:00 A.M., the vision arrived with the force of a cattle prod or lightning down the chimney. The wind had subsided and I was standing naked out on the picnic table, eyeing the three-quarter moon and trying to howl up a fresh batch of coyotes. I received a single, somewhat retarded response from down in the river delta near a den I had previously located. They were evidently done hunting for the night. I was actually hoping for a wolf, but I hadn't heard one in nearly four years, though the day before I had found a set of tracks in the drying mud of a pond's edge.

It was with this memory that the vision struck. Just before I had found the set of tracks, when I was well back from the pond, I had glassed a Hudsonian godwit, a rare shorebird. Standing naked now with my weenie shrinking from the cold, it occurred to me that, with a few notable exceptions, such as the Hudsonian godwit and the ruddy turnstone, the birds of North America needed renaming.

I shuddered at the enormity of the project. Most writers know only four birds—hawk, gull, crow, robin—and I was looking at more than six hundred species that required fresh names. I thought I'd better get started promptly, in order to finish before I kicked the bucket and my soul was hurled into the usual black hole in the cosmos. I went back in the cabin, dressed warmly, and headed east, fording a thigh-deep creek and passing a location I think of as the Place of the Bears. The area smelled dense and rank and I imagined for a moment that I was in the locker room of the Soviet ladies' Olympic team.

At dawn I named the Delphic warbler and, better yet, a smallish brown bird henceforth to be called the beige dolorosa. I dozed off under a tree and the nature of breakfast began to take shape. A nightwalker is entitled to a little wine, and there was a bottle of Barbaresco waiting. The meal itself would be a modest pasta made with three pounds of frozen squid I had brought from home. There were three tomatoes and a bouquet of fresh herbs I kept in a flower vase. A head of garlic and the somber character of Spanish olive oil would fill the bill.

As I headed home, I experienced a specific chafing problem known to many an amateur naturalist, so I had to walk splay-legged. The new project unrolled its path in glory. I had no intention of becoming a neo-Dondi/Gandhi, but by the end of this new calling I would be a small brown man in a green coat looking for brown birds. "Deep in his throat, but perhaps it is a bird, he hears a child cry," I quoted to myself, from a poem I had written at nineteen.

1990

THE RAW
AND
THE COOKED

WHAT HAVE WE DONE WITH THE THIGHS?

Where have all the thighs gone? Where are the thighs of yesteryear? This is not exactly a litany raised by many, but the heartfelt concern of a few. In recent memory I do not believe that I have entered a restaurant where thighs are allowed to stand alone proudly by themselves. I mean chicken thighs, though duck and turkey thighs are also lonely and neglected.

On a recent trip to New York via Los Angeles I tried to raise the thigh alarm in both places to showbiz folks in *au courant* restaurants.

"God, what I'd do for a plate of thighs, you know, grilled in *paillard* form with a sauce made of garlic that has been roasted with olive oil and thyme, then puréed and spread on the crisp thigh skin. Alice Waters makes them that way."

"I think that's Mike Nichols's agent," a lady answered.

"Once on safari in Brazil I ate a big platter of roasted thighs with a blazing-hot *chimichurri* pepper sauce in Bahia, then it was off to the jungle up the Rio del Muerto, where we were trying to catch a big anaconda for the new Disney theme park in North Dakota. I was lost for thirty days and ended up using duct tape for toilet paper."

"I think I saw part of it on PBS," a producer in an Armani power blazer said. "In Taos, where I met Dennis Hopper's cousin Duane. Duane Hopper. They're both from Dodge City, Kansas."

"Yeah, I've been there. The lady at the Best Western fried me three thighs for breakfast. With biscuits and pan gravy."

"Let me correct myself. That isn't Mike Nichols's agent. It's only Roger Ebert's agent. I heard R.E. just wrote a hot screenplay called *Naked Scouts on Their Birthdays*," the lady chimed in.

"I think chicken breasts are the moral equivalent of a TV commercial. I make Bocuse's *poulet au vinaigre* only with thighs," I insisted.

"The Budweiser Clydesdales are really getting dreary," she replied. "Dalmatians are cute in the snow."

"So are zebras." I watched as she ordered a poached chicken breast, insisting on flat-leafed Italian parsley on the side, as if it were intended to save this *filet de torpor*.

So I am a voice crying out in the wilderness. A casual inquiry to my brother, who runs the University of Arkansas library system in Fayetteville, and has contacts with Tyson, the world's largest producer of chicken for the table, revealed (hold on to your ass!) that they shipped 50,000 metric tons of thighs and legs to Russia in 1990! I fear I do not comprehend the mind that remains unstunned by this figure. It fatigues the brain, and deep in the forest on my daily hike I leaned against a lightning-blasted beech tree, a power spot, and imagined a thousand of these tons frozen into the shape of a prone King Kong in the hold of a giant freighter. I had gotten rid of one but had forty-nine to go. So many thighs, so many freighters.

Other notions began to spin off through the wintry air. Are we shipping our vigor, our strength, abroad? Would the ghost of D. H. Lawrence suggest that we fear thighs because of their proximity to the organs of reproduction and evacuation? Is it because we are still Mummy's children and crave the anonymous, tasteless breast? Is it a subconscious fear of AIDS? Probably not, as sixty percent of those under thirty in America have never seen a live chicken and couldn't tell a thigh from Jon Bon Jovi's chin. Once I prepared quail for an actress of some note who doubled as a vegetarian. She was appalled after dinner to discover she had eaten a "living thing."

"Not after it was shot and plucked and roasted at four hundred degrees for twenty-three minutes," I offered, suspecting Quaaludes.

Back in the forest I imagined the shark carnage that would occur if a freighter sank with such a cargo, the ship breaking up and the immense frozen blocks of chicken thighs slowly melting in the saltwater, down in the cold blackness of the sea bottom. Strangely enough in the old days in Key West I once night-fished with a Cuban for sharks with a live chicken, the big hook bound to the hen's body with twine. For reasons of squeamishness I did not hold the rod with the live chicken bait but drove the getaway car. Soon enough we were eating broiled shark steaks and tending a shark stew laden with garlic and fresh tomatoes. Much of the hen was still intact, though a bit of a mess to pluck. Not surprisingly, the shark had headed for the rear end, where the flavor resides.

I left the woods and made my way over to Hattie's Grille in Suttons Bay, my favorite restaurant in the vast expanse of northern Michigan, though there are three others that could also survive in the competitive atmosphere of Chicago, or the coasts—the Rowe Inn, Tapawingo, and the Walloon Lake Inn. Naturally there are other good places but they have largely neglected a responsibility of first-rate restaurants, which is to educate our palates. Jim Milliman is the owner and chef of Hattie's Grille, assisted by Alice Clayton, a bird-like young woman who is breathtakingly deft in the kitchen.

When I arrived during the afternoon prep work, Milliman was busy making three desserts, bread, and a pâté all at once. Then his wife, Beth, called and asked if he could whip up a white-chocolate mousse for her. He smiled and began chopping Belgian white chocolate. I poured a largish glass of Trefethen Cabernet, which is a steal, and was reminded again of the sheer speed that is demanded of the professional chef. I used to daydream of becoming one but the fantasy dissipates when reflecting on the exhaustion of preparing a dinner for ten. My own restaurant could accept only a daily party of four, at most. My hands are clumsy. I typed five novels with a single forefinger. Frankly, this limited my interest in revision.

Milliman doesn't go in for fancy names for his creations; his smoked whitefish pâté is called just that, and a lovely dish of his devising, medallions of Maine lobster in a tequila sauce, carries no frilly adjectives. He is particularly skillful with seafood—salmon, lobster ravioli, scallops, whitefish—though I enjoy his pheasant potpie, the garlicked veal chop on a wild-rice pancake, his chicken thighs braised in stock, cream, and shiitakes.

I was strangely silent sipping or gulping my wine, in hopes I would be asked what was bothering me.

"What's bothering you?" asked Milliman, who is accustomed to me in full babble about food matters.

I explained my concave and convex thigh thoughts, ranging through culinary history down to the sociopolitical implications of exclusionary food fadism, the penchant for fey minimalism in the upwardly mobile groups. I finished with, "Do you think this all stands for something bigger?"

"Absolutely," Milliman said. Then we discussed approximately a hundred good ways to cook chicken thighs, branching out into turkey thighs (I favor the nutrition nag Jane Brody's way of poaching them in vermouth with fresh vegetables and a head of garlic). For duck thighs and legs you need go no further than Paula Wolfert's *The Cooking of South-West France,* or to Madeleine Kamman. Alice Waters bones rabbit thighs and grills them with pancetta and fresh sage. I prefer my thighs with two wines I got from Waters's husband, the wine merchant Stephen Singer: any Bandol, or a Chianti called Isole.

On the way home I stopped at the grocer's for a slice of pork steak, a white-trash proclivity of mine. You pretend you're cutting off all the fat. It's the rare restaurant that offers pork steak. Doubtless it's being sent to China along with hard-to-find pig hocks. On the bulletin board in the grocery foyer someone was offering "Rabbits, Pets or Meat" on a three-by-five card.

This is a visceral world, I reflected, watching the carloads of deer hunters in bright orange milling up and down the country roads in the cold rain. I could have bought a thicker pork steak if my butcher hadn't been busy carving up deer carcasses. There would be a big kill this year, with extra permits given in lieu of extensive orchard damage. I have an orchard and couldn't shoot a deer for eating my young trees, but then I don't depend on the orchard for a living. On the rare occasion I deer-hunt I hike the vacant Lake Michigan beaches—where the deer notably aren't—to avoid shooting one. This is horribly dishonest as venison is by far my favorite meat. I'm forced to hang around local taverns with a long face, saying such things as, "If I hadn't lost my eye in the Tet Offensive [a fib] old mister swamp buck would've been deader than a doornail." Then I accelerate by asking for lesser cuts, the heart and liver, or the whole neck, including the bones, from which you can make a splendid carbonnade or *posole*. It usually works.

What we eat depends on where we live and how we have come to look at ourselves. An increasingly smaller part of our population has been raised within an age-old agricultural cycle where hunting and gathering are still a dominant, if waning, force in life. I find it disturbing to see recently all the lifestyle Nazis afoot prating about what one should drink, eat, read. Of course there is no dialogue; there never is after it becomes "news." Given a choice between the NRA and animal rights I'll choose a rowboat anytime.

In his wonderful new book of essays, *The Practice of the Wild*, Gary Snyder writes, "Our distance from the source of our food enables us to be superficially more comfortable, and distinctly more ignorant." Snyder is a Zen Buddhist, and I doubt he would condone hunting except by Native populations. The point is our "distance." I question the virtue of not knowing where your food comes from, whether it's the chicken on the conveyor belt clucking its way toward the knife, the steer waiting for the stun gun, the fish gasping in foreign air among hundreds of others. On the goofy outer edge, researchers at Yale discovered that plants react when a shrimp is killed in their presence. Of course there is nothing so immediately rewarded in America, in the arts, entertainment, or public life, as a shrill and limited consciousness.

To be Christian, or something, maybe the Russians need the thighs more than we do. Once they're dead they may as well be eaten, and for reasons involving the lack of soul we're not doing the job. I just worry that the Russians don't have the proper condiments—the fresh garlic and herbs, peppers, hot sauces, BBQ sauces, the wild mushrooms, leeks, and cream.

1991

THE DAYS OF WINE
AND PIG HOCKS

Certain modestly substantial thoughts may rise to the surface on tidal swells of enervation. During an extended period of book publication, interviews, and a nine-stop tour, all of which took nine weeks of precious life juices, I awoke in a hotel in Minneapolis quite nervous about the uneaten food one sees in the movies.

This perception began rather early, say in the late forties, in a small village in the Great North, where the local cinema charged twelve cents for those under twelve. Claude Rains or Charles Boyer would be dining in a nightclub across the table from a frilly jam tart busy making a lipstick moue. The table was laden with food, yet they would bounce to their feet to dance, leaving the food uneaten as they swirled through the tightly packed floor with nary a backward glance at dinner.

I suspect uneaten food so strongly caught my attention because there was a taboo in my family against getting up from the table before your plate was clean. Also, I did not know that movies were not constructed in continuous time. Claude or Charles and the lady with puffy shoulders might have returned unbeknownst to me and laced into the chow. I do recall that it wasn't until Tony Richardson's *Tom Jones* that we actually got to see folks eat with gusto on the screen. Naturally they ate a lot in the French and Italian films I saw in college, but not in our language. Despite the rage at the time for my distant relative, the Swedish giant Ingmar Bergman, he drew dismal last in the food stakes. I can imagine the screenplay gloss: "Leif Sturlson's yawn is anguished as he gnaws on the bread crust dampened by sea air. The Baltic rolls on in sodden fury."

Back to the hotel in Minneapolis, the Radisson Plaza, where a bronze plaque announced that Gorbachev had stopped by recently for an hour: a largish idea began to form as I ate my one-pound bran muffin—the size of a softball—with a double side order of country sausage (yin and yang). We are fond in the heartland of "farm-fresh country sausage," doubtless made in a converted warehouse on the Mississippi, for gut-flushing capabilities. I chewed at the muffin like a grief-maddened cow. Instead of all things coming together, all things were coming apart. Between me and Deborah Norville on the TV was the abyss. There was the sudden, firm resolve that I would not pass this way again. Better to stand in the dark basement behind the furnace for two months, an early form of punishment, than go on a book tour. Henceforth this hour would be known as "the muffin satori."

Now we all know that reality is consensual, and if you don't consent reality quickly dissembles. True coherence is a rare gift hard won by sages, while the rest of us live in a world stuck together by inferior glue. It occurred to me that food isn't a philosophical system or homosexuality a religion any more than heterosexuality, accumulating money, sport, literature, art, or music. Nothing is much like anything else. Nothing is a preparation for anything else. Getting over one thing does not get you ready for another. My four months in the virtual wilderness did not prepare me for a book tour; it prepared me for life in the virtual wilderness, for strolling among bear, deer, ravens, wolves, coyotes, loons. This was a reality I could consent to with my entire being, as airports lack a specific charm.

Well, "tough titty," as we used to say. In fact, that's what the coach said when my face (five bones) was shattered on the gridiron and an orthopedic surgeon had to quickly devise an aluminum mask for a game the next day. The number one murderer of writers is self-importance, as students of literary history know.

I abandoned the torpid muffin, sang "O, Freedom," and went off to the hotel gym, where I mostly looked out the window because the attendant's radio had announced that a friend of mine, Don Henley, had died in a helicopter crash leaving a concert in Wisconsin. A half hour later, when this mistake was corrected, I was glad so many people were alive. Splendidly enough, the newspaper interview at lunch was at Chez Bananas, a Caribbean soul-food place, and I had the restorative fish and black beans and rice with fresh salsa. Suddenly, the book tour didn't look bad at all. In fact, from my new vantage it held the promise of nourishment well beyond the predictable elixirs we use to rid ourselves of angst. I was anxious to finish a few meals.

If you travel a bit in this country, you know that there is no question that restaurant food in America is getting much better, well apart from the obvious triumphs of New York and L.A. After a generation of pioneers (Waters, Ogden, Forgione, Pawlcyn, Puck, et al.), a new generation of food obsessives spread from the coasts, from L.A., S.F., and N.Y.C., where there was no more room, into other cities and the hinterlands. On this trip I was especially taken by their youth, twenty to thirty-five or so, and their knowledge of French, Italian, and Oriental cuisines. Here are a few entries from my journal:

NEW YORK: Elaine's, straight from a late plane. Massive veal chop with garlic, plus double order of spinach sautéed in olive oil and garlic to acquire Popeye's strength. Bottle of Barolo and a couple of shooters of Calvados for grit. A bit turgid at 5:00 A.M. wake-up for TV show.

Left for Denver at noon with no appetite for airline lunch. Luckily Irene (Houghton Mifflin publicist) sent me off with rye bread and a container of Matjes herring, the smell of which my seatmate did not enjoy. Tough titty. Two confused days. Splendid after-reading meal at Sfuzzi, evidently a small Italian chain, with first-rate meat, produce, oil. The place smelled right! I was with a half dozen blurred people, and on the way back to the Brown Palace we somehow got trapped on the course of the Denver Grand Prix, which was to begin in the morning. Harrowing escape from the police.

Frenzied anger in Seattle, where I was put on the thirty-third floor of the Sheraton rather than the second floor of the Inn at the Market, which houses one of the best restaurants in America, Campagne. Canceled tour by phone, then read room-service menu and was intrigued by an item that announced a seven-course Japanese breakfast! Oh boy. Watched the phone ring eleven different times and dared a look out the window, only to discover I no longer had vertigo, which had been a life-long affliction. Two marvelous dinners at Campagne, including the best mussels short of the Breton coast, and a tasting of Bandols. Two fine lunches at Salute in Città, including the great restorative, *puttanesca*.

In Milwaukee a kind of sabotage had been planned in advance. Before my song and dance I was taken to a Pomeranian restaurant, Stemmeler's White Coach Inn—so German I feared owning a Toyota—where I was served a three-pound pig hock, first poached, then roasted. Certainly the best pig hock of my life, which is akin to saying my favorite grotesquely overweight girl whom I still somehow love.

A peculiar high point in Jackson, Mississippi, oddly a wonderful place. Actually drove through a tornado from the airport in an open BMW convertible. Very wet. After my pas de deux, went to Hal & Mal' s for dinner, also to Willie Morris's wedding reception. Down south they drink like they do in Russia. Kissed a lovely woman's hand with a modest flirtatious glance (Charles Boyer), only to discover she was the governor's wife! Was so embarrassed I could scarcely eat, but luckily Evans ordered eight appetizers, including the best of the trip, a deep-fried jalapeño stuffed with fresh crabmeat. Danced with southern belles until 3:00 A.M. Fine Sunday dinner prepared by traveling chef, Grissom, including a tasting of thirteen wines. I liked them all.

A break for bird hunting in Michigan and Montana, where my twin English setters, Tess and Joy (named after my tale-spinner friend Joy Williams), chased ruffed grouse, woodcock, Hungarian partridge, and sage hens through open windows onto the platter. Teary, deserving friends bowed to Nature in thanks for her gifts, and also to our fellow creatures, the bird dogs.

In L.A., straight from the airport, the best, so far as I
know, antipasto table in America, at Orsini's on Pico, followed
by a sea bass roasted with rosemary and garlic that weighed
exactly as much as the pig hock in Milwaukee. Igor, my favorite waiter, seemed to understand this symmetry. An inimitable
twenty-course Japanese meal in the private dining room at
Matsuhisa. Studio meeting at which I did not distinguish
myself.

Back to New York. Wonderful duck confit at Mark's, a
slice of Ray's eggplant pizza, another pig hock at the Ideal Lunch
on Eighty-sixth because the block looks as if it's about to be torn
down. Fine *choucroute garnie* at the new Quatorze on Seventy-
ninth. Stomach on the fritz. Carlyle scales register fifteen-pound
weight gain. The perils of public eating. Back to the wilderness
at dawn.

Perhaps it remains for me to write a movie in which people actually have a bite. But then screenwriters have scant control over their
product, and those in control, flopping around in their mad frazzle of
phone calls and errands, undervalue food. In some respects the movies are a frontier industry and food is devoured in order to "get on
with it," or in meetings so powerful that cupcake wrappers are eaten
by virtue of inattention.

I have rejected all offers to direct, which would certainly open
up new territory. The galley of the Gulfstream IV is too small for someone who takes food seriously. Perhaps, though, I should write something modish called *Rocco & Family*. Rocco begins as a Pacino-thin
LAPD detective with a multiphasic personality. In a rage he shoots
his three sisters mistakenly at a Marina del Rey brothel/crack house;
his sisters are supposed to be working at Hughes Aircraft, and he has
been puzzling over how they can afford Maseratis. Rocco flips into
another personality, wipes the prints from the pistol, and starts hitting the restaurants. The drama is in the fact that he never quite fin-
ishes a meal before some dim and inchoate memory tries to work its
way through the murderous fuzz of his mind. He orders a pizza but

leaves a single slice. He throws the last bite of an Italian-sausage hero to a bald dog. A clue leads him to Italy, where he is accompanied by an unseen concertina player. We see him eating skewered rabbits and *llengues de porc amb salsa de imagrana* (pig's tongues with pomegranate sauce), *piccione selvatico* (wood pigeons) by the dozen, bushels of sauced *funghi*, quarts of grappa while prone. Finally, while eating squid stewed in their own ink, he sees the faces of his sisters in the dark sauce. Etc. The story could go a lot of places, doubtless ending with Rocco stumbling down a beach in Santa Monica with gout even in his earlobes like the late A. J. Liebling. Anyway, it's a start on a food movie.

1991

ONE FOOT
IN THE GRAVE

It hit hard in Chicago. I was on the briefest of layovers at O'Hare and was trotting along the H concourse, looking for a vendor selling one of the famous local hot dogs. I began to crumple in pain, then whirled, thinking someone at Security might have shot me in the foot using a silencer. Ordinarily one hears a telltale bang, and if it's a machine gun the noise sounds like an air hammer.

But there was no blood coming out of my foot, at least not yet, and I doubted that my boot had that automatic sealant found in new tubeless tires. I backed up against the wall and felt the emergent sheen of cold sweat. My right foot arched and flapped against the floor, and I let out a cavernous moan like a wild ox in the canebrakes or, better yet, a wolf with the steel teeth of a trap buried in its paw. This moan, not incidentally, drew the frightened attention and quickly averted glances of those passing by.

I barely made the plane, and the remaining ten-year-old Percodan in my Dopp Kit didn't work. At home there was the question whether the boot should be cut off. My wife stood ready with one of her dozens of garden implements. She never liked the boots—a gift pair of Lucchese lizardskins—and was eager to slice one to the arch, but I thought of them as irreplaceable. Strange, but whereas five hundred bucks seems reasonable for a great meal, I could not conceive of spending that much for an article of clothing or footwear. To purchase a fine meal is to purchase a fine memory, and on my deathbed I will not care how I looked in the mirror, or to others, for that matter, but I will rehearse with pleasure the tablespoon dipping inaudibly into the kilo of beluga.

Thus it was, the boots saved from an attack of gout, the third in ten years, and perhaps this attack was telling me to develop an interest in clothing. Severe as the pain was, it does not deserve a soupçon of sympathy. Barring the cases where the sufferer is a victim of bad genes or simple ignorance, the disease is earned and totally devoid of emotional resonance. Unlike migraine or back pain, you can separate your mind from gout. It is in the foot, and in bed, after the hysterical removal of the boot, with the foot propped up, you stare at this blushing, throbbing appendage and do not say "Why me?" because you know so poignantly the answer.

Actually, and this may be a strain on those who didn't know me thirty years ago, I must paraphrase the late quasi-warrior John Wayne, to wit: I beat the Big A (anorexia) but lost to the Big G (gout). The fact is that I was somewhat athletic and thuggish in high school, and when I discovered I wanted to become a hybrid mixture—Rimbaud-Joyce-Dostoyevsky-Keats-Faulkner—I simply stopped eating in Boston, New York, and San Francisco. I wanted to look hollow and drawn and live in a garret, which was easy, as I was without funds. The writers I loved weren't muscular and burly and, since I hadn't learned to write myself, the least I could do was stop eating so I would look like a writer.

In those days a modest wind blew me this way and that. Rain knocked me into a crouch. I could jump nearly as high as my head but there was little use for this talent. Largish women craddled me in their arms, trying to get me to take nourishment. "Non serviam," I said, cribbing from Joyce, though unsure what it precisely meant. "Silence, exile, cunning!" The man didn't include eating, though years later I felt somewhat cheated when I discovered the pleasure Joyce had taken at the table.

Were it not for a daily Italian-sausage sandwich (with onions and peppers), I might very well have fainted and fallen off a subway platform onto the dreaded third rail. Naturally I would not be here today were I not forced to come to my senses. When I returned home to Michigan as a frazzled geek of a beatnik, my father advised me to start eating or I would soon become "nothing." He broiled me a whole chicken, serving it with a six-pack. "Get started," he said.

It is no mean thing, as we know from the modern-living pages of newspapers, to achieve victory over anorexia, and the urge toward this victory may very well have pushed me too hard in the other direction. Frankly, this is what happened, and I don't need to go very deep in the well of the past to be precise about the etiology of the recent attack of the disease. Besides, as an ex–private detective I know how events become fuzzy and witnesses unreliable. But then, I can remember what I ate on my seventh birthday (a whole jar of herring), so the record here is fairly lucid.

It all began when my youngest daughter, Anna, had returned from Montana, and I had an urge to fix a coming home–going away dinner. I was leaving the next day for a trip to L.A. that was urgent to the free world, my free world. For a number of curious reasons there is little good beef in Montana except on the hoof, where it is difficult to eat. The cattle are fattened elsewhere, and Montanans are left to squander their frippish appetites on lean, range-fed beef, or the supermarket stuff that is always a bit watery. Since it was nearly three degrees above zero, I cooked thickish porterhouses on the grill, of which Anna ate almost seven bites before returning to her Walkman and a volume by the late Carl Jung.

Soon after arriving in Los Angeles, I attended the premiere screening of *Misery* and, afterward, what used to be called a banquet. The movie centered on the life of a writer who gets the living shit beat out of him, over and over, by an adoring fan. This subject piqued my rather nervous appetite. I can't abide buffet lines, and at the dinner the beef table was devoid of people, so that's where I headed. Soon after, I went to Dan Tana's, an old-fashioned Hollywood bistro, for a nightcap with Darris Hatch, a young Columbia Pictures executive from Milwaukee. Studio executives are normally celebrity-proof, but Bruce Springsteen was sitting at the next table and I noted that Darris's eyes had become wobbly, which in turn somehow moistened her lips. This made me feel unsubstantial, so I ordered *vongole*, with double clams, to go with my drink, and two bottles of Barolo.

The next day, after a brutal twelve-hour meeting, I went up to Mr. Nicholson's for dinner, where his splendid cook, Paul, who is also a caterer, made a simple pasta with cream and an even pound of fresh caviar. For some reason my consciousness had refused to accept the known relationship between shellfish, fish eggs, and gout. Consequently, it was simple enough to devour a *seventeen*-course shellfish feast at Matsuhisa the next evening. While eating this incredibly presented fare, I quoted to the man sitting next to me, Mike Nichols, Richard Sandor's notion that our lives are a series of automatisms interrupted by a subtle amnesia. I also advised him that the Ivy out in West Hollywood served first-rate crab cakes with a salad of Maui onions and fresh herbs. I had eaten them that day at lunch while escaping to Santa Monica to see the Big P (the Pacific Ocean), as it is known in the area.

Sunday was a day of hundreds of yards of walking. I stay at the Westwood Marquis near UCLA because of the adjacent botanical gardens and because if the Big E (earthquake) occurs, I would be next to the medical school where I could make myself useful to fallen coeds as a chaplain. I walked so far that day because Bruno Baretto, the Brazilian director, was having a *feijoada* prepared for me at the home of his companion, Amy Irving. *Feijoada*, as everyone knows, is the Brazilian feast comprising a black-bean stew of a half dozen smoked meats, in this case transcendently cooked by Rémy, a native of that great country.

On Monday there was yet another twelve-hour meeting. Contrary to media reports, folks in the movie business often knock down a workday unknown in New York except to Wall Street chiselers. By now my nerves were peeled, and my right foot seemed a bit oversensitive, which I had falsely attributed to a misstep off a curb while watching an escaped parrot poop on a designer limousine outside my hotel. I went back to Dan Tana's that evening for the *cioppino*, one of my favorite dishes, an elaborate shellfish stew containing lobster, clams, shrimp, mussels. Colman Andrews, whose book *Catalan Cuisine* I revere, had recently given the restaurant a so-so review but had failed to eat its signature dish, the tureen of *cioppino*, chock-full of the fruits of the sea, tomatoes, and garlic. It is a health-giving dish, unless its contents shoot straight to your foot with their dark ammunition of purines.

And that is that, not discounting a hotel breakfast of roast beef hash. On the plane the boot could not quite contain the foot, but I knew if I pulled it off I wouldn't get it on again, and I couldn't make my way between concourses at O'Hare with a stockinged foot. I was poleaxed, as it were, and within the shimmer of pain I quite naturally thought, once again, of changing my life. "Don't do it," my soul yelled, though there was the vision of the boy who could jump very high and very long in a movement that was a mere splotch on human radar.

There is no point in describing the pain to you, gentle reader, because you have your own pain to deal with, which frankly compares unfavorably to my own. The presence of a housefly that might land on your rose-red foot makes you cringe and whimper in a way that disturbs your dogs. The colchicine, the drug that purges you in the first few days, creates a dullish imitation of Alzheimer's, a paradigm of extreme old age where you limp toward the bathroom calling out for pets that died in your youth. And in the middle of this, the thought never leaves your mind that it's your own fault. You are the pig that can't be dragged away from the trough. Can it be that I am the actual, secret, illegitimate child of Julia Child and James Beard?

What to do about it? The recommended low-purine diet suggests a total of *nine* ounces of fish, poultry, or meat per week. You also must avoid sweetbreads, anchovies, sardines, liver, kidneys, and gravy. I had abandoned the daily allopurinol pill, which prevents gout, under the exalted notion that a drug that permits continued bad behavior is not a good long-haul practice. I still believe this, but after six weeks of a low-purine diet my faith is shaky. The human obsession with the obvious in diet and exercise is strikingly at odds with the perversity of human behavior. Some of us were merely weaned too early and have been catching up ever since.

Unfortunately for me, I don't get any cheap thrills out of virtue. When I cooked my birthday dinner, a first course of grouse followed by elk with a morel sauce, I quickly ate my broiled Tuscan vegetables and polenta and then went outside into the cold wintry night. I peeked in the window at the slobbering revelers and felt the slightest, passing twinge of virtue.

Weeks later, while running through the streets of New York in the middle of the night, I found myself pausing overlong beside restaurant ventilators, the cold air laden with the odor of the cooking dead animals we love to eat, just as we, one day, will be dinner for the gods. I shall return to this life after a prolonged tune-up, bearing in mind that a dozen oysters is ultimately better than four dozen. And perhaps I shall buy my first tailored suit.

1991

JUST BEFORE DARK

The greatest poverty is not to live in a physical world.
—Wallace Stevens

It was only ten degrees above zero, and in the light cast by the small flashlight hanging from my neck I could see that the olive oil had congealed around the edge of the skillet, though the center of the pan was hot enough to cook the Italian sausages. Next to me, Peacock tried to chop a head of garlic with his gloves on but then took them off in favor of speed. I pitted the salty olives, then noted that the temperature in the capers jar penetrated boneward. Some of the basil had also frozen, but we plucked away the fresh parts. After I hand-squeezed the plum tomatoes I dashed to the live-oak fire to get the feeling back in my fingers, quite happy to see that the kettle of pasta water had begun to boil.

To the southeast the first glow of the full moon spilled over the Animas foothills. Peacock said that in deference to my gout he would add only one tin of anchovies to the *puttanesca;* I said that for the same reason he could have eighteen pieces of sausage while I'd settle for three. It occurred to us that this might be the coldest temperature at which the dish had ever been cooked. Americans seek records! When we mixed the noodles and sauce, adding red-pepper flakes and a container of Romano, we heard the guttural yowl of a bobcat from up the canyon. The noise grew fainter, as if the cat did not share our enthusiasm for the odor of the dish—doubtless its first exposure. After every few bites you had to put your serving back in the kettle to re-warm this mountain-whore's sauce.

It is strangely true that when you lift your head from your work, no matter how glamorous and eccentric the work may be, it is still a paradigm for "making a living," and if you travel to a location far from the usual tools of contact—magazines, television, newspapers, cinema— you are liable to come down with at least a moderate case of vertigo. Life is just what it is. It has no opportunity to be anything else until we make a move and discover how many other things life can be beyond our rather deadening routines. There is an especially apt Jewish proverb that says you shouldn't dig your furrow so deep that you can't see over the top.

I was down in the Animas Mountains in New Mexico's bootheel with Doug Peacock, the ursine grizzly bear expert. As we grow older we more closely resemble our dogs, and since Peacock doesn't own any dogs he has increasingly gathered the appearance of his beloved bear, *Ursus arctos horribilis*. We were visiting the Gray Ranch, which was acquired last year by the Nature Conservancy. The spread, as it were, is a little more than five hundred square miles, some 320,000 acres, an irregular, twenty- by forty-mile shape rising upward from the Mexican border. Not yet open to the public, it is a singular piece of property, a virtually intact high-desert ecosystem to be found nowhere else. As I watched three bald eagles and one golden eagle feed on a dead antelope in the middle of a forty-thousand-acre grama-grass prairie, my breath was tremulous and short, because I had seen something breathtaking. To the left I could see the snowcapped mountain on whose slopes I had slept the night before, in a canyon that contains Double Adobe Creek.

The vertigo had begun on the way over from Tucson. We had stopped at the huge playa (an arid basin) where Peacock had once seen fifteen thousand crows right after a rain. The rain had served to activate worms and insects in the desert soil, and he sat there watching enormous black clouds of crows descend throughout the afternoon and evening.

We had walked a couple of miles out of the playa in search of these winter crows when the wind shifted precipitously to the northwest, and within moments the temperature dropped more than twenty degrees on an already cold day for Arizona. I noted that the oncoming bank of swirling dark clouds looked just like snow clouds in northern Michigan; then we began to laugh as the snow came down hard, gathering ornately on the desert fauna. The snow also made it pleasantly obvious to me that we wouldn't be driving over the mountain trail that crossed the Chiricahuas that night, which translated into a stay at the Copper Queen Hotel in Bisbee, where we had dinner with William and Marilyn Eastlake. Eastlake is widely revered by other writers, though not necessarily by the editors and publishers who man the cash registers rather than keep the faith.

There was another touching near reprieve when we reached ranch headquarters and Vivian Walt and Bill Cavaliere, who caretake the place, said that in light of record-low temperatures they expected us to stay in the ranch house. I observed king-size beds, an ample liquor cabinet, and a satellite dish, and there was mention of a freezer full of venison. Peacock let off with a manly chuckle, saying we were heading up the mountain where we would "throw a bag on the ground." Not wanting to be a wimp I brayed that I had come directly from northern Michigan and this weather was nothing, neglecting to add that, other than streamside naps, I had not slept outside in Michigan since childhood.

So there we were, heading up Double Adobe Creek in Peacock's decrepit old truck, discussing the overwhelming peopleless landscape and our giddy love for Italian food, which would be consummated after a hike.

An adjunct wonder to an obsession with the natural world is that you don't have to become involved with exercise as a parody of work. As an instance, on my project to rename all the birds of North America (seventeen new names so far), I will have to walk thousands of miles. If you hike several hours in swampy country looking for bitterns, loons, and herons, you can ignore all aerobic notions, and when you reach your cabin there is the reassuring sound of golden tequila pouring over a squeezed lime, and a wood fire burning down to coals on which you will grill a side of ribs or a T-bone, food that is not allowed during sedentary periods.

Before unpacking, we headed up different sides of a feeder creek, the dense riparian thicket of a long, narrow canyon. I felt a wonderful mindless eagerness toward exploring the new territory, a palpable return to the curiosity of childhood, when the responses to the natural world are visceral. The pulse races to an unrecognized welter of tracks (javelina), then softens, determining where mule deer and a single, large bobcat stopped to drink. Walking at twilight owns the same eeriness of dawn. The world belongs again to its former prime tenants, the creatures, and within the dimming light and crisp shadows you return to your own creature life that is so easily and ordinarily discarded in other pursuits. I have always loved best this time just before dark, when the antennae stretch far and caressingly from the body. I heard the flap of the raven's wings before I saw it and exchanged a series of greetings before heading back.

After dinner there was a mild concern about keeping warm, which was overwhelmed by the beginning of the full moon's transit. Keeping warm meant a specific imitation of hibernation—one sleeping bag stuffed into another, coat, hat, gloves. I slept near the fire and could hear, a hundred yards away, the groans of Peacock trying to digest his hasty eighteen pieces of sausage. Because of unfortunate war memories he will not sleep near the vulnerable light of the fire. When camping with him, I'll occasionally call out to check him on the time, which he reads by the stars. He's invariably within ten minutes of being correct. If you sleep out two hundred nights a year, you become a student of the stars.

The clarity that arrived was even better the second night, when the temperature rose to a balmy twenty. We had moved camp to a grove of sycamores, and their smooth bark gleamed white above my head, a reassuring totem of the physical world. Across the creek I could see the tufts of bear grass and the dark blotches of live oak against the sere grass. The wilderness does not make you forget your normal life so much as it removes the distractions for proper remembering. I was sleeping on the home ground of Cochise and Geronimo, and it was not difficult to imagine their ghosts scampering up the mountainside in the gait particular to the Apaches and other true mountain natives who considered, without irony, the earth to be their mother, and whose presence in the southwest is, and was, absolutely imperceptible in the landscape compared with our own.

In an age when our government bilks itself out of potential environmental funds by jumping in bed with all manner of swindlers, we are very fortunate to have a private, nonprofit organization like the Nature Conservancy. They have land-acquisition and support projects in every state and are a singular organization in terms of saving land that desperately needs saving. Those who still love the land should tithe to it in one form or another.

Back in Tucson there was the natural anxiety brought about by what is known as consciousness. I have suggested before that what the wilderness actually prepares you for is more wilderness. You do not spend four days in Lutèce to get ready for a long period at Burger King. For reasons of vertigo we often avoid experiences of the highest order, and the wilderness is a specific failure as a nostrum for the modern world.

Tucson and its sunburned traffic quivered the stomach and brainpan, and there was no cure but to swerve into a supermarket and buy a couple of legs of lamb, three free-range chickens, five pounds of sirloin, five pounds of Guaymas shrimp, and a mixed case of Tuscan wine (sunlight generates a taste for tequila, Pinot Grigio, and Gavi de Gavi). After building a fire out of mesquite and ironwood, we marinated the lamb in garlic, white wine, olive oil, and chopped cilantro and cooked the shrimp. As an afterthought, we made a quart of hot Argentine *chimichurri* as a sauce to serve with the roasted lamb. Peacock whipped up a fresh chile sauce for the chicken while his wife told him about all the phone calls he should ignore. It became apparent that the food was too much for the three of us, plus two children, so Lisa got on the phone and soon the house was full of environmentalists who, being active people, ate everything we cooked. It was oddly disturbing but pleasant to be around people with a higher purpose than their immediate lives.

Later in the week I was in another Nature Conservancy project, a bosque along Sonoita Creek in Patagonia. It is a superb piece of wildlife habitat and has the additional advantage of being within a mile from the Stage Stop motel and a splendid restaurant called the Er Pastaro, manned by a native-Italian owner and chef, Giovanni Schifano, who was a general manager at Regine's. This way you can watch all the birds you care to, then eat food you rarely find outside Rome or Florence, and sleep warmly, if not transcendently.

1991

COOKING YOUR LIFE

There is more to life than lifting the bandage. Birds, for instance, and all manner of flora and fauna. At dawn in Los Angeles, I remembered how the coyote itched his ass on the wild rose then trotted off, not looking back. The bear wallowed on the sandbar in the river, soothing his blackfly bites; turned turtle, he shimmied his back into the mud, then pretended he couldn't quite get up again, weakly pawing the air as if rearranging clouds. I prodded him with a whistle, and he knew in a millisecond that it wasn't a bird, twisting in a concussion of mud and water, gone into the greenery in a finger snap.

That was a two-bear day—the other will come later. After a dense, muggy week with bugs so thick the woods were intolerable, a rare summer front came through from Alberta, announcing itself violently with a thunderstorm at twilight. I gathered in lots of wood, and cooked pork with green chiles and *chicas* (dried sweet corn). As a bow to the exertion to come the following day, after the weather broke, I also made Navajo fry bread using duck fat, a heretical gesture, and I tried to remember if I had ever seen a duck in Navajo country. Nope. There must be some on the San Juan River up near Mexican Water, but I didn't see any. While I ate, lightning hit a tamarack, which exploded with fire and then was doused by rain so intense it rattled the window. What a piece of luck to see lightning strike a tree! The pork with green chiles was a tad fiery, and sweat dripped off my nose in unison with the duck fat dripping from the fry bread, an animal-fat tip of the hat to symmetry.

In the bar that night the patrons were drinking by flashlight—the storm had knocked out the electricity in the village. In the small circles of light, the faces of fishermen and pulp cutters were swollen by bug bites and everyone was toasting the weather change. A pretty tourist girl danced in the dark, but when someone got direct with a flashlight she'd stop, her hazel eyes flashing green like my Labrador's. When she passed by me, I caught her scent, a sweetish mixture of beer and lilac. I headed back to my cabin with an unreasonable lump in my throat, the black, windy sky carpeted with stars. Before I slept I remembered the Lorca line "The enormous night straining her waist against the Milky Way."

These are actually hotel thoughts, and the texture is the same whether in New York or Los Angeles. If you can get your thoughts dancing around enough, images will arrive rather than a rehearsal of abstractions. "I don't understand why I have to wait a whole year for French royalties"; or, to a producer, "If you know so much about writing screenplays, why don't you write your own?" That kind of thing; thoughts dumb enough that you'd be further ahead jabbing a hat pin in your ass.

But if you settle down, perhaps sitting on two pillows facing the bare wall of the room, you can adjust your environment, even calm down enough to enjoy the city, despite it being mostly an occasion for shopping and random violence. If I'm too addled for *zazen*, darkening the room and watching Mexican TV works quite well, as does listening to a Puerto Rican radio station in New York. When the nerves are sufficiently peeled, Mozart will push you to sobs that ill prepare you for the next business day. Taking along hiking boots is essential. New York, of course, is a splendid walking town but Los Angeles is underrated, especially Santa Monica. There are a lot of dickhead jokes about the absence of walkers in Beverly Hills, but then the area is far too monochromatic to be of interest unless you're greedy, and greed can be better satisfied by car. Beverly Hills would be like walking a golf course without clubs. Memories, however, are more reliable than walking when you are once again stuck in a pressure cooker of your own devising.

Dōgen writes about the metaphor of the *tenzo*, the head chef of a Zen monastery, extending the idea into how we "cook our lives." It is a somewhat shattering moment when we realize that our lives are made up of the particulars of what we do every day. If there is a se-

cret ingredient, it has not been convincingly discovered. Women are
better at this realization than men. Men like to think of every morning as a fresh start, while women are more prone to believe that they
have just finished a night's sleep. For instance, on long road trips I
have a weakness for biscuits with sausage gravy, a nutritional holo-
caust unless you're bucking bales or hand-digging well pits. When I
order this dish, covering it with a fine pinkish haze of Tabasco, I remind myself that the following day is a fresh start. I feel girded for a
day of hard thinking and easy driving through Kansas or Nebraska,
or wherever, and there are fair odds I will repeat the breakfast the
next day. Continuity can be soothing.

Back to memories and cities. My recent problems with gout were
less a reminder of mortality than they were a cornball baritone from
the clouds saying to reduce the size and nature of the feedbag that I
am hanging around my neck every day. Recently, at a dinner in
Hollywood, I ate far less than Bill Murray, who, as a Chicago boy, is
not averse to "troughing it up," an Illinois idiom. We were at the
Muse, an odd name for a restaurant said to be favored by Madonna,
and I was seated directly across from Winona Ryder, a fetching and
intelligent lass who, distractingly enough, was more interested in
books than food. It is a little difficult to concentrate at a table for
nineteen, especially when you are the announced center of attention. It precludes the favorite French conversation topic at dinner—
food. There is a plaintive urge to grab a joint of beef and head for a
dark corner, but then I've never seen a beef bone at a Hollywood
dinner except when I was cooking myself. There is a theory that
cuisine emerges from the landscape, and this isn't cattle country.

I suspect that, finally, one recovers only inasmuch as one can
recover every day. After dinner, and tucked into bed (by myself), there
was a spate of insomnia as a result of actual hunger, a rare sensation.
The Westwood Marquis has twenty-four-hour room service and I was
tempted by the notion of bagels with lox and a bottle of Meursault,
but I decided to gut it out. The core of insomnia for me is invariably
the emotion of feeling put upon, and there is no more comic emotion
in the human repertoire. Feeling put upon is in the same category as

gout—a brutal self-affliction. I had recently invented an epitaph for a minor character in a novella: "He drowned in the sheer junkiness of his life, the sum of all his tastes, the incursions he allowed."

The epitaph amused me so much that I quickly dismissed two irritations—the nineteen-dollar toilet paper that is being marketed in Beverly Hills (cashmere thread is woven into the paper) and the memory of an intensely mediocre six-hundred-dollar meal in New York. The dinner was so breathtakingly inept that on the way to the hotel I had the driver pull up to a Ray's for a slice of pizza with eggplant. I'm not naming the restaurant because so many others deserve this lame punishment. I am not the catcher in the rye standing before restaurants trying to prevent doomed experiences.

With these vexations out of the way, I took my mind back home, usually a location of modest serenity, but there had been a recent photo of two cormorants with horribly twisted beaks, a mutation caused by the amount of toxins that industry continues to pour into the Great Lakes. I had to turn on the bed lamp to get rid of the cormorant image. I checked my notebook for a Lewis Shiner quote: "Pollution is simply alcoholism on a global scale. It grows out of the same kind of self-hatred, greed, and impatience, the same kind of delusions about control." There, that pinpoints it, and there was the image of the industries that border the Great Lakes as reeling and drunken, raising their big blotched asses and spewing chemicals into the once pristine lakes. It was difficult to be upset with Saddam Hussein for doing the equivalent on farther shores.

There was the sudden though dimmish memory of a plate of fruit I had called up for breakfast and didn't eat, also a glass of carrot juice I had ordered, tasted, then poured unattractively in the toilet. Pouring carrot juice in the stool of a mirrored bathroom is no way to start a day. The fruit, however, was still in the suite's refrigerator, and I glided out of the bedroom not very much like a big brown mountain lion. It was definitely not biscuits and sausage gravy, but still colorful, tactile, standing for life herself. There were blueberries, melon, strawberries, and the dreaded kiwi, which causes bunions on snails. On came Mexican TV with a baritone singing while he smoked a

cigarette like Robert Goulet used to do. What happened to Gogi
Grant? And out came a modest glass of white wine.

The blueberries worked immediately, taking me back to last fall,
when I hunted my twelve-year-old half-blind bitch Lab for probably
the last time. She tired easily, so it was a brief hunt in the middle of
a late October sleet storm. She waddled along the two-track just before dark, paused with her butt trembling to look into a dogwood
thicket. The grouse rose upward and turned, and I shot it going away.
She gave me a retrieve typical of her late years, wherein she bites into
the bird for a juicy little taste.

Back at the cabin I fried her the heart and liver for a snack, which
she ate with a wild wagging of tail. In the bird's chock-full crop were
aspen leaves, desiccated wintergreen, and blueberries. Late in the fall
I could smell the ripe heart of summer. I pushed aside the Provençal
daube I had prepared for dinner. I put the contents of the crop in the
bird's cavity for aroma, adding a thatch of fresh sage leaves, then
rubbed the skin with butter, lemon, and pepper and roasted it. Lucky
for me, I had a container of woodcock stock to make a sauce, also a
noble Tuscan Isole to drink. I gave half the breast to the dog, who
wheezed and farted with eagerness, smiling her peculiar doggish
smile—her ears draw back, her eyes squint, and she shudders with
pleasure, her blind eye reminding me somehow pleasantly of my own.

Naturally, I slept like a dog in the hotel, waking up happily to
order bagels with lox, onions, tomatoes, capers. Rather than read the
morning L.A. *Times* with its freight of mundane horrors, I turned on
MTV and watched an improbably beautiful black woman singing the
refrain "Everybody dance now." I did an obligatory jig, totally unlike
M. C. Hammer, the only man I currently envy.

On the way to Columbia I was glad the company had moved to
Culver City. When I used to cross the mountain from Westwood to
Burbank, I was beeped at for not driving fast or skillfully enough. I
blew the Santa Monica light, barely nicking a Fed Ex van, which was
hard to see, and made a hasty escape down a side street. I was thinking of the second bear of my two-bear day. I had hiked overlong in a
dunes area near Lake Superior. The cool wind had strengthened

through the day and I wanted to see the big lake in turmoil from a high vantage point. I nearly turned around because the sand had begun to needle my face. I climbed the lee of a radically steep dune by pulling on the roots of the vegetation above, the wind blazing into my face at the top so that my eyes were nearly closed. I was utterly startled to come face-to-face with two ravens, which are ordinarily difficult to approach. They loosened their toeholds on a dead pine and drifted away with pissed-off squawks. I smelled a rank smell and looked down the dune face at the ravens' symbiotic buddy, a very large black bear who whuffed, then churned away with a power that would be the unapproachable envy of any athlete, of which I am not, so I watched with jubilance.

1991

IGNORING COLUMBUS

When the Big Light goes out, you hope it will be turned on again. It is immediately apparent that you are not entering a restaurant while you are being gurneyed into an operating theater. Case studies reveal that it is common among acute schizophrenics to believe that doctors are, in fact, aliens. This occurred to me at age seven, when I had the first of a number of surgeries, and recently I was reminded of it during a sinus operation. Acute schizophrenics are also virtually immune to cancer, the singular advantage to that hideous disease so far as is known, although the aliens have been rather muddy on the subject with the notable exception of R. D. Laing.

My last memories before being launched chemically into the void were about dog who, though recently dead, decided to go along on the trip. I had held her while the vet gave her the "hot shot" and clearly saw life herself leaving in undulating shimmers from her mortally ill body. It was reassuring to see that life actually was a noun rather than a collection of puffy adjectives. The next morning I dug a rather deep hole in the barnyard, put in a layer of green cedar boughs, and laid in the old girl wrapped in her favorite blanket. Around her head I placed a grouse, a woodcock, and a deer bone to feed her on her trip down the long Ghost Road.

Her decision to join me in the operating room was her own. In that she was a Labrador, I could always talk to her about matters that tend to bore my English setter, especially food. While spinning along in the ether, I mumbled something about revising my version of a barbecued Texas brisket that had possibly been my good-bye dinner in that I didn't know at this point whether I'd wake up. It befits a gentleman to ascend with beef grease in his scuppers. Curiously, the Bible does not mention the menu for the Last Supper.

What you do is buy a largish fresh beef brisket, perhaps nine to twelve pounds, reminding the butcher *not* to trim the fat, which you can effectively do after the cooking. In a well-sealed aluminum tent in a roasting pan, you place the brisket fat side up, pouring on a quart of your favorite BBQ sauce, whatever amateurish bung drainage that may be. It's your brisket, though the sauce must have plenty of cider vinegar, a stick of butter, and an ample handful of hot-pepper flakes. Cook gently in the oven for three hours, say at 275 degrees after you bring it to heat. Finish the meat briefly over hot coals while you defat and reduce the sauce, which has grown exponentially and deliciously with brisket juice. As an accompaniment, I favor a fresh fruit salad, and a casserole made of rice, cheddar, sour cream, and a dozen minced jalapeños. I served this to the potential mourners with a case of Concha y Toro Cabernet, with which I have replaced Bolla Valpolicella as a table wine, once Bolla hit fifteen bucks from a low of eight several years back. You will also need a case of beer for the crude at heart.

In the anteroom, well before I was given a soupçon of narcotic, I fell asleep still trying to digest this meal taken the evening before. Of course, I was flying in the face of the recent gout lesson, and enraged sinuses resemble gout in the face. We are often like autistic children, unable to connect experiences, especially if we want something interesting to eat.

So there I was in outer space with waning beef thoughts and my dead dog trotting along beside me, when my mind turned to a specific fear brought about by Rice University astronomers who had announced their discovery of an "object" at the outer edge of space that is the size of a hundred billion suns. We're not talking dollars here, but suns. Why did they wait until a few weeks before my operation to announce this discovery? Why hadn't this cosmic lump been noticed before? I brooded over this immensity daily and wrote my personal science adviser, David Quammen, but he hasn't as yet answered. Naturally the object is a black hole, a clumsy euphemism at best, and not a hole at all but matter so dense that a quantity the size of a marble would plummet through the earth and out the Yangtze River.

Fortunately, this fear was allayed by the image of Lauren Hutton presenting her not quite astral body for a pelvic repast, as it were. We all are aware of the banality of the unconscious, however, and L. Hutton's lambent, glowing body was replaced by the image of Columbus in one of those goofy hats that look like an upside-down Victorian pillow. Columbus! That miserable fuck! How could it be that my sworn and lifelong enemy would present himself now, the princeling of our contemporary hell, the perpetrator of the colonialist hoax we are still enduring? In the midst of a twinge of anger I lost consciousness.

Of course, Columbus himself is relatively innocent of all the difficulties I ascribe to him. At base, he was just trying to make a buck and was the first of many Spanish and Portuguese sadists blown westward by giant bedsheets. The whole thing is remotely a culinary crime, as the avowed intent was to look for the spices of the East, but then perhaps that is similar to blaming child abuse on Adam and Eve. It's just at this dislocated point of our national soul history, it's apparent that we don't know where we came from, we're not sure why we're here, and now that we're here we don't know what to do about it. This messy state never would have come about if we had stayed where we belonged.

And there's no particular point in stating that both the Chinese and Vikings beat Columbus to the punch. It's a moot quarrel anyway, when the notion of discovery is contrasted with the estimates that there were anywhere from nine million to fifteen million inhabitants in North America when Columbus hit the bug-infested mangrove swamps of San Salvador.

There is a splendid new book coming out by Peter Nabokov called *Native American Testimony,* a chronicle of Indian-White relations recalled totally from Native American testimony from 1492 to the present. The book makes a fine alternative history of the United States, all without the implicit or explicit manifest destiny tripe, but then many Dutchmen will tell you that they discovered Africa. It is interesting to note that before Columbus there was an Indian "village" of from forty thousand to sixty thousand souls near East St. Louis, Illinois, called Cahokia.

At the onset Nabokov notes the way Native Americans observed our peculiarities. "When a Hidatsa comes into the cabin," Goodbird observed in the summer of 1914, "he is given a place to sit, or a chair . . . he does not get up and pace about. If he should do so our people would think he acted foolishly." But whites, Goodbird noticed, "pace back and forth in their rooms. We Indians think it is because the white man's mind is working while he has nothing to do; that he himself may be idle, yet his mind keeps working."

Nabokov also discovered that the Yaqui Indians of the Southwest were puzzled by our thought processes. The Yaquis called whites *gentes de razones*. One tribesman explained, "Yes, you are a people of reasons, you always have reasons for this, reasons for that."

There is a blushing point in the book about food, the humorous complaint of a native holy man. "When you come to my cabin I always say to you, 'Go and Eat.' . . . But when I come to see you, I never see any food in any of your dwellings; and it is only at certain definite hours that I can find any food; then the bell rattles, ding, ding, ding! And all must go then and eat, or all will soon be out of sight."

Of course everyone is welcome to admire Columbus and watch the network and PBS documentaries featuring the stentorian voice of James Earl Jones or the right-wing bleats of Charlton Heston— "Some called it Tuesday! The scurvy-ridden sailors of the *Pinta* butchered an albatross," etc. It's always one thing or another in history. There are no blanks. The reason why the young and the older, before fifteen and after fifty, turn to religion is their perception that we are not designed for comprehension. Only in the strident middle of life do we have things figured out. Ultimately, though, spirit will get you through times of no ritual, but ritual can't get you through times without spirit.

Meanwhile, back at the hospital, I awoke after several hours to my wife's pleasant face, and the notion that I was utterly trapped in a zoo for sick people, a splendid metaphor for life, but in this case as real as raw meat on the floor. There was a discussion of whether I would have to stay for the night, during which I remained calm then announced I was leaving as soon as I could walk. Home is a far, far better place to bleed. This is a natural, suitably childish attitude for one who has spent months in hospitals as a result of injuries to eye and spine.

There is a lot of mystifying talk nowadays in the New Age and "male" movements about power, or what they call empowerment. It has occurred to me that people are nasty enough when weak, let alone powerful. When my mother asked on the phone if I had "learned from the experience," I said I had learned not to play football at sixteen and get my face crushed. It was a powerful experience, somewhat on the order of an auto accident when you figure out that an auto can be a different kind of Kalashnikov. It was impossible to draw conclusions or build a shrine to so obvious a wound.

During a solitary convalescence at my cabin, I immediately set about curing my rubbery jitters with some violent food. Since the pampas were distant I would become a bull of the forest by making a *chimichurri* sauce with parsley, oil, vinegar, lime juice, ground chiltepins (the hottest edible pepper), a half cup of fresh serranos, and a half cup of diced garlic. I roasted a three-pound lake trout over wood coals and ate it with a side dish of my own devising, a corn salad made of greens and dried *posole* from New Mexico, ladling on the *chimichurri*, which cleared the sinuses and freshened the brain. I repeated the meal with chicken and ribs, heading into the backcountry as far as I could walk between meals. The last night, during a thunderstorm, I was blessed to hear my first wolf howl in several years, the possible cause of an unpleasant aftereffect of the operation—back home my wife had awakened me with a slug several times because I was howling like a basset at the fire whistle, a coyote at sundown, a wolf at a moon sodomized by a golf club. During the day, however, my sunny disposition returns, and I am ever eager to confront the life challenges of the kitchen.

As an afterthought, I have made a resolution that could pass for a conclusion. I will stop using my fax as a weapon and then avoiding the phone calls in response. The world is chock-full of reality, and nobody's perfect. Even Buddha himself needs a quarter for a phone call. So what if I feel as if I had a baby through my face.

1991

EATING CLOSE
TO THE GROUND

Lord Death is a real big eater. In dimmish moments when I think I will not be here with you always, it occurs to me you will not always be here with yourselves. Simple as that.

Perhaps you are wondering what brought about this religious bent of mind? Two brushes with death, my own and another's, the latter the most vivid young woman I have ever met, owning a density of grace and beauty that the world ill deserves but is given occasionally by the gods. Her name was Teresa. We shall not see her, but we shall join her. Enough said.

The other brush owned a bit of the comic if you were not a participant. I organized a ten-day wedge of walking in between trips to New York and Los Angeles. To be sure, walking solves or resolves nothing, but it does abolish or erase the questions. It's not that you don't give a shit, but that the ordinary concerns disappear into the sky and the landscape. I am talking about wilderness walking, or at least walking in areas of pronounced wildness where human intervention does not exist except for an occasional contrail. Of course it is best to ignore the contrail, from which you can extrapolate an entire doomed civilization.

After a dawn bowl of granola with buttermilk to atone for New York gluttony, I drove to an unpeopled area about a dozen miles from my cabin. I was a bit troubled by the weather, as the wind was clocking this way and that, first off Lake Superior and the temperature would drop to the forties, then around to the southwest and the temperature would quickly rise to seventy or so, arousing blackflies, mosquitoes, and deerflies in an amount that made you wish you were back in the cramped and bilious gut of New York (in a suite at the Carlyle with seven Audubons on the wall and speedy room service).

Within an hour or so I had worked my way out into a region of violently hilly dunes and cliffs, with forested pockets and hillsides covered with yellow primrose, beach pea, hawkweed, and sea rose. The exertion was such that the granola fuel soon dissipated, and a hoofprint tended to remind me of venison chops and a flushed grouse the coming feasts of autumn. At cliff's edge, staring down at Lake Superior far below and wishing I had bought a canteen, I noted the approach of a solid fog bank and at the same time heard an immense noise approaching from the west that was either thunder or a million-pound bear. I sat down to watch the drama as the thunderstorm swept around Grand Sable Point on a collision tack with the enormous, swirling fog bank that stretched a dozen miles to the east.

Frankly, if I hadn't been fresh from New York, it would have occurred to me to get the hell out of there, though that move was already tardy. The storm would have been horrifying if seen through a car window, but then my car was miles away. I more or less bared my heart to the elements for want of anything else to do. The fog beat the thunderstorm by a scant minute, and I rechecked my vest pocket for the compass, scrambling back from the edge, not wanting to take a five-hundred-foot dive. Quite suddenly I wasn't Dersu the Hunter but Jimmy Dumbo, searching for cover in a fog so dense I was running into solid whiteness. I tripped into a deepish sand pocket blown into an oval by a millennium of strong winds. The first strokes of lightning were giant strobes in the whiteness, and I found myself facedown, digging like a badger, my body jellied by the volcanic thunder, which had a rock-crushing crispness. The next lightning strike was so close my body tingled in the sandpit and the air smelled like the fog was on fire. The thunder that followed was too loud to hear, and the dune absorbed it with a shudder. At that point I gave myself up as dead meat, turned over, and watched the belly of a cloud swirl past ten feet above me. The next lightning and thunder were farther to the east, and I felt a specific drowsiness. It occurred to me that I was dead and had not yet understood the symptoms. I closed my eyes and found nothing in my head, then felt rain falling in sheets. I turned back over, scooped out an airspace for my face, and waited out the squall that was now a hellhound that had passed me by.

Nature can be some fun. I did not get up until I felt the sun on my neck and the deerflies had begun to feast on the back of my head, where they had successfully burrowed through my wet hair. Blake said, "Everything that lives is holy," to which we might add, "Everything that eats is mortal." I crushed the flies against my scalp and stood up, noting that from my sandpit vantage the earth was at eye level. The storm had veered out to sea and eventually would trouble Canada. Close by, near a single blush-pink sea rose, a yellow and black butterfly perched on a dried coyote turd.

Back at the cabin, I discarded my intention to write a scholarly column on Native American food. It was too late in life to pretend that I know more than I do. I heated a bowl of Chiracahua stew I'd made the evening before, an almost vegetarian (more atonement) recipe of pintos, squash, dried corn, chipolte, ancho, and chiltepin, garlic, cumin, and, alas, salt pork. Jane Brody, the arch–health ninny of Gotham, seems unaware that salt pork made Arkansas what it is today, not to speak of Missouri and North Dakota; brave, big people who were unafraid to change T. S. Eliot's line to "Sometimes I think that gravy is a great brown god."

I still felt a tad storm-flayed over lunch while sorting through a dozen volumes on Native American cookery. After a long walk you never return to quite the same world, and my day had been filled with less than a fine excess. The occasional ringing in my left ear seemed to say that though life doesn't bear repeating, it is difficult to let it go. Civilian religionists have always scorned foxhole Christians, but then incoming artillery, tumors, and lightning bolts are memento mori that no one gets off earth alive.

Quite naturally these dire portents pushed my mind over a nether edge toward survival thoughts of sex and food. Screwing was out of the question, as the creature world is sexually unattractive, not to speak of evasive. Were you a superhuman who could run down a doe, you'd be far too tired to close the deal. This left me with dinner plans, which revolved around several small, fresh whitefish to be cooked over an oak fire, a tomato salad, corn bread, and a wild rice sent to me by Louise Erdrich. Not quite by design, this was a Native American meal. Unknown to most of us, these folks gave us corn, tomatoes, beans, potatoes, squash, and chile peppers, among other things.

Throughout the afternoon I devised an elaborate diet from the sources at hand. There was the ready notion that indigenous food would make me truly healthy, also impervious to the kind of inattention that almost got my dead ass blasted off the planet that morning. I made long lists of attractive food possibilities, but then with a predinner drink my enthusiasm waned. When involved in any self-improvement notion I invariably screw the lid on way too tight. Try to think of the human organism as a sturdy rubber band: if you stretch it too hard at a sharp angle, you'll develop a snap-back problem. As a renowned amateur self-therapist, I am an expert on this snap-back syndrome—I shall never again eat a pound of foie gras at one sitting unless, of course, it is offered to me. I compromised by telling a cedar tree I would eat this food five days a week, with the other two dedicated to French and Tuscan classics. Beans and rice would pleasantly alternate with *bollito misto* or *tête de veau*, or a hundred others.

As an additional loosening of rules, I would offer myself the native food of an entire continent, much of it readily available by mail order: salmon, Dungeness crab, and halibut from the Northwest; buffalo loin from the Great Plains, where I'd also travel to shoot sharptails and sage hens; crawfish and oysters from the South; nothing whatsoever from the Northeast, where the Natives were having clambakes before Jesus loomed large; chiles from the fabled Southwest, and perhaps a rank javelina carcass plus fifteen kinds of Papago and native beans. Gary Nabhan, the author of two splendid books, *Enduring Seeds* and *The Desert Smells Like Rain*, has started an indigenous seed bank where many desert foods are available, including tepary beans, which have sixty percent more protein than pintos. I'll even bake bread from amaranth flour and chew mesquite seeds for dessert!

From my own area, which is Odewa-Chippewa (Anishanabe), my setters, Tess and Joy, would help me fetch a half dozen types of game birds, plus I could hunt deer, moose, raccoon, squirrel, beaver, the wily opossum, muskrat, and woodchuck. Bear are a personal taboo, as in the past year bear dreams have supplanted wolf dreams. I would also pick and eat fresh or dried thorn apple, chokecherry, grape, bunchberry, strawberry, wild cherry, currant, blackberry, and raspberry. The Chippewa were given to throwing a handful of dried berries into venison stew along with wild onion and garlic, a move also practiced in Soviet Georgia.

There. You shall have monthly reports. I don't want to deal with the beverage problem. Canadian whiskey sounds passably wild but isn't, though tequila is made from the agave cactus. I've never drunk a homemade wine that wasn't loathsome, so any strictures in this area would be unfair and prevent the likelihood of more immortal poems. Also, I can't listen to the news without a beverage—the dark tales of how Republican rapacity mated with Democratic desuetude, monitored by a press with moral Alzheimer's, has imperiled the republic.

1991

RETURN OF THE NATIVE, OR LIGHTEN UP

I get real tired and hungry trying to figure out the nature of existence, the nature of nature, and the apparent stillness at the heart of being. Just recently I lucked out on the subject of time when it occurred to me that time wasn't something we spend, rather it dissolves around us like the waning of late afternoon light. Death becomes relatively easy to handle when you think of the earth as a five-billion-year-old minefield. Nature still has me flummoxed, and I fall back on Thoreau, who referred to her as that "vast, savage, howling mother of ours." Next month we'll deal with God and music.

There is a specific need to lighten up, maybe go dancing, even if it's out in the barnyard by myself. An old fear has resurfaced that my anima has become so heavy I'll plummet through the surface of the earth where the crust is thin. Bird-hunting season is in the offing, which should help. There's nothing like ignoring your livelihood to make you feel better. Effective hunters learn to leave their "selves" at home, no doubt a skill that emerges from survival instincts. Once while skeet shooting, a friend had hit seventeen in a row when I asked if he thought his wife had ever cheated on him. He missed the next six.

Recently I was torn away from my cabin like a largish piece of Velcro for yet another trip to L.A. This is only to say that my Native diet has been somewhat truncated through no fault of my own, though with a certain relief after a week's practice. Frankly, it is excess at times that makes the spirit soar, a lesson we must keep relearning. Some of you may have forgotten William Blake's dictum, "The road of excess leads to the palace of wisdom." Jimi Hendrix, are you listening?

But before I lighten up I must get rid of an average abscess. While dressing for dinner in L.A. after doing either ninety or twelve laps of a pool—I lost count—I turned on the TV and watched a few minutes of a program about the sexual abuse of children, then flicked to a news program that featured a Desert Stormlet parade, including a sound track of a yokel braying about freedom. This was no way to get ready for dinner or the screening of Madonna's *Truth or Dare* that followed. Another snit ensued, and I wondered why most movies remind me of sitting through a two-hour banjo solo. This one in particular seemed a deification of banality. Has rock music become the Rock Cornish hen of the arts, a severely limited life-form, genetically trivialized, bearing the same relationship to actual music as body building does to the intricacies of track and field? I pose this as a question to you, gentle reader.

At the screening there was an urge, anyway, to drop a pound of Limburger in the air-conditioner blower, slide out the door, and head into the hills with the other coyotes who can't tell the difference between one-hundred-grand autos. One of these coyotes said he regretted the passing of cocaine and the present dearth of garbage. Now showbiz folks eat their dinner rather than merely casting the old teeth-chattering glances at the food. The tendency of chefs to intricately decorate and arrange their offerings came into being during the cocaine years to titillate the ladybugs. When I went to Michael's in Santa Monica after it first opened, I thought I was looking at a topographical photo of a flower arrangement. Now that showfolks are no longer snorting their paychecks, they have turned to somewhat sturdier food, which is approached in a manner almost as humorless as that of New York. I long for the days when a friend tilted his plate vertically, thinking in his drug haze he might be eating a painting. When the contents fell off like an actual Schnabel painting, he wept at the destruction of beauty.

But it's time to lighten up and forget that as a young man I purposely broke my fingers to avoid the tyranny of the guitar, piano, dulcimer, and lute. I grew my own warts by keeping toads as pets, avoided iodized salt in hopes for goiter. I stopped short of binding my own feet. "We have faith in our poison," Rimbaud said, and all energies were directed toward becoming a monster of Art. In contemporary parlance the syndrome is known as a "one-issue person."

This is only to identify the problem in the effort to lighten up. We, quite fatally, become our youthful dreams, and the intemperate energies toward the written word spread to my fishing, hunting, and cooking. Fly-fishing for trout had to be expanded to tarpon and marlin, and why settle for woodcock and grouse when there were more than a dozen other game birds on the continent? The Dagwoods of America usually concentrate on the outdoor grill and perhaps an otiose chili con carne, but a few are catapulted into studying hundreds of cookbooks well past midnight. There is also a sexual tinge when you have read your Kant, Nietzsche, Schopenhauer, and Kierkegaard in the tenth grade before you've seen your first naked girl close up and real, felt the first heat flowing out from beneath a lifted sweater in a '54 Chevrolet.

This is what ruined my Native American diet—the lust for all the things of this earth, rather than just a few. As my wife never said, "You're just too damn protean for your own good." But then I may go back on the Native diet when I reenter the vast, dank forest of the Upper Peninsula tomorrow.

Last evening we cooked a shipment of seafood FedExed by Charles Morgan in Destin, Florida. Since it's important to cook everything when it's absolutely fresh, we went through the entire container. Not wishing to be monochromatic, I grilled an appetizer of baby-back pork ribs using Matouk's, a Caribbean fruit-based hot sauce. We moved on to soft-shell crabs *meunière*, then kebabs made of chunks of cobia (a rarely shipped Gulf fish) marinated in Mozambique piripiri and skewered with peppers and mushrooms.

The main course was an oddity taken partly from fiction. I had just read James Hall's splendid new whopper mystery, *Bones of Coral*, which is based in the fatally tarnished, rabid netherworld of Key West. (I once read in the personals column of a local Key West magazine: "I like cop piss, old tires, and wet cement.") Hall mentions the fresh grouper sandwich at the Full Moon Saloon, and since I had eaten twenty years' worth of these splendors, that's what we made. Huge ones on toasted onion buns, with tomatoes, red onions, lettuce, tartar and Pickapeppa sauce. This all required a dozen bottles of Lindeman's Chardonnay and Pinot Grigio and a case of Molson, then lemon cake, Alembic brandy, Armagnac, coffee. A three-hour snooze before I rose and washed the dishes to prove myself a worthy fellow.

This dinner lacked something of the Native. In a way it was a reward for having a tooth pulled the day before. That's what it was. Just call my dentist. The meditation point involved is whether it is better to climb a hundred mountains or climb the same mountain a hundred times. This is not about ladies but a shimmering stew of phenomenology and the experiential, a topped or a topless world, the vacuum between the Virgin and the Garrison. An excitable boy tends toward the hundred mountains, while the wise man ignores the conundrum as yet another barrier to satisfaction before the inevitable giant asteroids strike the planet. The Defense Department is actually addressing the asteroid problem, but I fear it is too little too late.

During my dawn walk, which is frequently delayed by sleep, I designed a punishing meal for the Supreme Court for their refusal to read the Constitution: a bottle of Riunite apiece, Mom's lazy-day leftover casserole—green beans in a mixture of Velveeta and mushroom soup—Spam and instant mashed potatoes, green Jell-O with tiny marshmallows and maraschino cherries. Sit there until you clean your plates. No TV.

My mind drifted away from vindictiveness when I spotted a rare indigo bunting, taking me back to the somewhat shameful unraveling of my Native diet a few weeks before. It was the last evening at my cabin before the L.A. trip, and I had driven to the Dunes Saloon to make calls and have a couple of modest nightcaps. After a full week of eating Native, I had become so serene I could hear my own blood, the thousands of tiny blood rivers running through my carcass. It was real hard to carry on a conversation. Back at the cabin, I lay on the picnic table watching the northern lights, which were pale blue and pink cosmic rivers of light. The sound track was a pack of coyotes chasing a deer, which I could hear snorting off in the swamp. The coyotes gave up on the deer and crossed the logjam in the river. My not very frail body began to lift upward, gently turning toward the northern lights, and I leaped off the table in alarm. This was no way to get ready for an L.A. trip.

I started the generator—engine noise is an effective way to dispel the spirit world. The situation demanded an immediate narrowing of the doors of perception. In the cabin my battery-operated Zenith brought in a rock station. I pranced around to a Doobie Brothers song to establish contact with the mundane, then a Don Henley number, followed by my rank nemesis singing "Like a Virgin." I popped open the fridge with these songs in my heart, forgetting that there was nothing but a natural fright wig in there, a fridge that would delight a fruit bat or one of those no-fat ninnies who currently plague us. There was a single possibility, however: a very unnatural five-ounce chunk of lean salt pork tilted against a pan of corn bread. I had been using small wedges of the pork to flavor my Anasazi and tepary beans, but now my childhood called out rather shrilly, and there was an image of the oak barrel of salt pork in my grandfather's cellar. I remember the density of the salt-pork gravy on cornmeal mush, which is now referred to as polenta. This gravy is especially good with the buttermilk I had been wasting on granola. Dare I? Of course. I browned small chunks of pork and made a roux, then whisked in the buttermilk with a hearty dose of Tabasco, ladling a full cup on hot corn bread, washing it down with V.O. ('84). Another half hour of dancing, a tentative good-night peek at the northern lights, and I was a well man, safe from unwarranted space travel, though there was a recidivist urge before falling off to sleep to run through the thicket along the river.

1991

LET'S GET LOST

It's a very odd feeling just before dark to find yourself misdirected and misplaced in a large patch of remote forest that you didn't previously understand was quite so large. It's not a matter of bearings, as the bearings disappeared hours ago back at the edge of the woods. The clearings are distinctly shaped in the twilight, probably worth hunting out the edges, but offer no familiar clues. You attempt to walk in one direction, toward the setting sun, though that isn't the direction you intended to go, but the river is over there and an overgrown two-track that will be barely visible in the growing dark, and the two-track is only a few miles from the car. Not incidentally, your compass is in your other coat, the heavier one, in the car. As the sweat cools and chills your body, the heavier coat would become valuable indeed, though not so valuable as the compass.

Your bird dog's bell is faint in the distance, as if she too had quit hunting and was looking for the car, or perhaps she is frightened. The previous dog had always headed for the car, or walked on your shoes, when there was a bear in the vicinity. On a hillock in a clearing there is a diseased, leafless tree that, against the sky, looks like the skeleton of an immense bird readying itself for flight. Quite suddenly you don't even recognize your thoughts and look down as if to recheck your presence, patting yourself on the head as your father did to you. There is a vision of cooking the kill, a grouse and two woodcock, over a wood fire, but the night would be well below freezing and damned uncomfortable. It's all quite wonderful, if a little frightening. If I don't enjoy myself in this life, when am I going to enjoy myself?

I don't advocate or defend hunting and am no longer even slightly interested when it is brought into question—I would willingly wear a hair shirt emblazoned ATAVISTIC if it were demanded of me. Part of the pleasure of being lost is that no one else can locate you either. A main desire in my "agenda" as a man and artist is not to be located. As my hunting over the years has diminished to a few species of game birds, I have devised a number of other secret activities in the natural world that replenish the soul. Perhaps they will finally erase hunting. Of late I have begun to envy a group of brook trout that live in a small spring far back in a marsh I visit regularly. If I lie very still, they return to their lives, which are without human scrutiny, a splendid idea. The central melancholy item of late is that there are so few places left in this United States where one can become convincingly lost. And I am not particularly snobbish about the activities of others—certain of my friends watch baseball and football on television, which I view as on the order of staring up a pig's ass. Hey, go for it. However, I'm mad for basketball.

On this particular morning, before getting lost, I had made a bear stew for a friend. Now, I would not shoot a bear for a cool million in cash for religious reasons, but this bear was already dead. I could tell because five pounds of the animal was handed to me in a frozen package, a definite tip-off. As the meat thawed there were indications of the dread freezer burn, an infirmity that wouldn't matter much in the intended recipe.

The evening before, still on my Native kick but yearning for something French, I had devised "Franco-Papago" tepary beans using duck legs and thighs (politically correct), duck stock, lots of garlic, salt pork, fresh sage and tarragon. I ate an indecent amount, which stood me well in my directionless wanderings. Through sympathetic magic I had acquired the nonchalance, simplemindedness, perhaps stupidity of a duck.

The bear, however, presented more challenging problems. An older bear tends toward the flavor of a popular boot grease: rank, tallowish, rather sour at the edge of the palate. Slow cooking in a Dutch oven was the obvious choice, especially since a portion would be my dinner after the solo hunt, and I could cook it in the oven for a long time at 275.

There was a memory of a stay down in Durango, Mexico, many years before. On a hike in the mountains I had come upon some vaqueros eating a stew made from a bear that had killed a calf. They gave me a bowl, and it tasted like a violently strong version of ordinary chili with beans. I ate the bowl impassively, though my eyes must have bulged and my ears certainly rang, washing it down with a tin cup of mescal, a local version of lemonade. I ended up using a full cup of garlic on my bear, an equal amount of serranos and jalapeños, a half pound of Anasazi beans, cumin, and Mexican oregano.

When I finally made it home from being lost, my cabin smelled like a saddle-and-harness shop down on the border. Lucky for me I was bone cold and trembling with hunger. It was a rendition of lifestyles of the poor and aimless and reminded me uncomfortably of the hero of my novella *Brown Dog*. That night when I delivered the stew to Mike, the proprietor of the Dunes Saloon, my behavior was somewhat surly and ursine, though I do recall dancing solo to a Patsy Cline medley on the jukebox with tear-moistened eyes. Cline plus whiskey has always done this to me, as she, along with Edith Piaf, so obviously and uniquely meant the words she sang.

The good news about the bear stew is that it set fire to Mike's blood and gave him the sexual energy of the few remaining nineteen-year-old athletes who don't take steroids. His wife was indeed thankful, though she rejected the stew out of hand, saying that it smelled like a well pit with something dead on the bottom. My own wife wasn't as lucky, what with being exactly 257 miles away. And neither was I because, after a nightmare about being a captured bear the Germans were giving a lobotomy to through the right foot (seriously), I awoke at daylight with a high-medium case of gout in the right foot.

How could this be, when my friends Guy and Russell were arriving that very afternoon from France and Montana for bird hunting? I headed for the colchicine, a remedy that includes blurred perceptions, fuzzy thinking, intense drowsiness, and diarrhea, but then my rock-radio horoscope said, "It is better not to think too much today." Back in bed with pain pills there was a flashback to a recent family reunion to which I brought a fifteen-pound Delmonico roast and a case of red wine, also a dinner of seven types of grilled sausages I made for my visiting brother, plus a party *asado* the next day of two whole rough-cut fillets, a butterflied leg of lamb, a loin of pork, and five pounds of shrimp. This kind of eating within four days was possibly a contributing factor to the gout, but like cigarettes and cancer there was no one-on-one proof. More likely it was that I had lost twenty pounds, which tends to concentrate the purines in the blood. Many folks had noted that my face, which normally resembles a pleasant beige bowling ball, had begun to acquire a hollow look that revealed the ravages of a life of art. A Native friend warned that Black Elk had said, "The power of the world always works in circles, and everything tries to be round."

After a few hours of rest and shallow, errant thinking, the pain subsided, and I limped to the kitchen. The menu for the weary travelers included an appetizer of grilled woodcock, then on to a wild-rabbit cacciatore with fresh tomatoes and basil. During hunting season we favor the cuisines of France and northern Italy because, frankly, they are better than anything else, though they falter somewhat in the health aspect. This is what may be called "destination eating," something you do purely for its own sake, an ideology of pleasure rather than function.

Most of the table talk revolves around what Thoreau called *gramática parda,* the rather tawny grammar of earth: the past twenty years of hunting and eating together, sex, wine, the plans for the next day's hunt, memories of fishing, hunting, and eating in the Keys, Montana, Mexico, France, Costa Rica. There's an unfortunate pop-psych term current nowadays called "male bonding"—an offshoot of the confused male movement. I certainly have nothing against the movement itself other than the silly rip-offs of Native American language and customs, and the making of a civil-service program out of our sacred relationship to the earth. Evidence is that we hunted and fished for at least a million years, and many of us gave it up only in the last hundred. It is a blasphemy against the natural world to reenter this reality all painted up like MGM redskins, with basso gargles and growls, carrying a spear, of all things.

But then, along with the Germans, we have a weakness for constructing otiose ideologies out of anything at hand, from trickle-down economics to race to murder. Your entry into the natural world should be sacramental, drawn from a religion without verbs. In one of the scant few wise books of our time, *The Practice of the Wild*, Gary Snyder states: "The rules are matters of manners that have to do with knowledge and power, with life and death, because they deal with taking life and with one's own eating and dying. Human beings, in their ignorance, are apt to give offense. There's a world behind the world we see that is the same world but more open, more transparent, without blocks."

1991

PRINCIPLES

In geologic time everyone now present on earth will be dead in a few milliseconds. What a toll! Only through the diligent use of sex and, you guessed it, food can we further ourselves, hurling our puny *I ams* into the face of twelve billion years of mute, cosmic history. With every fanny glance or savory bite you are telling a stone to take a hike, a mountain that you are alive, a star that you exist.

A few of you of a critical bent and a firm memory of third grade are asking, "What about shelter and clothing?" Not at all an interesting question, and to which I pose another: Would you rather camp in a pup tent at Lutèce with Elle Macpherson or spend your pathetically short time on earth with real estate agents and haberdashers?

Now that we have returned to earth from the nether reaches of the cosmos, we can address certain dilemmas of dislocation and free-floating anguish, to wit, is there an American cuisine? Of course not. Have you forgotten the melting pot, a notion that also tends to be sprung on us in the third grade? Melting pots don't produce specific cuisines, or do so only inasmuch as directed by region and ethnicity. In terms of eating, you are far luckier if your grandmother is French, Italian, or Cajun rather than Scots-English, Irish, German, or Swedish. The frontier tended to be pork-ridden and verminish after the game was gone. Farther west, no buffalo cuisine evolved except among the plains natives because we slaughtered seventy million buffalo within a scant thirty years for their tongues and hides and to make the area safe, as Phil Sheridan said, for "spotted cattle and the festive cowboy." Cuisines don't evolve in thirty years, or out of movement for that matter, but out of bioregions maintained in good health by their inhabitants.

Societies like our own and Germany's, burdened as we are by a soul history dominated by the fetishists of pragmatism, tend to eat for function—a meal is mere fuel for the realities. It is interesting to note that now that our drive toward dominance has become somewhat enfeebled in the direction of a service economy, the food is getting better. You are liable to find an acceptable, if not good, restaurant in any American town of more than ten thousand. Travel is not nearly the culinary mud bath it was even ten years ago. In fact, our past wretchedness is no doubt the cause of our current relative inventiveness. The truth—that most of our best efforts still fall short of a French truck stop—must not discourage us. For those of us who have just passed fifty, our daily prayer should be that our guts hold out for the coming new age of American food.

I just came to a painful, jolting stop, remembering a college trauma. A kindly professor drew me aside while I was in the process of flunking out of graduate school and told me that, while I might someday be a poet or storyteller, it was certain that I would never be a "thinker," that I was far too interested in the "textural concretia" of life itself. In a trice I hitchhiked the thousand miles to Greenwich Village and had an Italian-sausage sandwich with fried onions and green peppers. By the next day at lunch, Kant and Wittgenstein had dissolved in the marinara on the fifty-cent spaghetti plate at Romeo's. I returned to Rimbaud, Apollinaire, and Char for wisdom, abandoning forever the academic pursuit of trying to answer questions that no one ever asks.

Just recently I made a difficult three-day trip to Paris. As you have no doubt noted, scarcely anyone calls it Gay Paree anymore, evidence that the myths of our youth have been further dissembled. How I craved to go there as a midwestern high schooler (Haslett Rural Agricultural High School, now a suburb) flunking chemistry while trying to read Sartre's *Being and Nothingness*. The book was inscrutable but that meant nothing, as I intended to carry it into a Left Bank café and meet a dark-eyed girl wearing a turtleneck. Back in her garret I would drink wine while she bathed in the sink without tearing it off the wall. Errant details always ruin fantasy. The sink *does* tear off the wall and she dies from knocking her head against a table leg. I'm convicted of murder and spend the rest of my life on Devil's Island. The bell rings and chemistry class is over.

Frankly, Paris has always somewhat frightened me. I hadn't been there in fourteen years, and on three brief earlier trips I had been broke, traveling on the generosity of friends. Once at Faugeron's I estimated the bill to equal three months of my income. When alone I feared ordering a meal because they might spring some sort of five hundred percent tax on me. People were so beautifully dressed and appeared to be on important missions, even while sitting at cafés. Despite two years of college French, I could not bring myself to say anything, though I was an expert at the menus. Paris is far and away the most gorgeous city on earth but it chills the blood when you're broke. Only up in Normandy with the familiar smells of hay, earth, and cow shit did I feel comfortable.

On this brief trip I discovered both of us had changed. This time I flew first class (expense account) and was somewhat nervous that someone I knew would discover me doing so. As the wag Garrison Keillor has pointed out, midwesterners hate to be discovered at pretension. Naturally, I was caught by an intellectual acquaintance who glared at me, said hello, and headed for steerage. I could barely swallow my first drink, but got over it when it occurred to me that I no longer believe that a plane is more, or less, likely to crash into the ocean because I am a passenger, a specific relief from ego.

At my not very humble quarters at the Plaza-Athénée, I napped from the overnight flight, waiting for lunch and my first meeting with a prominent actor. In three days our meetings took place at lunch, dinner, while taking walks, and at nightclubs, actually accomplishing a full hour of work. Such are the ways of the movie business where ninety-nine percent of anything accomplished is derived from mutual wordless assumptions. In this case the sole irritations were the paparazzi, who grew in number until by the third evening I was close to a pointless violence. Rather than being perceived as a sensitive writer, I was mistaken several times as the actor's "security," probably due to my moderately burly physique and crummy midwestern clothes. This has happened before, and I merely pat my breast as if carrying heat, perhaps the 9mm Walther I stole from Hunter Thompson ten years ago in Key West after he ruined a beach picnic by shooting dead jellyfish.

But anyone can have meetings. It takes real attention to eat well. The first lunch at the Lipp was late and bit rushed. Since it was a hot day, I ate an enormous plate of their famed *choucroute garnie*. In that the French are not exactly pro-German, this is considered to be strictly an Alsatian dish. We lightened up that evening by going to the Stresa, where *choucroute* bloat allowed me only pasta *al aglio e olio* and a wonderful salad of chicory and watercress.

Very early (jet lag) the next morning I managed a three-hour walk, got lost, and finally took a three-block cab ride to the hotel, after being misdirected several times by friendly folk. Since it was hot again we went to Gourmet Ternes, owned and operated by the former head of the butchers' union in Paris and reputed to have the best beef. In consideration of the heat I skipped the *rilletes* I desperately wanted and had a lentil salad and an enormous chunk of filet. So much for American beef pride—this was as good, if not better, than the Palm or Bruno's Pen & Pencil. We delayed dinner until late waiting, waiting for the heat to subside, which it didn't. At the Voltaire I went ahead with foie gras and *tête de veau*, a preparation from the tongue, cheek, and brains of a calf, with a wonderful sauce *gribiche*.

During the next day's dawn walk my whole system seemed to be backing up, as it were. A wise man would have fasted and communed with pigeons, but at lunch at Fouquet's I started simply with an eggplant flan and coulis, letting down my guard with a confit of goose thigh accompanied by potatoes fried in goose fat. The saving grace is that these restaurants are not of the "all you want to eat" variety. Dinner at Bellecour moved gracefully into the top ten of a lifetime category, which is no mean thing. I had not heard of the chef, Gerard Goutagny, who is a genius of the simple—which, of course, is tremendously complex. I had a salad of poached ray on a bed of *passe-pierre*, a kind of wild seaside string bean, followed by the roast pigeon I should have communed with, followed by a grand fresh fig tart.

For some reason, at dawn I felt crisp and lean with nary a stomach burble. On the way to Orly it occurred to me, as it had on my three previous trips, that the singular French gift is to allow each ingredient to taste like its essence while marrying it to another. Their poet of the Resistance, René Char, said that "lucidity is the wound closest to the sun." This is certainly true of their good restaurants, where clarity of intent informs every move.

Naturally when I got home it was hot so I barbecued an Amish chicken using Sweet Baby Ray's ("the boss sauce") as a base. I have heard that Paul Bocuse heads for barbecue shacks in America. A full day out of Paris I headed for my cabin for detoxification. Since it was hot in the Upper Peninsula, I made a mouth-blasting Thai curry out of a low-cal turkey thigh. That evening at the tavern there was much talk of a huge marauding black bear that had entered the village, destroying the beehives of Stan, Mike, and Willard. Rich had brought his hounds to town and was running the bear. We could hear them baying in the distance through the screen door of the bar. The trouble was the bear was too big to "tree" and was safe in the night. Suddenly I was a very long way from Paris.

1991

THE LAST BEST PLACE?

Even the greatest thought may at first appear too diaphanous and flimsy to embed itself in our memories. Lucky for us we have writers to record these thoughts before they fly away like a Delphic warbler on its final trip south (it does not know that the floating nubbin it will land on in the Everglades is the upper lip of an alligator, or that the high-tension wires feeding the air conditioners cooling the minions and minionettes of Palm Beach will be a fatal, body-blasting— literally—encounter).

Recently, on a long drive to Montana, purportedly "The Last Best Place," I lost approximately forty-five minutes of great thoughts because the pause switch on my tape recorder had been joggled by unknown forces. Perhaps Sony should install a Klaxon similar to those that go off on airplanes when the flaps aren't down during takeoff. Suffice it to say, this empty tape, unlike the Dead Sea Scrolls, cannot be re-created, another specific piece of evidence that the Electronic Age has atrophied our sensibilities so that Memory herself has gone the way of the alphabet, typewriter, blackjack, and accordion.

I do recall a single item, which you may find falls a degree or two short of greatness. It centers on the image of dead bodies in the parking lot of a restaurant in Minnesota where the food was so gruesome and humiliating that patrons committed suicide after exiting. Rather than ruing the needle in the eye that is a bad meal, I turned my thoughts to cholesterol, which has now surpassed the Budweiser Clydesdales in the banality sweepstakes. It occurred to me that cholesterol problems are caused, as usual, by the failure of imagination. The highest cholesterol rates center in the upper Midwest, the land of the egg-and-gravy gobblers, as it is known worldwide to nutritionalists. Yet if you have a trace of imagination you can take fifteen minutes off from a busy day, enter your own or Farmer Brown's henhouse, lay down on your back, and arrange a deep halo of straw around your face. Soon enough an obliging hen will perch ("squat" is unsavory) there, and you will witness a miracle of nature—a 101-degree (chicken body temperature) egg will ease itself out, albeit somewhat grotesquely, with a pop, then plop on your face. This will deter further egg binges, though a number of Republicans in the Senate, Specter and Hatch among them, may find it stimulating.

On to Montana to do the houlihan, whatever that is. I'm not sure it is "The Last Best Place," the name accorded it by a compendious but eminently readable anthology of the state's writers, overseen by William Kittredge, an eminently readable writer himself. By the same schemata, in terms of population demographics California is entitled to a forty-thousand-page anthology, a big sprawling bitch of a doorstop indeed. I've been spending a month in Montana nearly every year for twenty-five years, which adds up to two years of sporadic tenancy and, of course, makes me an unqualified expert on the state. Don't go there if you need a job, and don't bring in any more cows, as the public lands are swinishly overgrazed. I don't say the latter as an eco-ninny but as a thirtieth-generation farmer. Our government is an environmental slumlord.

The Montana trip began on the first day of an experiment in human behavior—my own, in fact. I craved to become a blank, to relearn the language I knew before I was born and the one I will speak after death; to become empty and serene as the night sky, not counting the stars that whirl, so we are told, in a billion-degree torment. The source of this impulse was more Rousseau/Thoreau than Buddhism, which has a defined sense of humor about such hubris. I wanted to become as simpleminded and happy as my bird dog, and the first step, after studying her behavior, was to ban thinking, reading, TV, movies, and, most of all, writing. The life unexamined is frequently worth living, or so I thought.

It seemed impractical to ban eating because others would then notice what I was up to. Anyone who has been involved in self-improvement schemes as long as I have is either an utter fool or has learned to keep his own counsel, to admit to no one, not even your therapist, that you aim at even a minimal behavioral change. This gives you an excellent fallback position: no one knows if you fuck up. Of course God knows, but He is presumably concentrating on some of the hotter world trouble spots. As an instance, when watching a satellite-TV diet program and hearing that the Lord helped some blimp stop eating four dozen eggs and a gallon of ice cream a day, I was sent back to William James's *Varieties of Religious Experience*.

Another reason for visiting Montana is that our two-year-old grandson lives there. Not yet able to stand on his own two feet, he lives with his parents, my eldest daughter and her husband. Despite my occasional visits he does not recognize me, which I find somehow comforting. The other day a radio psychiatrist admitted that nearly all of us haven't been emotionally honest since we were three years old. There was a touching moment of mutual recognition when I broke my secret regimen and I sat down with him to watch a Bert and Ernie *Sesame Street* video. He could tell I wasn't trying to cozy up for quality time but actually wanted to watch my old favorites, Bert and Ernie, so strikingly reminiscent of male relationships.

I should add at this moment that I take back my previous comments about the improvement of restaurant food in America. It is purely the luck of the draw. We arrived after two and a half days on the road in a state of heartsick biliousness. Both my daughter and her husband are accomplished cooks (she had worked at Dean & DeLuca in New York), and our first bridge back to culinary reality was a lamb couscous with winter vegetables. Each evening brought treats of similar dimension after a full day bird hunting or floating for trout on the Yellowstone River. I remember veal meatballs with fresh tomato and basil, a Harrington ham from Vermont, crabmeat and pompano from Florida, two roast Hutterite chickens, and a single truly great meal of grilled sharptail grouse accompanied by a fresh chantrelle risotto and tomatoes Provençal, from Patricia Wells's excellent book *Bistro Cooking*. The wines that evening were a Berganze di Berganze and a Salice Salentino ('85) suggested by Stephen Singer in San Francisco. We finished with an astral old Calvados, Sire de Gouberville, sent

from France, clearly the best of a hundred Calvadoses I have tasted
(translation, drunk in quantity). For a night off we had an excellent meal at Ira's over in Bozeman, the only other real option being
the Grand in Big Timber, run by Larry Edwards of former Chico Hot
Springs fame.

It's more fun to eat when you're hungry. On this trip, part of my
ambition toward emptiness included booking a guide, Danny Lahren,
for twelve days in a row. After nearly twenty-five years of hunting
and fishing in Montana, I scarcely needed a guide but very much
wanted the obligation to do something every day to avoid the dread
thinking, reading, writing, TV, movies. I admit I broke this vow once
when Russell Chatham, whose house up in Deep Creek we were bor-
rowing, gave me a video of one of Roger Ebert's seven-star hits called
Debbie Does Dallas, which I presumed was a French farce, knowing
Chatham's tastes. To my wife's shock the movie turned out to be pure
porn. I rolled restlessly on the couch, exhausted from a fifteen-mile
hike searching for Hungarian partridge. After I dozed off, my English
setters, Joy and Tess, barked angrily at the screen, presumably for femi-
nist reasons, or at the sight of something akin to a depth charge in a
seafood store. In the morning, on the way to the mountains, I FedExed
the film to Orrin Hatch, to fill in some specific gaps.

So for two weeks we ranged over Montana—high, wide, and
handsome, as they say—in a successful search for trout and game birds,
staying a couple of nights at one of my favorite hotels, the Crazy
Mountain Inn in Martinsdale. Both the town and hotel are delightful places, and, frankly, you can stay there a month for the price of a
night at the Carlyle or Plaza Athénée. The Crazy Mountain Inn also
has the best chicken-fried steak with cream gravy in the world, a somewhat narrow category, I admit.

On the last day there was the startling sight of a coyote near the
road, crouched and crippled with a bloody rear end, evidently hit by
a car. Not fifteen feet away an immense golden eagle sat on a fence
post waiting for its lagniappe meal. My mind said "metaphor of the
poet," but it was quite simply a coyote staring at his death.

Ten additional days in Michigan's Upper Peninsula and I had completed the experiment in my mental deprivation tank. Reaching home, I leaped for Rilke's *Selected Poetry* (Stephen Mitchell translation) and read it straight through to purge the dumbness out of my bones. I listened to *All Things Considered* and watched CNN *Headline News* simultaneously. I wrote a poem and called smart people.

However grim the world, we are what we have evolved into. That's natural to us. In Paris there had been a cold sweat when a French journalist reminded me that several years ago I said in a moment of ire that I had become a writer to avoid shitting through my mouth like a politician. You can't take this out of the context we live with every day. Mark Twain had the notion that there is no distinctly criminal class in America outside the U.S. Congress. We may add the executive branch. There is currently a dimension of cynicism in Washington that sends even Hollywood scampering to the puke trough. The world is our wake-up call, but we need places like Montana on occasion to avoid drowning.

1992

THE MORALITY OF FOOD

If I were twenty-one again and knew what I know now, nothing would be different. Life that was once a blur is now a blur with vaguely sharper edges. A poet—this is where I began and where I still see myself on the rare occasion that I use a mirror—can be likened to a CAT scan machine or, better yet, a magnetic resonance imager. The emerging wisdom, however vital, is too ordinary to be attractive— somewhat on the order of fire is hot, ice is cold, and dead is dead. This spring on a mountainside in Wyoming a considerable poet, Peter Matthiessen, said to me, "I have never learned from experience," a sentence of stunning bravura and honesty. Me neither. I tend to prefer the truth of the imagination and the heart's affections, and an actual experience is nearly always forgettable. But perhaps this is better, after all, than the computer maven on television who said, rather flatly, that "in human relationships you have to factor in the emotions."

This brings us to George Bush. I have an office pool betting on the date of his invasion of Cuba to save his ass in the coming election. Since I am the only one in my office, I get to win. It's only a matter of time, and a dream told me it would be on the eve of the coming NBA finals between the Bulls and the Lakers. We are at the tether end of an era of greed and political chicanery not experienced since the 1920s and, before that, the 1880s, when a congressional vote could be bought for twenty-five grand. The price has gone way up, even considering inflation. If only the environmentalists could raise a couple hundred mil to spread around Washington, they might get somewhere. Of all the various terms for bribery, "PAC" is the freshest minted.

Of course, when drowning in a mud bath the human soul must howl "mud bath" or lose that soul. You can also lose your soul by howling all the time. And if you forget how to dance, you don't howl well. How do you learn and relearn to dance within a suffocating welter of moral ambiguity? Got me by the ass. But you better. Any other first lesson is appropriate to your mortality.

You can tell I spent two of the last four weeks in New York City. While there, it was my pleasure to talk to a bunch of unequivocally bright people. My head did a lot of spinning because, frankly, you can get out of practice for this back home. I had to do a lot of napping and tell the hotel operator to hold the calls. I began to wonder if people who live daily in this maelstrom of intelligence get the same pleasure from it. It also occurred to me that these people, deprived as they are of daily contact with the natural world, have made food an intimate part of *their* natural world, *their* dance. In the density of this atmosphere, both pleasures and disappointments are intense. An intelligent New Yorker pissed off about a bad meal is a sight to behold. Back home we are more cowlike, humble before the sawdust in the meat loaf, the tang of bouillon cubes in the sauce, the cans of mushroom soup that are deemed appropriate for a thousand casseroles, the steamed "prime" rib painted red, the ocher-colored Jell-O flashing marshmallow eyes from a thousand salad bars, the barrels of "au jus" behind steak houses, the pale frozen vegetables served in the middle of harvest season, the beef from which pink water trickles, where even the batter is battered, and stomach nostrums outsell condoms ten to one. My beloved Midwest, stuporous cousin to the Rhine and the Ruhr!

Meanwhile, back in New York there was an embarrassing incident after a fine lunch at the Mark, where the conversation was so intriguing I limited myself to a salad of duck confit and a little white wine—actually a big salad and a bottle of white wine. Afterward, passing the Whitney on the way to Books & Company, there was a hot dog cart with its pungent odor of sauerkraut, a Midwest gourmet item. I looked around to make sure no one from the luncheon was passing by. After the second bite I saw two of them headed my way and darted into the entryway of the Whitney with blood rushing to my head as if I had been caught whacking off in the choir loft, as once had happened to a boyhood friend. Lucky for him, he was and is insensitive and thought his act heroic. He currently is a leader in the Michigan political rage to truncate all aid to poor people. In fact, there is a bill under consideration in the state legislature that would allow Republicans to beat poor folks with oak cudgels on Monday afternoons during the dark winter months.

Of course, I'm being unfair. Nothing is black and white except black and white. In fact I ate improbably well in the Detroit area on my way to New York. I had agreed to talk about myself to a gathering, an activity that requires a lot of nutrition and beverages as the years pass. I actually made a song out of my recent book of essays, *Just Before Dark*, and warbled it to the assemblage, arms and feet akimbo, in the manner of Goulet, Torme, and Manilow. It was suggested that this indicated a man in extremis. Not so: torpor makes one shameless, and I'm not interested in what I've written after I've written it, let alone in chatting it up.

Fortunately, I blocked off time to visit two establishments that rise like bastions and sentinels of the culinary in the Midwest: Zingerman's in Ann Arbor and the Lark in West Bloomfield. If you've ever taught composition you know what an amazing bunch of stuff rises like bastions and sentinels, but these two are utterly genuine monuments to the range and possibilities of good taste.

In the Lark there is a curious amplitude and grace, warm colors and light spirits, which you identify with Europe at its best, rather than fine restaurants in New York and California, where self-consciousness can sodden the air and the help is straight out of *The Mikado*. The Lark does not present consensus food. The menu and the wonderful monthly newsletter seem eccentric until you've eaten there, and they are totally the product of the owners, Jim and Mary Lark, and their superb chef, Marcus Haight. There is similarity in attitude to the splendid Chinois on Main in Santa Monica where, after entering and reading the menu, you wonder if you are in for foolery or are in the hands of a mad genius. Since I entered the Lark in a fuchsia slump, I was caught off guard when a trolley of pâtés and oysters arrived. How gorgeous and direct with nothing, including my appetizer of pasta with fresh chanterelles, looking like it had been wrapped at Bloomingdale's.

There is a moral stance here that reminds one of Robuchon's revolutionary notion that food should taste like itself, that it need not wear a wig and earrings. A roast Maine lobster with elephant-garlic hollandaise tastes real good, as does a copper cataplana of large white Gulf shrimp, clams, mussels, and chorizo, as does a veal chop with porcini mushrooms, as does the utterly prime beef and lamb, and the Salzburger Nockerl Austrian soufflé. I drank a Dunn Howell Mountain Cabernet that was as good as those old, wonderful '68 Heitz Martha's Vineyards. It hurts deep to know that I live a distant 280 miles to the north. Frankly, they cook a lot like I do at home at my best. My recent little wild pig stuffed with garlicked fruit, after an appetizer of sweetbreads and morels, would work well in both places. The Lark would be as chock-full of patrons in New York and Los Angeles as it is just north of Detroit. On either of the dream coasts, it would be a pleasurable and enchanting relief, like a warm rain after a good movie.

Considering their origin in a college town, Ann Arbor, you wonder what torments led Zingerman's to such grand efforts. To recheck this notion I had to look again into Toynbee's thoughts on his adversary theory of history; and, further, the idea that great cuisines tend to emerge from economics of scarcity. To my mind, there is nothing quite so bleak as college towns with their morose, Germanic quasi-traditions and metronomic social milieu; they remind one of jury-rigged macrocosms of mental supermarkets producing generations of bung fodder for the economy. I readily include Cambridge, New Haven, Berkeley, East Lansing, not to speak of Ann Arbor. (Excluded are universities in big cities where a student is shorn of snot-nosed feelings of exclusivity.)

Zingerman's, however, *changes* Ann Arbor in the manner that Wallace Stevens's jar on a hill in Tennessee changes the wilderness. If I were ever sentenced to a gut-wrenching year of teaching (you don't get to turn out a convincing product all by yourself), I'd merely buy a house down the street and be quite happy. In Zingerman's, I get the mighty reassurance that the world can't be totally bad if there's this much good to eat, the same flowing emotions I get at Fauchon in Paris, Harrods food department in London, Balducci's or Dean & DeLuca in New York, only at Zingerman's there is a palpable feeling of warmth and goodwill, lacking in the others. This is doubtless because Zingerman's educates its patrons through its clerks and a monthly newsletter on the important matters of the cheeses of the world, olive oils, teas and coffees, spices, condiments, salamis, and vinegars. In business ten years, owners Ari Weinzweig and Paul Saginaw have an obsession for the best, and it is consoling to stand with them in a walk-in cooler and look at stacks of imported prosciutto, great wheels of Parmigiano-Reggiano and English farmhouse cheddars, drink a double espresso, eat a meat-filled pastry of Sephardic origin. In the cellar I watched a young man plucking the meat from a hundred roasted free-range Amish chickens, fresh killed daily and brought up from Amish farms in Indiana, to make the lowly chicken salad! This is a moral act in my book. Nothing can taste good without first-rate ingredients, as Alice Waters pointed out, and that's been adopted as a war cry of Zingerman's.

I took a couple of their sandwiches with a side of garlic potato salad back to my hotel on a cold, rainy afternoon. The first down the hatch was an andouille with roasted hot peppers; the second included Amish chicken, Roquefort, and red onion, and was grilled. While eating them I mourned the fate of our country with serenity. We are all peasants with upturned faces looking fearfully east toward Washington. For more than a decade they've been pissing in the national lunch bucket and flogging the bottom dogs. Meanwhile the Democrats, as Norm Mailer brilliantly pointed out, remind one of motel furniture, the kind of stuff I was sitting on and looking at. The East indeed, whence cometh our next hell. I'm betting on Cuba.

1992

CONTACT

Late on the eve of my departure for Apache and Papago country in the Southwest, I had an occasion (boredom) to watch a feature on reincarnation on the Arts & Entertainment channel. The program was morbidly silly, with none of the female nudity one hopes for in late-night satellite scanning. My youth was pre-*Playboy*, far before the photographic organ-grinding of the present, and my interest in naked women is a holdover from these times. A farm boy down the road owned a nude photo of an actress, I think it was a youthful Barbara Stanwyck, which was the envy of the neighborhood at a nickel a peek. We would spring our little woodies and drift across the hay stubble toward the woodlot, all atremble with hormonal torment. One also looked at the back of the photo hoping for the fabled backside.

Back to reincarnation and the mysteries of continuing reoccurrence; it all must be true or the program wouldn't have been on such a tony channel. To be frank, I zoned out, imagining the modernized cave I was on the verge of living in near the Mexican border, then a segue into dozens of past lives where I was invariably a starving infant, which certainly clarified present adult hungers. In most of these previous lives I was merely pitched off a cliff, thrown in a river, or abandoned on an ice floe, never bulrushes. In the Apennines in ancient Tuscany my tiny body was left with a family of wolves who tried to feed me masticated rabbits, but I had no teeth and died anyway, thus explaining a fondness for wolves, rabbit stew, red wine, and garlic. On a cliffside of the Baltic, Viking women wrapped in deerskin without undies stood over my little head praying to Odin before I was booted into the air, watching puffins and shearwaters on the way down before I plunged to my death into a flock of swimming sea ducks, a ready explanation for my interest in both women and bird watching. I was also the toilet-bound miscarriage of a hatcheck girl and a screenwriter working for D. W. Griffith, which identifies a notable lack of success in this area.

Once you get the hang of this past-life thing it is real hard to stop the process. So far I have been limited to the infant human form dramatically truncated by circumstance, though I'm sure when I become properly attuned I will discover I have been flowers, trees, caterpillars, snakes, even a dreadful maggot, though let's hope not a piglet roasted for a Republican fund-raiser.

So great was the stress of this revelation that I slept fitfully, woke early, and immediately set about making a restorative *posole* of elk shoulder, antelope shanks, and deer heart. This would be a soup course, to which I would add an appetizer of roasted doves and a main course of sautéed largemouth bass from Florida, for a group of arriving guests. It did not occur to me that none of them were likely to have eaten this exact meal before, admittedly a somewhat eccentric menu. The menu, though, helped me in the difficult process of discovering what I had been thinking about. For instance, why does it drive me crazy to cook the same dinner within the same year. An enervating habit at best that represents a false striving for originality at the cost of sanity.

Which brings us to the theme for today: how not to be crushed lifeless by habituation and conditioning. To be honest, there had been a recent birthday, a nonevent that seems to occur at varied times each year owing to the artificiality of time perception. Birthdays are soul chasers, ghost bounty hunters that track you down to ask the usual question, "Qué pasa, baby?" When you are younger you are able to thumb your nose, with the reasonable, though often strident, notion that things are going to happen in the coming year. A writer, however, like others in the arts, is in an isolated category. Unless he is witless, he knows very well that all but an infinitesimal amount of writing is tracking fish on a dry riverbed. Serious writers, an artfully self-designated group, may justly scorn newspapers, but in terms of future readers they may just as well have been published in fish wrap.

Still, the direst of notions is endurable if you are properly obsessed with your work and with trying to reinvent the form, as long
as you have a life to go along with it. Just recently I had the idea I
should reread all my work and see how it affected my appetite. I
chickened out, as it were, knowing that this is a "root hog and die"
world, and it is best not to be crippled by self-judgment. The life that
goes along with the work is best designed as a river that doesn't turn
around and look at itself until it slows down at its unwitting but utterly natural destination.

The week before my mock reincarnation reverie I had driven
south to Georgia and north Florida to quail hunt with old friends.
This trip included the childish excitement of sneaking your bird dogs
into a good motel where dogs are not allowed. The older, experienced
dogs seem to enjoy this process, observing the etiquette of quick entries and not barking, of furtive meals enriched by restaurant leftovers.
Dogs get bored, too, and a road trip, which in their dimmish memories has a hunting destination, is a wonderful break in routine. Typi-
cally, they sleep all the way on the two-day trip back home. A word
to the wise is to not get boozed up, run out of dog food, and feed the
mutts a dozen roast beef sandwiches in the Arby's parking lot. The
change in diet has an explosive effect when added to the leftovers of
your Italian meal. You discover that the motel can add damages to
your credit-card number. Hey, we're sorry. We left a twenty for the
maid.

Anyway, on the long trip down I noted that the country had
gotten much smaller since my bogus dharma bum days, or so it seemed
in an incautious moment. But then it occurred to me that cars, airplanes, even houses, are designed for convenience, rather than actual contact with the bioregion, the landscape one travels through
or lives within. The reason why our country seemed so grand, vast,
and mysterious in my youth was because I was hitching, and there
were frequent long periods between rides when I was in actual contact with the locale. You could smell the foliage on the mountainsides,
hear turbulent rivers and the peculiar blurred screech of the red-tailed
hawk, the buzz of cicadas, the alarmed rattler coming to life when

you lifted a hay bale. My fascination with Nebraska began at sixteen on a hot afternoon when I walked off the road, no Interstate then, across a pasture of Herefords, and cooled myself in the Platte River, then napped in a dense grove of cottonwoods. When I awoke in the cool of the evening, I was surrounded by curious calves, and the cottonwood branches were full of irritated crows whose roosting area I had invaded. I ate a piece of bread and warm rubbery cheese from my pocket, and thought of riding a log down the Platte to the Missouri. This Nebraska is unavailable on the Interstate.

In New York and L.A. the meals are more interesting than the meetings, even though with the meetings there is the promise of a check, basically an abstraction in itself, one that will disappear into a paper trail as opposed to hidden C-notes in the billfold. Hunting birds is as far, experientially, as you can get from a meeting, and also has the specific advantage that you get to eat what you shoot. One need not call a Jungian to understand that this experience has several hundred thousand years of resonance behind it.

When you drive out of the North for quail you drive out of winter, which in the South is an imitation of our spring. In a scant two days (I don't entrust bird dogs to the airlines) you are wandering in the peculiar cover of pine and briars and seed-bearing flora that plantations have discovered is the best for the natural propagation of quail. If the day is very warm, your attention is at the maximum because the habitat holds the stray moccasin and rattler, creatures about which your northern setter may have a fatal curiosity. Bird dogs are rather single-purposed dingbats and tend to bring out the mother in you. At day's end you pick off the ticks and groom out the burrs, somewhat on the order of monkeys in the wild or at zoos.

It is not widely understood that when a dog smells a bird and points, this act is an abbreviated stalk, genetically transferred, and emphasized for steadiness in training. If you're a goofy writer you speculate that there would be a downside to owning a sense of smell that developed. If someone farts in the kitchen, a sleeping bird dog in the far corner of a living room is liable to rouse himself. The sense of smell that identifies quail brings the dog to a stylish stop, and the other bird dogs that haven't yet caught the scent have been taught to honor this point at a distance. You then step forward and flush the quail, which travel in coveys. The shooting itself is quite difficult but resolves itself with experience, perhaps on the order of what it takes to become a very good tennis player.

After a pleasantly exhausting day of hunting, you are not interested in the mail, phone calls, newspapers, TV news, or the outside world in general. You take care of your dogs, shower, then cook, the latter prolonging the glory and texture of the day, partly because you have a genuine appetite. During the week we prepared such goodies as roasted doves and quail with a foie gras sauce; a small wild pig with a garlic fruit sauce with a roast teal for a starter; and some grilled barnyard chickens with a paste of garlic and rosemary added late in the cooking and with an appetizer of stone-crab claws. I attribute my lack of a gout attack to my religion and the fact that we also cooked collard, mustard, and turnip greens, plus dozens of vegetables that are never available in good condition up in Michigan. Though my friend and host Guy de la Valdene was raised in Normandy, we experimented by drinking a couple of cases of good northern Italian wine, my notes on the latter having been eaten by my dog when I left her in my room to go dove hunting.

Sad to say I returned home from this other reality with a lump in my throat, which gradually passed with a renewed decision to "grow up," a procedure I have had to make a thousand times when returning to work, this time on a novella and a screenplay. I remained paralyzed, however, until a lucky day when I read Angus Fletcher' s *Colors of the Mind*, a book of conjectures on thinking in literature. This is an immensely brilliant and difficult book and is recommended to anyone with a brain at anchor. The other lucky stroke that day was that my youngest daughter, Anna, gave me a professional Saladshooter, and for the first time I made a skillet of hashbrowns that turned out as a perfect, golden pie. We err when we stray too far from the life of the mind and the potato.

1992

COMING TO OUR SENSES

I took a very long fall that had apparently been waiting for me way up Hog Canyon. The ridgeline looked good for Mearns quail, and I scrambled up in defiance of gravity and good sense, forgetting that the backcountry is always trying to get you to self-destruct. A loose rock perched on another rock, no doubt for eons, was my downfall; I slipped, whirled, spun, slid, then plummeted, ending up on a pile of sharp rocks, deep within which the dread Mojave rattlers hibernated, perking up their little snake ears to the commotion, perhaps thinking that a stray ungulate wired on locoweed had met its doom.

My peerless guide, John Haviland, came at a dead run as if to a funeral offering free lunch and booze. He stuttered in his shock, "Ba-ba-what?-hurt-rammed-rocks," a glyph for what was to become my new name—Baba Ram Rimrock.

So I lay there waiting for the wet spots, the warm emergent blood smelling of sheared copper. My bird dog leaped over my body without particular interest on her way to new cover. Quite suddenly I did a kip-up, a gymnastic procedure, landing on my feet. Strange to say, there was not the slightest of bruises beneath my torn clothes, a fact I attribute to my finishing the fourth draft of a screenplay about how a man became a wolf.

When John and I reached the nearest bar, I called my employer, Columbia, and they agreed to spot me to a DNA test in hopes of pinpointing the cause of recent disturbing body phenomena. Haviland, an old dog hand, aptly pointed out that he had had an English setter (male) survive a leap off a seventy-five-foot cliff, so my experience, though troubling, was scarcely unique.

Of course, everyone knows that old Goethe saw "such a price the gods exact for song, to become what we sing," a rather sad note for the man writing an exhaustive study of fireplugs or rock singers. Just this morning, loping up a border canyon, I was disturbed by a peculiar odor that grew stronger with the miles. Near a seep trickling from beneath a mass of boulders I saw the large, feline tracks, and nearby, beneath a manzanita thicket, there was the spore of a mountain lion, the scent a mixture of pee and scorched fur, which brought me, finally, to my senses.

I've spoken of this to no one yet, and because of the lead date, by the time you read this column it will have gone one way or the other. I may be lost to the ages, but an aspect of this transmogrification is not to care about such trifles. My cohorts at PEN are welcome to split up the shreds of my immortality. The obvious downside of this condition—say, public toilets and that sort of thing—isn't what it might seem as you have become more curious than judgmental. There was an embarrassing moment in a supermarket yesterday, the fabled Reay's of Tucson, where with Peacock I was buying thirty pounds of protein for a barbecue. A mature woman in tennis togs of startling attractiveness passed the cheese display, and my body became spasmodic with an involuntary humping motion. No one noticed except a very old lady who raised her cane, pointed it at me, and said, "Bang," a living precursor to feminism.

Once you get outside the city limits of Tucson the Southwest is considerably more foreign than Europe, on par with Brazil or Tanzania in terms of initial estrangement. The life-forms of the desert are unfamiliar, the initial impression vertiginous when studied at close hand—a cholla, so contorted and angular, is a case of botanical hysteria to a flatlander from the northern Midwest. A different kind of caution is in order, and there is the grace note of a new landscape to draw off your accumulated poisons, a world so strange and wonderful that the poultice effect is instant. It is possible to keep your mind's mouth shut; though, of course, any new place can be destroyed by routine and conditioning in moments if you are unwary. All around us nature answers her own questions and none of our own. The misery is created by asking the wrong ones. If you are looking into a cave far up a mountain wall, it is not the time to wonder why this magazine takes twenty-seven days to send the check. Then you are no longer looking into the cave but back in the verminish suckhole that passes for life these days.

Last night on the American side of Nogales (the Mexican side is far larger), I ate dinner at Las Vigas, a Mexican steak house of surpassing pleasantness. One of the best dishes is *machaca*, which is traditionally made by rubbing a brisket with an assortment of ground, dried chiles, and sun-drying it up on a roof above the bug line. When you are ready to use the meat thus preserved, you cook it slowly with beef broth and fresh chiles until it softens, then you jerk it and continue the cooking until it is almost dry again. The result is a transcendent intensity of spicy beef flavor, a little reminiscent of Szechuan dry-fried beef, a difficult and time-consuming dish to make well.

Years ago, in La Paz, way down on Baja, I ate the local desert beef, tough when not butchered thin, but utterly delicious. Around here the local, cheaper beef I buy, ungraced by the feedlot, is similar: lean, somewhat tough, but with poignant flavor. I sliced some at a quarter inch, grilled it over coals in the fireplace, slapped it on a hot tortilla, adding Ubel Murietta's fabulous private stock salsa, a one-dollar supper, not counting the equally fabulous Joseph Filippi Cabernet.

This all set me to thinking, as my relatives say, whether I ever could go back to those big, fat, larded prime porterhouses except on rare occasions. The flavor of this beef is produced by the variety of dry-land feed during free grazing in this bioregion. Unfortunately, in the upper Midwest, with its relative density of moisture and rich pasturage, you don't get the same flavor result. Our wandering, mountain-bound ungulates are not limited to alfalfa, timothy, vetch, and fattened on corn. When there's not enough grama grass down here they'll eat a variety of wild fodder as extreme as mesquite pods.

Which doesn't exactly bring us to overgrazing of public lands, though we're pointed in this direction. In a month of hikes, I've noted that National Forest and BLM lands in the area are in much better shape than they were a half dozen years ago, in contrast to parts of Utah, Montana, and southwest Kansas. I tend to agree with Mel Coleman, a Colorado rancher, who has offered striking leadership against rangeland abuse, in addition to producing wonderful beef under his trademark Coleman Natural Meats. There has been a lot of grotesque posturing on both sides of the fence. The bottom line is that the 263 million acres of public land used for private grazing does not deserve to be abused any more than it's permissible to deface the Lincoln Monument. If you do not believe land can lose its soul, look at land that has lost it.

I have managed to generate a degree of shame down here from not speaking Spanish. When you are dark complected with a thick, black mustache and also spend most of your time outdoors, it is difficult for others with this appearance to believe you don't speak their language. Despite college French and Italian, Spanish seems unyielding in its erratic, rapid-fire lack of consonants. Years of listening to Les Paul and Mary Ford, Freddy Fender, and Johnny Rodriguez on country-music stations hasn't helped, and neither has close attention to Los Lobos. At a calf roping I think I heard a vaquero say "chinga lo caballo," but I'm not sure. So during the evenings I sit with a Spanish dictionary beneath the radio tuned into a Mexican station, throwing mesquite logs on the fire, watching two feral cats I've adopted chase scorpions. Naturally, nothing in Spanish on a menu escapes me, and there is this image of a man going from country to country speaking a nonsense language made up totally of food items.

Today was the last day in the field, with hunting over until next September, but then my interest had long ago waned, other than hunting as a metaphor for attentive walking, watching the dog for fascinating cues from javelina and bobcat tracks to the peculiar little holes Mearns quail make in search of tubers. There is also the pleasure of physical exhaustion; because of the severely rumpled terrain, a three-hour hunt down here equals two days in Michigan.

By late afternoon the temperature had dropped twenty degrees and my drying shirt was stained with salt lines, my hair nearly crusty. My partner, Haviland, and I had just blown a covey rise, and I had lost my dog. I climbed a hill that was questionable in cardiac terms and looked south at least fifty miles into the wilds of Sonora, Mexico, where vast thunderheads were forming. Far below me at the bottom of the arroyo I could hear John's call, "Point," which sent me again on a skidding descent, hitting varied cacti on the way down with resultant pinpricks of blood. Tess was stretched out before a gnarled oak stump surrounded by thick grass and mean cat's-claw. It was apparently a false point, and after a determined effort to flush the quail I asked Tess, "Where's the bird?" and she darted her head into the barbed cat's-claw and retrieved it. I felt I had robbed a coyote, bobcat, or hawk of a meal, and during the hour's cold walk back to the car I was a dumb, chilled beast without a thought other than a yearning for a quart of water, three fingers of whiskey, a brace of roasted quail stuffed with sweetbreads and leeks. My joints had lost their grease, and it was painful to note that the dogs, despite their exhaustion, hunted all the way back to the car, coursing up and down the hills as if they were immortal. Even more disturbing when we reached the car was the feeling that I'd rather stay up there in the remote canyon than return to what we seem to have agreed is the real world. The notion of "coming to our senses" is never what we expect.

1992

WALKING THE SAN PEDRO

I am at one with my sentimentality, I thought, walking a long way along the San Pedro River straight into an oncoming thunderstorm, a gift of El Niño out of the Pacific, crossing Baja and Sonora and heading straight at me, of all people. Only a sentimentalist can think a storm is, perhaps, picking him out, sort of like Lord Byron giving instructions to the deep and dark blue ocean, also that he be buried with his beloved dog.

The Nature Conservancy is trying to save key areas of the 140-mile-long San Pedro River, the astounding richness of its riparian thicket in a state, Arizona, where most such thickets have been lost for the usual reasons (it wasn't the Natives; guess again). The watershed itself contains more than four hundred bird species, of which, on a good day, I might identify a dozen without my not very dog-eared bird guide. For sentimental reasons I don't like to lug books into the wild, and on this day, for equally sentimental reasons, I was looking for the gray hawk, of which only twenty pairs still exist in the United States. That's not very many, say about the average class size of an Ivy League university, but definitely a higher quality, though nature can't be graded on a curve.

Jack Turner, the famed mountaineer and Himalayan guide, gave me the "I am at one with my sentimentality" idea for a T-shirt while we were speaking of the current and endemic disease of "nature as pure fun." There had been a lovely photo in an outdoor magazine of a silhouette of an arch up in the Canyonlands but marred with a geek, no doubt garbed in spandex, loping across the top. Certain sports, say mountaineering and rock climbing, cycling, and trout fishing, have reached a state of exhaustion via equipment and technique, pointillist scrutiny. Sucked dry, pure and simple. (Cooking is in the same danger.) It is some consolation that Reinhold Messner has soloed every peak over twenty-six thousand feet and without carrying oxygen. Now the sport is something like trying to be a poet in Ireland while Yeats was still kicking strophes.

While hiking Guajalote Flats (wild turkey) with Turner, I had tried to dislodge, nudge away the pain of discovering the recent death of my favorite living musician, Jim Pepper, a Native jazz singer and saxophonist of fatal simplicity and grace. "Water-Spirit feelings running around my head, makes me feel glad that I'm not dead," Pepper sang.

After Turner left to camp three weeks alone up in the remote Escalante country (after Bhutan you're not concerned with snow and cold), I drove over to the San Pedro, listening to my Pepper tape in the gathering storm, the view to the southwest owning that peculiar dense gray of a chalk-dusty blackboard. There's never anything behind a blackboard, just more blackboard, or so I thought back in school, where I never wanted to be anything else but elsewhere.

There was only one other car in the Nature Conservancy parking lot, containing an elderly couple who were eager to advise me to stay put, that a storm was coming. We chatted about birds, then they recommended an "all you want to eat" cafeteria way up in Tucson. I wasn't all that natty, and they must have thought me a likely candidate for a cheap, ample meal. I thanked them and promised to try the place, making a mental note to check out the eating habits of the elderly. Years ago in Paris I had watched Englehardt, the diamond merchant, eating lunch, and he wasn't cutting back. And then there was Curnonsky, the revered Prince of Gourmands, who had virtually collapsed at the trough. I think that in his last year A. J. Liebling even had gout in his earlobes. If one were to do a column on such a grand and austere topic, the magazine should send one to France, or better yet Italy, grand deluxe, since the classiest hotels and restaurants are full of old folks racing to spend the money their heirs would blow on glitzy sporting equipment.

I headed into a path along the San Pedro at a pace beyond my normal capacity, wanting to get at least five miles from the nearest human sign. My thoughts were sunk in the memory of a group of old Italians who ate several times a week at the Prince spaghetti house in Boston when I worked there as a busboy at nineteen or twenty in between stays in New York. I was real hungry when I applied for the job, having been fired and not paid after two days at a car wash for reasons of general inattention. At Prince I quoted some memorized Ungaretti to the manager in an attempt to establish myself as friendly to Italians. The manager had hung signed photos of Julius LaRosa and Jerry Vale above his desk, and I said that my mother listened to Arthur Godfrey every day so I was familiar with the splendid LaRosa. That worked better than the Ungaretti quotes, which were full of the poetic self-laceration normal Italians don't favor ("Have I fragmented heart and mind to fall into the service of words?"). The manager took me down to the basement kitchen, having observed that my trembling was due to actual hunger. I remember that on the stairs he paused to ask about my interests and that I had answered trout fishing, the French symbolists, and the stream-of-consciousness methods of James Joyce and Djuna Barnes. "Trout you can eat," he said.

Carmen, the chief cook, served me chicken cacciatore and fried eggplant, neither of which I had ever had before, plus pasta and what must have been a twenty-ounce glass of red, which made me dizzy. I slept four hours in a linen closet and started work on the evening shift. During the months I worked there, the cooks remained very friendly, no doubt because I was a goofy farm boy who would bring in Pound's *Cantos* so they could help me with the passages in Italian. The cooks stumbled on Pound's Tuscan but were faithful in training me in matters of Italian food, including scungilli, *trippa*, the necessity for voluminous amounts of wine and garlic. They took me to a belly-dancing place where I saw a very young Helena Kallianiotes perform, a fact that astounded her twenty-five years later. But that night we all got quite drunk and wept at the music and belly beauty.

Now, so many years later, walking the San Pedro, I had become teary over the past, Jim Pepper, and the number of vermilion flycatchers there were flitting in the thickets, one of the brightest colors in all creation, and the way the birds could hold almost stationary in the gathering wind. Then I was brought to instant panic by a massive snorting noise and a rumbling bawl. Sharing the dense thicket with the birds was an immense, stray bull, blowing snot and making a not very tentative paw into the earth, which seemed bludgeoned, his ponderous weenie moving in the wind gusts. I noted he had to be part Simmental, which was irrelevant, and that he shouldn't be here. But he was. I waved my walking cudgel and began singing. He roared again but then became subdued by an old Sons of the Pioneers number, "Tumbling Tumbleweed," and went back to feeding. I moved on in a hurried circle, an anointed Orpheus.

The trouble was that I ran into him again two hours later in a driving rainstorm, having forgotten the slight but real danger he posed. This time I was close enough to smell his gassy grass breath, the green fumes, and his hot, rain-soaked pelt steaming in the mesquite glade, the soul of "otherness." In the meantime, driven by my brain and what I had come to see that afternoon as a mind profoundly misshaped by imagination, I had fallen into a riverbank weeping fit. I had pumped along at a coronary pace until my clothes were soaked with sweat and then had seen my sought-after gray hawk in a cottonwood top. I plumped myself down to watch him (or her), and my heart still raced. *So this is my last picture show,* I thought in the manner of a sentimentalist, then predictably observed that it was a good place to die.

There was a suitable amount of thunder, amok songbirds, the rare gray hawk's primaries ruffled in the wind gusts amid pale-green cottonwood gusts. My heart slowed, including the romantic whirl that always includes surreal tinges—"I have eaten truffles like apples, peyote like Oreo Minis, also ten thousand udders; caught twenty-pound pike and trout, two-hundred-pound tarpon (not that big) and marlin, but never wrote a million-dollar screenplay or won the Prix Goncourt or kissed the foot of a princess with a star of amythest in her heel, and I didn't make herring this winter because I was in Arizona." Jim Pepper's up there, or wherever, with Patsy Cline singing the verbless duets of the spheres. Also by dying here I would miss my wife's meat loaf, my favorite proletarian dish.

Lucky for me I got lost in the gray hawk who lifted and set his wings, letting the wind shoot him downstream. How could we drive this hawk out of this world by greed and carelessness? How could we disappear into ourselves and forget our subject matter, the earth?

On the long way back I bowed with impunity to the bull and swung my cudgel at flying tumbleweed. I was wet as a fish and parched at the same time, opening my mouth to the driven water. I thought of Baudelaire, revered in my late teens, who told us to "be always drunk" ("*toujours ivre*") on "wine, poetry, or love." But he also said about the poet, "*Ses ailes de géant l'empêchent de marcher*" ("He cannot walk, so borne down is he by his giant wings"). Possibly sentimental bullshit. I had just walked for four hours, with time out for weeping.

1992

BACK HOME

Distraught, I fled north with little more than a frozen wild pig's head in the cooler for nutrition. The distraught part left me, per usual, when I crossed the Mackinac Bridge into the Upper Peninsula, my *querencia*, as it were, the place where I feel safe and strong, perhaps noble and true, though those virtues become less important the moment I decided not to run for vice president of the United States.

Luckily the wild pig's head was accompanied by an extra set of jowls, a tongue, and a tail, as I intended to make headcheese from a very old family recipe, a dish strongly favored by stalwarts such as Mark Twain, J. P. Morgan, Ulysses S. Grant, Teddy Roosevelt, and Walt Whitman, though it was spurned by Lascelles Abercrombie, Aubrey Beardsley, Martin Buber, and probably Gandhi (the jury is still out on the last).

Culinary purists might question the tail, but then I use all the animal if I care to, and what's more, I still do my own stunts. Strange to say, though, as the head, extra tongue, and jowls began to poach—not exactly a visual treat—orthodoxy swept over me like a heatstroke and I couldn't drop in the tail, which was reticulated like a joke snake stuck in the freezer to scare Mom or the little woman. I'd save the precious tail for a pot of beans and chiles, or perhaps leave it on a remote stump to puzzle a raven or coyote.

The cabin hadn't weathered the winter very well. Among things that didn't work were the generator, the propane refrigerator, the well, the pump, the lights, and the toilet. When the pump was fixed, the toilet blew out due to a frozen valve. It always amazed me that ice could break a pipe. Once in our barn back home I was lucky enough to be there on a cold night—twenty below zero—when it happened. Shrapnel flew, as it were, reminding me of Vietnam, where I didn't appear, having been blinded in one eye in my youth. (The story on the blinding changes somewhat whimsically, the most recent being that I fell off a barn roof on an upturned railroad spike. Next week it could be Mother Teresa's spike heel.)

Meanwhile, back at the cabin, so many things are happening that my head would spin if it cared to. Workmen speed around the property directed by my Finnish hired hand, Eddy Hermanson, who, because of recent cataract surgery and heavy white frost, has requested a coffee royal. This is a simple concoction favored by millions of Scandinavians: coffee, sugar, a couple of fingers of whiskey. Oddly, perhaps because of the early hour, this is not considered drinking but medicine. These are stern folk, and you would be thought a tosspot if you skipped the sugar and coffee. Rules are ancient and stringently observed, and one never hears the kind of modish self-improvement chitchat I had overheard a few weeks before in the Côte Basque—"I straightened out my agenda, and now I feel good about myself." This Brie-in-the-Cuisinart kind of language mush tends to put me off my feed, and I was barely able to finish my veal kidneys *en croûte*. The guilty party was a handsome, well-tailored woman, obviously from Anaheim. Now that "the time of healing" has begun in the L.A. area, they should include a run on the language.

Despite three days in a dysfunctional cabin, I remained brown, round, and serene, while in former times I would have ricocheted off the log walls. I studied the rain, then the dense, cold wind, as I made pork and broccoli with pasta (a head of garlic), a couscous using a massive turkey thigh, winter vegetables (and a head of garlic), and stewed squid with a head of garlic. After I finished my work, which includes three hours of walking so the work won't continue to kill me, I read James Lee Burke novels, a recent wonderful discovery, and James Villas's stunning new *French Country Kitchen*, which I also read as if it were a novel, pausing to brood over splendid plot twists, the movement from region to region in search of prey (a good meal). Villas owns the unassuming style of a master, with a depth of knowledge of French food that is always used to illumine rather than to show off.

It was quite a campaign making headcheese in a cabin on the blink. Bob Kerrey is rumored to have said of his campaigning that it was like spending three months going through a car wash backward. My procedures weren't quite that Olympian, though they required a strength of character far beyond anything Dan Quayle has encountered in his office, at Rotary, or on the golf course while trying to defend Greed as God's will.

Since the cabin was darkish, I hauled the cauldron and head out onto the picnic table, where I could sluice away the mess with river water. As I have implied, a poached pig's head in the shrill light of a cold windy day is not exactly a centerfold. At first I tried to distance myself by pretending I was a brain surgeon, but that act of imagination was sullied by the fact that while my palms where hot and greasy the backs of my hands and rest of me were getting cold. Curious ravens wheeled and drifted far overhead. A brain surgeon doesn't normally work under these conditions, and almost never on a poached head. In the interest of speed, my gestures became crude, ripping and tearing to get at the precious meat within the jowls, the nougats surrounding the neck bones. I dismissed the question of whether it was a girl or a boy pig, snacked on a few morsels, and imagined a group of Nebraska farm girls going through the same thing during butchering in the fall of 1912, singing "You Can't Be True, Dear" or perhaps "A Spanish Cavalier" or the dread "Green Grow the Lilacs."

I stored the picked meat in the cooler and began to cook down the heady broth, redolent of the swamp in north Florida where the creature had lived its feral life, scampering and rooting, shaking rattlers and moccasins like a terrier before it gobbled them, finding edible roots from secret knowledge contained in its genes, wallowing in an algae-lidded pond to cool off in the August heat. I put the kettle of broth outside to cool off before defatting, ate my stewed squid, and headed for the tavern to meet what politicians call the constituency. It was a profitable evening, deciding as we did that the United States Congress and the executive branch must move to Joplin, Missouri, to remove their distance from the people, and to shear away their imperial purple and grotesque privilege.

On the way home on my two-track I flushed a young bear, and there was a flash of panic that the critter might have drunk my pig stock. Bears love pork, unmindful that they are distant relatives to the pig. The bear had failed to reach its target, and though it was after midnight I finished off the recipe; defatting the broth, warming it from jelly back to liquid, adding herbs and a little vinegar, dicing the meat into a ceramic tureen, adding the broth, and placing it into the cooler to seize up again, all by the light of a kerosene lamp. I pretty much felt like a pioneer as I added maple logs (long-burning) to the fire and slid off to sleep, dreaming I was a green man happily encased in a tree with an eyehole outward on a thicket.

The wind shifted to the south, and the weather began to warm just after dawn, now smelling of the burgeoning forest rather than the raw clarity of Lake Superior. After my obligatory and dreary oatmeal I headed for the woods for my first total day off in months, driving a two-track to a favorite place some fifteen miles from the nearest people, where all day I wandered in spirals that must have looked like circles to a goshawk high above me. I was quite happy, as it was the first goshawk I had seen in a long time. Lunch was a tin of cheap sardines, a dozen Nabisco Premium Saltines (I made a mental note to forgive Henry Kravis, as these crackers are fine), and a couple of quarts of cold water. During an after-lunch doze in a thicket full of birds, I paused to reflect on how these creatures are built in such a way as to appear rather ungainly when they mate, but then what would Woody Woodpecker or the Road Runner and their cronies think if they watched one of our sex videos (that Clarence Thomas never saw)?

When I awoke I was part of the ground that someday I will actually be a part of in a somewhat delaminated form. There was suddenly the troubling idea voiced by Tom Robbins: "It is questionable, for that matter, whether success is an adequate response to life." I thought how most writers seem utterly exhausted with their lifelong affair with themselves. In both New York and L.A. I had closely observed what happens to these members of the Famous Guys School, the permanent scowls waiting for permanent deference. By older I mean age fifty-five. Since I am fifty-four, some precautions had to be taken, though I'm not actually famous, more like an offensive lineman for an off-brand football team like the Kansas City Chiefs. I began to think, prone in the thicket, of the Mackinac dictum I had begun to devise the year before to avoid hauling my professional activities into my solitude. Included in what I had to give up when I crossed the Mackinac Bridge were being right, an incredible energy waster; holding the world together by thinking about it; and abandoning what I thought was my personality, a tiresome collection of rehearsals. The last was the hardest, Dōgen's notion of "no contriving reality to suit the self." This is brutally difficult, as indicated by our political life, where the effort has been given up.

This kind of thinking nearly ruined my afternoon walk until I got lost in a swamp and my beastly nature took over. Far, far away in what direction did dinner call? A delicious-looking snowshoe hare scooted by. I climbed a hemlock and saw my big red Toyota Land Cruiser in the distance. *Of course it's easier*, I thought, *to sort life out in the wilderness*. Historically, this is the way it's always been done. But then no matter how shabby and irresolute life can be, I had to believe what Rilke said: "It's only in the rat race of the arena that the heart learns to beat." It's a little difficult to haul your wilderness to New York and Los Angeles, but that's what has to be done.

Back at the cabin at dusk I cut a grand slab of my headcheese, made Chinese-style mustard to accompany it, and a salad, then took it all to the table with a heavy loaf of Chamberlain's sour rye and a sixteen-ounce glass of Valpolicella (I allow myself only one glass of wine at dinner, so I make it count). Like the walk, the headcheese was everything I hoped for without thinking about the end result.

1992

REPULSION AND GRACE

Within either the classic Greek or Elizabethan concepts of drama, disasters of either business or marriage do not transcend the comic framework into the arena of tragedy. Tragedy is saved for those of "high degree" who fall from a "high place" because of hubris. (Marriage and business were not thought to be sufficiently high places, more like an ordinary porch with a bad step.) The fall of the tragic hero is understood to be a fortunate fall, as the dire straits of the hubris-ridden hero reconfirm the eternal verities by which we survive, verities that have largely disappeared. Thus we no longer have tragedy, though we have a vast oversupply of pathos.

Just in case you're wondering, these were my thoughts while fleeing the brilliantined wastes of Gotham, where I had essentially been fired and rehired three times in three days, the age-old shuddering elevator of showbiz. The fall itself was out of bed at the first crack of a pearlescent dawn, gooey with smog and the burnt fur of ozone. Just an hour before, at 4:00 A.M., I had put the deal back together over the phone. It was to be a Day of Eating and Thanksgiving. A rule of thumb for grown-ups is to contain your infections and never leave a city in a state of delamination, an admixture of panic, hysteria, and a lump of coal beneath the breastbone. This is not the kind of soup you want to carry onto an airplane and back home, where you would be liable to distress normal folks with your act as the Rodney King of screenwriters.

When I hit the floor, somehow rather gently, perhaps like a thickish leaf, I instantly remembered that sleeping monkeys don't fall out of trees, also that I had never fallen out of bed before. This was a classy hotel (the Carlyle), and I noted that the area under the bed was clean as a whistle, not a fuzzball in sight, which gave me a sense of the order and rightness of things. One of the dozens of the usual interior voices also told me that all emotions must consciously be sieved through the idea of grace, that we live in a universe and on an earth with meaning. Another voice, a bit more trenchant, told me that when the world woke up, it was time to make arrangements to go to my age-old hideout, the Cornhusker, in Lincoln, Nebraska, where Sanity herself, if never more than an inch away, is in fact in the air of Nebraska like an odorless perfume.

I set off for a hike through the delightfully empty streets—not even the fiber-laden joggers are out and about at 5:30 A.M. In the dense, misty greenery of Central Park I bowed to the six directions and recited a prayer recently learned from the Siberian Yakaghir:

listen you
invisible one
my scream's a storm
covering the world
leave this man
this sick one here
leave this man
alone.

That should do it for the time being, I thought, as I began to run and jump in concentric circles. While catching my breath after a minute of this untoward activity, I brooded on an event I had been lucky enough to witness the week before. *In the thickest of thickets seven miles from my cabin, I hear a loudish, grumbling whuff, and a bear flushes out ahead of me. I come upon a patch of beaten-down ferns where the bear has been rooting, and under a dogwood a movement catches my eye. It is the largest snake I have ever seen this far north, and it is contorted and flopping, mouth engorged, trying to swallow a good-sized toad ass-first. I am repelled and glance away but then I can't very well pretend I haven't seen it, so I stoop down close. The snake's mouth has split a bit near the jaw hinges from the effort and is bleeding. The toad's forelegs, shoulders, and head are still outside the snake's mouth. When I draw to within a few inches, the toad begins to blink at me. I blink back involuntarily. It is all so sudden, I think. What a wonderful epitaph.*

I left Central Park, making a modest detour to pass the finest shopwindow in the city, Lobel's, where my canines visibly lengthened at the meat display, the rising sun glistening off the teeth in the window's reflection. I cut over to Lexington and picked up six ounces of bargain sevruga, unable to resist the bargain, even though beluga is better. Back at the hotel I called my erstwhile producer, Douglas Wick, and invited him over to discuss stress at the power breakfast I had ordered up. To join the caviar on its bed of ice, I had selected a large fruit-and-cheese platter, ham steak, a lemon sole, soft scrambled eggs, hard rolls, coffee, and a bottle of Meursault, obviously a breakfast of champions. After eating his share Wick said he had an appointment, though I knew he was bustling back to the Regency for a snooze.

Perhaps I should have been hosed down with lithium, but the breakfast didn't make me drowsy. In fact, I had a hot dog waiting for the Met to open for the Mantegna show. Unfortunately, the mustard and onions cascaded down my natty outfit. I didn't notice this, despite all the amused stares, which I interpreted as New York bonhomie, until a kindly old lady helped me clean up.

Mantegna made my heart soar as I trotted uptown to my soul-and-mind doctor, Lawrence Sullivan, who has helped keep me alive in spirit all these years. For some reason, after I have written a novel, screenplay, or long poem, I have given away my mind and it is difficult to get it back. Walker Percy calls it the Reentry Problem, while George Romero and the Haitians call it something else. After Sullivan, I decided to skip a formal lunch in favor of a quick frank at the sacred Papaya King and a five-hour nap, the exact number of hours I had been walking, but as luck would have it I spotted some friends from Books & Company at Brighton Grill & Oyster Bar on Third Avenue and went in to say hello. It is impolite to watch others eat, and I noted there were a half dozen types of oysters offered, a rare thing in the neighborhood, so I ordered a dozen Chesapeakes and some beans and rice with andouille sausage, a delicious prelude to an afternoon nap.

Back in my room there was the troubling thought that I might fall out of bed again, that maybe once it starts the act becomes a habit; thus I anchored myself with covers smack-dab in the middle of the big bed, listening to the oysters gurgle to the sausage, which whispered to the frank touching the fading caviar and sole. Just before New York I had spent three days in Chicago visiting the latest reincarnation of Jimmy Hoffa (Nicholson), and we had eaten lavishly and well at Gibsons, including a steak the size of the M volume of the *Britannica*, certainly one of the top-four steaks of my life (the other three were at the Palm, Bruno's Pen & Pencil, and Gallagher's in New York City). The next evening we went to Tufano's and tasted everything, splendidly down-to-earth and delicious, though I had to go solo on a big bowl of tripe and garlic.

As I dozed off there were a number of troubling thoughts, including the possibility of gout. There had also been a number of cards and letters over my last column asking what I had done with the pig tail I didn't use in the headcheese? (I took it to Beverly Hills and used it as a surrealistic riding crop to fend off unruly actresses.) Even more troubling had been a long, very secret meeting with a venture-capital group in Chicago, which made a seven-figure offer to get me to abandon this column and join a think tank in an effort to come up with a new and vastly profitable religion. These wealthy folks were Apocalyptic Pessimists and noted that the public imagination had run amok, the country utterly bifurcated with an orgy of greed and contempt for the poor and people of color on the top side, while the lower fifty percent were a growing class of social mutants. Their essential offer was the purchase of my imagination to help create a syncretic religion out of Buddhist, Christian, pan-nature traditions, to be marketed to the upper classes, guilt-free and profitable—sort of an EST with balls. Curiously, no mention was made of food and wine, wild animals, fishing, dogs, sex, or dance. I walked out of the meeting, even refusing the ten-grand honorarium for hearing them out. I had to continue my struggle with the ordinary, an obsession with the commonplace: day and night, God, marriage, food, stuff like that. And there was the suspicion that once you became an android there was no turning back.

When I got my wake-up call at 6:00 P.M., I was still giddy from a nightmare where showbiz had forced me off a cable strung two thousand feet above an enormous hydroelectric project. As I plummeted down toward the sluices of the dam and the immense turbulent river to my death, I heard a creaking of pinions in my shoulders, which slowed my descent, and I flew laboriously downriver into a pine forest, landing in a tree. I backed away to see what I was, discovering that I had become a black bear with the wings and the head of a huge black bird. What a relief! Such a creature can handle anything.

There was a message from Russell Chatham, the artist, who was in town for the night on his way to Russia to fish Atlantic salmon. We had a fair number of drinks and finished my breakfast caviar; then we went to San Domenico and met the editor of a fine magazine. Given my day's feeding I had intended an evening's fast, but I didn't want to be a wet blanket. During the year before, I had been to San Domenico but had been troubled by the death of a friend and missed the point. This time I caught on as we proceeded through a soup of white beans and plump mussels, roasted eel, a simple pasta of basil and fresh tomatoes, roasted squab in garlic sauce, a number of bottles of Tuscan wine, a tasting of fine grappas.

I'm suggesting that this is a civilized way to leave town after days of turmoil and anguish over your livelihood. At dawn I flew to Detroit, where I picked up a test car for a trip into the interior, fifteen hundred miles on back roads to reach Lincoln, Nebraska, which is less than half that far away out there in what's known as flyover country, the actual heart of this country, driving through a sea of grass, then a sea of corn, a sea of wheat, then back north to the upper reaches of Minnesota, where the forest is a vast green sea, its treetops rippling like green water in the wind.

1992

OUTLAW COOK

I recently finished a novella, and the process so depleted my imaginative energies that I barely knew what to eat. One evening I came perilously close to eating nothing at all, somewhat like digging a big, densely empty hole in the day and leaving it unfilled. Ten thousand nitwits will tell you that nature abhors a vacuum, not one of them having experienced anything that might tell them what the pithy gist actually meant, such as the sharpness of hunger that comes after a day of hard work, say, making up three pages of a brand-new world of unslaked vixens and forty-nine-hour nights. It is the usual stasis of anticyclone, and it makes you as hungry as you are incompetent to address the problem.

So what do you do? You don't just stand there like Lord Byron at his fatal Missolonghi, or drift between cupboard, fridge, and freezer like a newlywed girl musing on her recently perforated hymen, wondering why the food doesn't come all ready on the plates like it did at Mom's. The simple fact is when your poet's eye has been in "fine frenzy rolling," your cooking is liable to become either rotten or distorted. At my cabin I got so jumpy after saving my young heroine from three older men who resembled my friends that I flipped and conceived of a highly illegal meal, a thirty-pound elephant's asshole shipped FedEx from Zimbabwe, cooked for three days in a rock-lined fire hole in a bleached gunnysack soaked in 151 rum, to which is added thirteen pounds of garlic and an equal amount of fresh hot chiles. Serve with plain white rice. A Bordeaux is a possibility. If you feel squeamish about elephants, an entire cow's udder is an acceptable subtitute. Perhaps Dean & DeLuca will ship you one. Or Hormel.

That sort of thing, almost what the lifestyle ninnies call a cry for help. Curiously I was saved from these dire straits by one of the quotes tacked up on the bulletin board above my desk—per usual, salvation is either within or close at hand, and you need not board a plane to track down a guru or one of the civil-service shamans who abound these days. Stuck there, between a fading "Quit smoking" and "I'm giving up control of the world and all its inhabitants," was a message from D. H. Lawrence:

> We cannot bear connection. That is our malady. We must break away and be isolated; we call that being free, being individual. Beyond a certain point, which we have reached, it is suicide. What man most passionately wants is his living wholeness and his unison, not his isolate salvation of his soul. I am part of the sun as my eyes are a part of me. That I am part of the earth my feet know perfectly, of me. That I am part of the earth my feet know perfectly, and my blood is part of the sea. There is nothing of me that is alone and absolute except my mind, and we shall find that the mind has no existence by itself. It is only the glitter of the sun on the surface of the waters.

This message from the deeps jarred me out of the nonsense of the Romantic tradition, the lineage of the artist as Western hero: "I am the Lone. I don't need no one." Quite suddenly I became just plain Jimmy again, and I turned to a stack of cookbooks, both recently purchased and arrived in galley form, which served, along with the Lawrence quote, to simmer me down from a hubris-ridden monster to a rather brown and lumpish middle-aged writer, immortal perhaps, but ordinary. Such is the speed of our culture that immortality itself never lasts more than a month anyway.

John Thorne is a curious soul standing quite alone, the seventh and most distant cousin of that great gaggle that forms the world family of food writers, almost as if he had invented his own environment and had no need of company, much less his relatives. Because he stands well outside, he knows all the family secrets, both good and evil. There is that air about him of the benighted accountant who was fired for saying that Donald Trump didn't really have any money. Thorne has long edited a wonderfully cranky newsletter called *Simple Cooking* and has published a cookbook with the same name. Now he has a new book with the preposterous but accurate title of *Outlaw Cook*, written with his wife, Matt Lewis Thorne. To think of Thorne as only a food writer is the same as considering Raymond Chandler just a mystery writer. In *Outlaw Cook* there is a dimension and resonance of experience almost never found in American food writing, save in that very rare creature, M. F. K. Fisher.

One hesitates to use an ancient (for our time) word like *neuroses*, but it does come to mind when reading Thorne. You wonder what series of psychic knots led him to something as ordinary as a kitchen for resolution, how the winding and unwinding of his mind made him fix on the commonplace, much in the manner of a Zen master, for nowhere in *Outlaw Cook* is food preparation allowed to be more that it is, or to stand for anything other than that intensest preoccupation with life processes, the true familiarity with which is always a long and painful road. As Thorne says, "All I wanted to do was to go into the kitchen and cook. Why did that prove so very difficult?" Here we must remember Umberto Eco's observation about America's obsession with imitation: that we are submerged, drowned in a culture whose media instruments moment by moment lead us away from the possibly genuine in the direction of a muddied approximation.

This is not to say that *Outlaw Cook* won't drive you daffy. After reading the section called "The Baker's Apprentice" I rushed outdoors with a throbbing head and vowed to the stars and northern lights that I never again would try to bake a loaf of bread. One imagines Thorne standing there in Maine during a February gale, the snow clotting in his eyebrows, manning his outdoor bread oven, fired meticulously with hardwood, all from a quite understandable mistrust of a society that is unable to produce a decent commercial loaf of bread.

This distrust further informs Thorne's opinions of food, chefs, and food writers who advocate recipes that don't emerge from ordinary (however unheard-of) principles, principles that can't be humanly absorbed and reproduced. For instance, Thorne is a bit snippish about Paula Wolfert, one of my favorites, who is forever discovering a dish or chef too incredibly remote for the rest of us. I never minded this tendency, which is only a mutation of xenophobia—"I was there first when it was best"—because if I can't re-create the dish, I don't care about it except as an oddity. I readily accept the fact that my périgourdian duck legs may not be as good as an old lady in Périgord makes them, but why should I care? The old lady is not painting Matisse, and neither am I. We are trying to make something good to eat. If someone wants to be a snobbish dickhead in terms of inimitable food mysteries, they are welcome. These are the same sort of snots one met in college, destined never to write anything because they couldn't be James Joyce. They end up making soda bread in Iowa suburbs.

Of course, the proof is in the pudding. The other evening my wife made Thorne's oven-baked potato-and-buttermilk pancake, and it was better than the best sunset, and so are his renditions of Chinese noodle dishes. The most recent pleasure, which helped me survive the brain wastes of the novella, was the chapter on pasta. "What is a meatball, after all," Thorne says, "if not a triumph of quick wit over brute reality."

I made a succession of his pasta recipes for breakfast at my cabin. (It is a significant bit of honesty that Thorne always properly attributes his adaptations). If I work from 7:00 A.M. to 10:00, I am not about to settle for the obscenity of bacon and eggs before a hike. Get your wretched oatmeal out of the way at daylight, and while you work, mull over in an out of the way place in your brain the possible simple noodle dishes you want to eat before you launch yourself into the forest. Heat a reasonable amount of fruity olive oil, chop either three, five, or seven cloves of garlic, and sauté until soft; tear up some fresh herbs—basil or sage are good options; add some pepper flakes and Greek olives or anchovies if you like; boil your half-pound or less of good imported pasta (San Francisco will do), drain and assemble, then strew on a handful of manly pecorino. If you think a waffle is better, you are beyond help. All of Thorne's versions construct a malleable iron in the soul that makes the day's pleasures and mud baths tolerable until dinner. Who gives a shit if you get fired when the belly is full, the senses tingling, a blue moon is coming, a thicket awaits your footfalls, your garlic breath awakes a sleeping bear or startles a deer into a circular prance?

Outlaw Cook is full of the thickish but angular prose of a good novelist, and there is a lot of it, rather than the minimalist recipe instructions of the quasi–food mavens. You could not be further from the captious hoaxes of food magazines that announce the twenty-five best restaurants in America, or how you can pig out on fiber and never fart in your Armani suit. Daily we come closer to the historical arena of that famous food quarrel of ancient Rome: whether the hummingbird's thighs are as tasty as its breast, whether it is better to pluck them alive or dead, or whether one minute or two is the preferable time on the grill.

It is humorous to note that since we have no consistent tradition we are doomed to freedom. Sometimes this works, sometimes not. Unlike Mitterrand in France, or the Japanese, our leaders don't know what to eat and can barely read or write. The dialectics of freedom are such that we delaminate unless we are constantly reminded of our separate ethnic parts. This has always been true since Jefferson, and only diversity and freakish good luck has saved us.

It was rather soothing after the rigors of Thorne to reread Elizabeth Romer's The Tuscan Year, an image, month by month, of a culinary heaven, where the cuisine emerges naturally from the rural ground like the hundred kinds of local mushrooms. It is a book without irony or doubt, simply food and a mode of life that nurture each other.

Another curious boon was A Taste of Memories from Columbus Park, a cookbook that emerged from the old "Westside" neighborhood in Kenosha, Wisconsin, assembled by Catherine Tripalin Murray. Lest you think I am daft, you are rich and can afford to order this book. It is a compilation of neighborhood memories and hun-

dreds of interesting recipes garnered from the families of Italian im-
migrants. We should bow down in thanks to these folks, without
whom we would be eating like they do in Kansas. There is even a
recipe for how to make your own prosciutto if you have a spare hog's
hindquarter. I intend to try it and will advise you in a year's time when
the results are ready and tested.

Meanwhile, our passions help one another survive. Way out
there fine young women with sleek limbs are saved by my fictive
advice. I can't really help B. Q. from Valentine, Nebraska, who wrote
to ask if he should drink his well water if there's brown scum in every
glass, though scum is a possible source of vitamin O. And D. F. of
Hobe Sound, Florida, should not substitute his after-work six-pack
of beer for six bottles of wine. Three bottles is adequate in warmer
climates.

1992

UNMENTIONABLE CUISINE

The doctors told me that I'd never write again, but here I still am, well barded and bigger than the biggest goat, all aflow and afloat in the wine-darkened mud puddle, the beer-belly yawp that is our public life. Where is the weatherman or weatherwoman, the weatherperson, to properly judge the dimensions of the shit monsoon that sweeps back and forth across the land?

On a recent wonderfully meaningless driving trip to Nebraska, it occurred to me that the country would be much improved for my purposes if it could be enlarged to the point where New York City was three thousand miles to the east of my farm in Michigan and Los Angeles was six thousand miles to the west. We have about run out of secrets of the good sort in this country and more space might do the trick; more hidden corners, more empty areas that the cartographers refer to as sleeping beauties, additional mountain ranges with hidden valleys where buffalo roam and grizzlies and wolves coexist in snarling harmony with several Native American tribes whose members, for good reason, have refused to learn our language. Anyone who attempts to photograph or interview them dies instantly from mysterious causes, yet I am welcome because they value my poetry and nutritional advice. Their maidens peel my garlic with trilling laughter.

Real secrets will emerge from a land that isn't veering toward being used up. This was the actual reason I was headed toward Valentine, Nebraska, way up in the Sand Hills where the ranchers have managed this section of the Great Plains with admirable skill. It is nearly all private land and possesses none of the exhausted bleakness of BLM and Forest Service land elsewhere in the West. The landscape, however vast, is insufficiently dramatic to attract the usual sightseers seeking cheap fixes, the kind of tourists who are thrilled by the Elmer Fudd-ish Mount Rushmore, a grotesque insult to a God-fearing mountain. A single glance will make you pray for an earthquake.

The Sand Hills are a splendid mood wrench, and when one's soul has been strained repeatedly through the culture's most soiled sheets—politics and showbiz—it is one of my dozen secret places to go. It is a sea of grass, and if you are attentive you can watch it grow, an act of great personal solace. All great secrets are as open as the gospels shorn of the banal and murderous freight of church history. As the sage told of his life: Before I was enlightened, I chopped wood and drew water. After I was enlightened, I chopped wood and drew water. Decay emerges from the scorn of the ordinary, or from the political distortion of the ordinary where greed and psychotic tribalism are the most esteemed virtues.

Back to secrets. I heard a number of them on this trip, including, on *Headline News*, the fact that our government has stored over a trillion pages of secrets! After a long day's drive, *Headline News* will remind you that an obsession with the landscape is a real healthy diversion. On country-music stations there is the frequently heard genre of secret wise words "my daddy gave to me." Sad to say, these are generally on the impact order of: *Don't eat yellow snow, draw two cards to an inside straight, let your naked wife dance for rich men, or forget your mom in the old folks' home.* The sort of advice that Queen Elizabeth and Ronald Reagan evidently gave their kids. *I shall not piss on the rope that hangs me*, I thought, turning off the radio in favor of various tapes, including Jim Pepper, Roy Orbison, and Tibetan chants.

Curiously, at the Iowa Beef Steak House in Des Moines, a secret arose from my brainpan as I was consuming a splendid rib eye and a bottle of Valpolicella. It was simple fare but damned good, perfection indeed after a seven-hundred-mile day. It is generally better to avoid inventive dishes in the western heartland. Recently my oldest daughter had called, advising against ordering cioppino in Montana. Anyway, at the Iowa Beef Steak House I watched a Grain Belt monster—a motorcyclist to boot—polish off his order of two fourteen-ounce Iowa pork chops in a trice, finish his meal with a quintuple whiskey, then do an expert wheelie out of the parking lot into the night. It was at this moment that the secret came to me, and I'd like everyone to write this down in their diaries: Never eat more in a single day than your head weighs. Startling, isn't it? Obviously, I *should* be starting a new religion.

Back at my motel, I rather excitedly called my wife with this secret. "How do you weigh your head?" she asked. "My people are working out the details," I replied, turning for comfort and warmth to my bedside travel book, *Unmentionable Cuisine*, by the renowned food scholar Calvin Schwabe. I won't spoil it for you by telling you the ending, but this book is chockablock with intriguing details and recipes from throughout the world, exploring with unmerciful wit the xenophobia of our food habits. For instance, last month I suggested in jest that a cow's udder was a possible substitute for an elephant's fundament in a recipe, and in Schwabe I discovered an appreciable French (who else?) recipe called *Tétine poelage*, which, as Schwabe implies, would be a certain hit in Jackson Hole.

Unmentionable Cuisine made my heart sore, as xenophobia is my bête noire (off rhyme). The mere idea of genetic or locational virtue has been, outside of religion, the main source of mayhem and death since the world began. If the Chinese wish to eat their festive pooches and cats, so be it, just as we must be tolerant that England ate a good share of its draft horses during World War I. Pancreas is favored by some, as are rats, mice, and varied forms of snake and insect cookery. This led me to reflect on the growing beef prejudice among certain groups of our culture—usually those quite remote from the agricultural cycle—in favor of white food (chicken breast and fish). These folks think they are going to live longer. Too bad it comes at the end. They are also ignoring the high longevity of the beef-eating areas of western Nebraska, west Texas, and New Mexico. One of the main causes of death is fretting about your diet.

The relentless fertility of Iowa and eastern Nebraska began to distress me, and it was a relief to leave the Interstate in Lincoln. Given sufficient time I would avoid these vehicle sluices altogether and once managed a thirty-day, seven-thousand-mile drive without

getting on one. A day looking at old photos at the Nebraska Historical Museum and two nights at the Cornhusker further soothed me,
as did eating at Laslo's, where I loaded up on skillfully cooked fish to
get ready for beef country. My only tantrum came on a walk as I mused
on the recent huge spate of feel-good books written out on the soft-
est edge of the environmental movement. We are ill served by sentimental fibs that ignore the human history of an area. Any day now I
expect by mail a galley called *The Earth, My Big Buddy*.

On the way up to Valentine, I stopped near the famed city of
Dannenbrog (the Danish capital of Nebraska) and visited with
Roger Welsch and his wife, Linda, who cowrote *Cather's Kitchen*.
Welsch is the real big fellow in overalls you see reporting from
the heartland on Charles Kuralt's *Sunday Morning*, a columnist
for *Natural History*, and an author of a dozen books on folklore
and Native Americans. In a curious way, he knows more than just
about anyone I've met but wears it so lightly that his peculiar
genius, like Will Rogers's, can go unremarked. After too many
drinks at Eric's Bar, where wit was rifer than at Elaine's, we cooked
T-bones, and I was awake at 3:00 A.M. meditating on a Jungian notion found in a bedside book to the effect that depression comes
from living too high in the mind. Of course. Someone should have
told me this when I was fourteen and trying to parse Nietzsche,
Schopenhauer, and Niebuhr while holding down a job on the football team. At first light I was deep within a thicket in Pawnee
country along the Loup River, returning to the house for a light
breakfast of eggs, potatoes, and fried *jackatrice*, a Czech headcheese
that Welsch had made. On my way to Valentine with a somewhat-
bilious stomach, I thought about Welsch's work and those other Nebraska triumphs—Willa Cather, Mari Sandoz, Loren Eiseley, and
Wright Morris—though it must be admitted that they jumped ship
in the first flowering of their talent.

I drove into the Sand Hills with the fervor of a hermit headed
back to an island remote from our collective madness, spending the
day on roads I hadn't managed to take in on a half dozen previous
trips, loitering, walking, chatting it up with meadowlarks and heifers,

deer, wild turkeys, a lone rattlesnake on the Nature Conservancy ranch along the Niobrara River near Norden, where they raise buffalo and Texas longhorn cattle. These grasses, varieties of bluestem and grama, have always depended on ungulates, whether buffalo or cattle, for their health.

On the way into Valentine, I made sure that Bill Joseph's Peppermill was still there, then checked into the Super 8 motel and reviewed my hundred pages of notes for a screenplay to take place in the area in the 1920s. I had two successive dinners at the Peppermill with my local cronies, Bill Quigley, Corky Young, and Cleo "Junior" Bloom, a retired rancher and Juilliard graduate. The massive, prime, well-aged T-bone went dreamily with a Trefethen Cabernet. We stared nervously as Quigley's wife, Ann, actually ate shrimp, which at this longitude and latitude looked like albino tomato worms. After a very long day's drive through the Rosebud and Pine Ridge reservations into the Badlands, I repeated the dinner, this time with a two-pound rib steak of superlative quality and flavor.

This was all close to what Rimbaud wanted—Christmas on earth every day—though in the middle of a sleepless night I took a long walk with a lump in my throat, sensing the soul history of the Rosebud to the north, then dreaming of a photo of the Night Chase family of Sioux.

1992

HEART FOOD IN L.A.

On a recent longish trip to Los Angeles—where the raw meat was thrown on the floor and I was left sucking the mop, a vilely mixed but accurate metaphor—it occurred to me that when one is utterly cornered and snapping at one's entrails like a fatally wounded coyote, about the best thing you can do is read a book. "Reading will carry you away," said Kari Loeschke, grade five, the winner of our local 1992 bookmark contest, a statement not the less wise for being so widely ignored, and frequently by the writer who ought to know better but most often doesn't.

So on the second day of a ten-day plummet into fear, degradation, hysteria, and near bankruptcy, I left my hideout at the Westwood Marquis and drove over to Dutton's, a bookstore in Brentwood, where, running counter to habit, I avoided the cookbook section in favor of stronger stuff. There was a palpable lump in my chest when a clerk found a copy of Pablo Neruda's *Memoirs*, a revered book of which I once ordered ten copies and gave them away, leaving me none for the past decade. I also bought a fresh copy of Rilke's *Sonnets to Orpheus* and the compendious *Collected Poems of Octavio Paz*, edited and translated by my prized student at Stony Brook back in the mid-1960s, Eliot Weinberger. I found out only last year that Eliot was never actually enrolled, just hung out for whatever knowledge was available—in other words, a pure student whose peculiar genius married very well with that of Paz. Anyone who wants to understand Mexico must also read Paz's *The Labyrinth of Solitude*.

On the way back to my rooms I stopped and sat by the carp pool at the UCLA botanical gardens, where I once met a brain surgeon who came there to "calm down" before he opened yet another skull for corrective procedures—certainly as demanding a profession as writing screenplays. I sat there and let the mud settle for an hour or so, finally so still that an iridescent-green hummingbird came within an inch of my blind eye, doubtless sensing the nectar there in the memory of childhood flowers. A catbird also approached, giving dozens of renditions, including cats, horns, Los Angeles traffic, the cries of actresses who would never get parts, all in mockery of my interior whining in this paradise.

Back at the hotel, I watched a band of feral parakeets swooping over the gardens near the pool in an attempt to drive away what looked like a red-shouldered hawk. I had forgotten my bird-watching monocular, which is also useful for looking at the ladies around the pool, ladies as beautiful as a head of white garlic beside a bottle of red Montepulciano. Then I smelled the new-book smell of my new books, the astounding freshness of the pages, the countless glyphs I was about to relearn.

It seems we are either lapsed or evolving, and every day you can tote up one or another. It is impossible to establish a holding action when, as Novalis insisted, "our bodies are moulded rivers." Or at least it is for me. My recurrent fantasy of simply owning an Amoco station somewhere north of the forty-fifth parallel has become dog-eared. I have always been troubled by Rilke's notion that "only in the rat race of the arena can the heart learn to beat." Cloistered virtue is just that. An Amoco station would simply be a lame trade-off for a hermit's cave.

After the parakeets disappeared in a slender, green cloud toward Santa Monica, I began to read Neruda and within half an hour the great Chilean had sedated the banal foment of Los Angeles all by himself. What power! The ringing phone, unanswered, and the android voice mail were less than neither here nor there, something akin to music too crappy to be despised. At one point I looked up to study an interesting cloud, one that enclosed with schizophrenic humor my powerlessness in Babylon. Everyone knows that writers are not es-

pecially valued out there, though novelists who also write screenplays tend to be indulged a bit. "Pride goeth before a fall," Mom and
the Bible used to say. My current entrapment deep within the trash
compactor was caused by my own hubris, greed, and ambition. Writers
are simply holes in the earth out of which is mined the raw material
of stories; in short, they are garden-variety versions of the Delphic
oracle.

This notion of being both mine and miner, a working stiff, made
me warm all over and I returned from the cloud, which was headed
for China, to Neruda and a conversation he was having with Lorca
about Rubén Darío where Lorca quipped: "In an adjective he gave
us the sounds of the forest . . . a master of words, he created constel-
lations with the lemon, and a stag's foot, and a mollusk filled with
terror and infinity. . . . He built a limitless esplanade of gin across the
grayest afternoon the sky has ever known." The book was an invisible tropical shower washing the mud away.

I would like to say the days rolled by, but they didn't. Interspersed
with what are called meetings, I returned to my Neruda, Paz, Rilke,
and Frederick Turner's splendid new A Border of Blue—a study of the
history and nature of our Gulf Coast, which arrived in galleys—and
also worked on notes on my new religion to be called, simply enough,
Bobo. The religious notes developed at an accelerated rate when I
spent the weekend at a friend's house and was able to develop their
suspicious extremities in a room decorated with actual paintings by
Bonnard, Soutine, Rouault, Matisse, Picasso, and, of all things, a
Chatham landscape. The main text of Bobo would be a novella,
Running Fucked, by my "other" and pseudonym, Bob Duluth, who,
while running out the entire forty-fifth parallel, collects his thoughts
on his Sony Dictaphone (as a Columbia employee, I get fifty percent
off). Nutritional and sexual theories will be included.

Under the extremest tensions, some writers turn to Dick Greg-
ory diets and become even more sallow and depleted. This has not
been my M.O., to be frank. There was a troubling moment at an

A-list dinner party where I was informed that my restaurant choices weren't "in" at the time. This sort of pathetic bullshit has been thrown in my face throughout the world. I don't care who else is there. I even like Chasen's, and its Republican habitués, who in other situations might gag a maggot but do not deter me from the fine food that has a genius for the ordinary. I also like Orsini's, Giordano's (gorgeous appetizer table), and, most recently, Ca'Brea, where the whole boned, marinated, and grilled chicken was a skull popper, one of the top dishes of the year. Having tried and failed to bone a chicken through its ass, I am aware that it's no mean feat, though it bears specific similarities to screenwriting. I asked Tom Sweet, the proprietor of Ca'Brea, and I think he said that the chore was farmed out to some Japanese ladies in the suburbs. I no longer take notes in restaurants as it makes everyone nervous.

Another recently opened triumph is the Monkey Bar, a true hangout, a semiclub with an excellent kitchen headed by Gordon from Aspen. The menu is somewhat eclectic but I ate there on three evenings without a soupçon of disappointment, trying dishes as varied as jerked pork loin with Cuban fried rice, the freshest broiled halibut, a kick-ass risotto with hot chiles, a superlative fresh corn chowder with nuggets of Maine lobster. The Monkey Bar is not a place for the rara avis of food snobs, who would be diverted by too many beautiful women in a crowd that appears singularly unsmitten by the guilt of success. The restaurant would be unthinkable in New York, where folks are loath to appear happy.

Returning to the hotel each night, tummy full, brown, and round as a floating Botero model, I'd read until 3:00 or 4:00 A.M., until the words drifted away from the sentences and the paragraphs slipped down to my chest, where they stuck attractively to the splotches of red wine. The TV remained off for the ten days due to the depraved and unendurable sincerity of politicians. I wept bitterly when Neruda died again, as he must, over and over for each reader. I dried my tears by grinding my face into the pillow and sticking it out the window, where the smog had cleared and the night's scent was oceanic, flower-laden.

*   *   *

Disappointments don't separate anyone. At dawn, hours from departure, I became homesick finally for my bird dog, Tess, and my shot put, a sport I have been developing for myself because it's so ordinary and represents nothing but itself. I packed my stacks of books and remembered an April fourteen years before, when both John Huston and David Lean were bent on filming two of my stories. It didn't happen but then the stories are still in print and in my own versions. The maudlin is never appropriate, nor can one approach this floating world like an aging midwestern linebacker.

The world wonders at the improbable vitality of our trashiness. The world is real tired, and we seem to be getting that way ourselves. There is a frightening mortality to it all, the sheer odds against a durable product in a collaborative medium, but then it's been done before, again and again, and will be done in the future. It is much easier to look back at good movies and forget the enormous effort behind the ninety-seven out of a hundred that turned out pretty worthless. There is an inordinate capacity in institutions, whether governments, universities, publishers, or studios, to turn pretty good wine, vintage or not, into distilled water that they hope everyone will want to drink. You have to hold out for the wine, even blood, nights that are actually dark, bears that aren't teddy, gritty women like you actually know, children who die contorted into question marks, the sun on people who never bought lotion, the human voice not reduced to prattle, animals who have never been watched, the man who cuts all the ropes so he won't hang himself.

1993

FRESH SOUTHERN AIR

Just this morning, at dawn in fact, I stood outside in my underpants in the dense, bitter cold, a blustery wind laden with snow out of the northwest, thinking about the new administration and the wild-duck soup looming as an obvious breakfast choice. It was a comfort indeed to finally have men at the helm without benign contempt for blacks, Latinos, Native Americans, gays, lesbians, artists, and women. All these folks have been getting a raw deal for quite some time now, so much so that I won't mind in the least when my well-deserved income tax edges back up to the fifty-percent mark. The only guilt I find really tolerable is in the aftermath of gluttony, common as Seattle rain or flies around a cow plot.

During the soup I had made the night before out of leftover mallard carcasses, I began to brood over the old notion of the dollar-a-year man, once a form of government service offered by the financially blessed to their beloved republic. I don't really make all that much, but enough so that a MacArthur grant wouldn't make a dent in the annual financial mud bath. The fact is that I liked the idea of being called a dollar-a-year man, and surely Clinton and Gore could afford fifty cents apiece for my sage advice in the area of nutrition and beverages. I would not dream of adding the sexual advice that is solicited from me in local taverns, also in New York and Los Angeles, not to speak of Nebraska. "Either do it or don't. You're going to regret it both ways." That characterizes my stock answer in the sexual arena, and also covers trips to the dog track, most restaurants, and perhaps life itself.

So, Bill and Al, send me fifty cents apiece, and pardon my familiarity. At least I'm not some relentless kvetch like Sam Donaldson. Also, I'm older than either of you and can call you what I wish. I worked valiantly for you in the aforementioned boîtes—in recent years it required a couple of drinks to even bring up the subject of politics, what with this notion that there was an invisible cloud of liquid shit sailing over us day and night. Now that the cloud has dispersed, we can all wash up and go to work, having finally perceived the real contents of trickle-down. And take note that I don't actually want to go to Washington, which I have found tremendously disappointing, except for the crab cakes, the National Gallery, and the intelligence of Bill Bradley. Besides, I have outgrown my cheapish suits during a long spate of taking in too much air and water, a neuroses I hope to overcome. One tended to gulp air and water during the past twelve years, needing to be grounded in basic elements to avoid falling off the country like dead meat off an upturned platter.

I actually stayed up until 4:00 A.M. to watch the election returns owing to disbelief and anxiety that television was pulling a monstrous hoax or late returns would turn it all around. After a fitful ten-hour sleep I hungered for the normal and had a Spam sandwich for breakfast, a long hike, then Campbell's tomato soup (with cheddar cubes) for lunch. I shall not pass this way again, as they say—an unrepeatable experience, once in a lifetime, a culinary bungee jump akin to Mengele's dentist chair.

Now to the advice itself, though I haven't received my buck yet. Tear up the bloody Rose Garden, which has become as tiresome as Paul Harvey and Rush Limbaugh. Dig an enormous pit barbecue and plant a vast herb garden. Build a kennel for bird dogs, preferably pointers and setters, also a skeet and trap range, a trout or bass pond to practice fly casting, and a big vegetable garden, as nothing humanizes quite so much as growing some of your own food. Feed the workmen who are doing this and do some of the cooking yourself— distance from food preparation poisons the soul with cold abstractions. I forgot the kiva for Native dances, and while you're at it paint the house green. It's been white too long.

On dozens of trips to the American South for sporting purposes, including Tennessee and Arkansas, I have noted a number of nutritional pitfalls and, in fact, have fallen helplessly into them myself.

For instance, when my brother John left Yale and New Haven for Fayetteville, Arkansas, he gained seventy pounds in seven years through an addiction to biscuits and gravy, a southern fetish. Now that he is back to a vaguely normal size, I accompanied him to his informal therapy group on this addiction. Biscuits and Gravy Anonymous is a little less dramatic than other twelve-step programs—you can push gravy only so far into metaphysics, and the problem is mostly a metaphor for itself. I piped up with an idea cribbed from the great therapist Sandor to the effect that gravy is a bicycle you never forget how to ride—you just have to stay off the bicycle. This notion was met with little enthusiasm, as the group did not mean to ban biscuits and gravy, only to control their consumption in all its multifoliate forms: sausage gravy, ham with many variations of red-eye gravy, even biscuits with chicken-gizzard gravy, or the dread gravy with gravy in a bowl, drunk, by general admission, when no one else is in the room.

One can easily imagine Gore and Clinton way back when in pinkish England yearning for the dish, but by reducing current ingestion to once a month the desperate procedure of jogging can be avoided. At this very moment I know nine ex-joggers with ruptured discs and five more awaiting knee surgery. One can scarcely sort out the world's collapse under tribalism and illusions of genetic virtue while experiencing back pain. During my own month in the hospital in traction I howled obscenities at one and all, and allow me to tell you that a nation cannot be led while under the influence of Percodan, Demerol, and the humiliation of hospital food.

Since everything is available to you, you should know there is such a thing as power food. Surely you remember when Mitterrand made sorry mincemeat out of Reagan in Bonn during a time when the Great Communicator's doctor had him on a diet of pullet breasts, yogurt, and fruit. Mitterrand, meanwhile, had been eating power food: foie gras, confit, rillettes of forest pork, pigs' feet, calves' brains and liver, sweetbreads, a daily dozen Belon oysters, game birds, mussels, plus literally shovelfuls of garlic. The results of the meeting could not be otherwise. One has to wonder if those who control the nutritional wing at the CIA were not sleeping at the switch.

And banish that dreadful fake French "continental" food at formal banquets, state or otherwise. People would be infinitely happier with a three-hundred-foot Italian sub from Manganaro's, with the contents of the cheese and dessert counters at Dean & DeLuca on the side. There are hundreds of ample soups and stews that can actually be served hot—daubes, bourrides, carbonnades, cioppinos, even the holy Mayan *menudo.* Beside each plate put a magnum of Woodbridge, a wonderful table Cabernet I've been drinking recently. I say a magnum per setting because there is no nastier experience than being trapped between two bores with an empty glass. If you want meat, place cutting boards laden with barbecued pork shoulders, beef briskets, ribs, and loins spaced out along the table so folks can carve their own. If you want to tip your hat to the vegetarians, have bowls of broiled Tuscan vegetables dressed with olive oil and garlic, also some poached Pacific coho, seviche, giant Costa Rican avocados brimming with Dungeness crabmeat. Come to think of it, there is a simple dish that would stay hot for large numbers—a French dish that involves stuffing a braised quail surrounded by a potato-and-leek purée back into the baked-potato skins.

On the subject of vegetables, avoid those undercooked miniatures that no one eats, and read Thomas Jefferson on the subject. Accept no foreign gifts but Bordeaux and Burgundy—the word will get around. Do not forget the greens of your youth—collard, turnip, mustard—they are an integral part of the choo-choo train of digestion, pushing the dangerous fats downward to the Potomac, though they slide better with an ample quantity of salt pork.

For entertainment before, during, and after dinner, invite Iris Dement to sing her "Our Town," segue into the Pro Musica Antiqua during dinner, then a "battle of the saxophones" afterward between Sonny Rollins and Jackie MacLean. Don't avoid guest clashes, as they keep people awake. Seat Billy Graham (a saint in his profession) next to Allen Ginsberg, Matthew Fox next to Ross Perot, Dennis Banks and Russell Means beside Kevin Costner, Marilyn French next to Warren Beatty. Since it is not politically correct to have dancing girls, try dancing boys and girls together in the form of any of a dozen ballet companies. Simply everyone likes to look at bodies. And don't forget daily and fully undressed naps. Most of the fatal mischief engineered in the world is accomplished by non-nappers, folks who can't let well enough alone, or so states a joint study by the AMA, the London School of Economics, and the Bobo Institute.

This pastiche of advice, with more to follow in the years ahead, is a sample of what you'll get for your dollar. Some of my critics think that over the years I have learned a little too well how to get the jump on hunger. Perhaps. But then I was never meant to be wise, and Washington has thousands of somewhat bilious wise guys. What's wrong with having the first vivid presidency since Kennedy and Johnson? The past twelve years were gray indeed, and now we need some technicolor.

1993

BORDERLANDS

Once again my birthday was allowed to pass unremarked by my government, the world's most powerful autistic child, big as all outdoors. Over the years I have sent them a fortune with nary a word of thanks. At any given moment I could be pitched into prison for no clearly announced reasons. My health has been shattered by dread. Luckily this is only the mood of the moment, because it is this precise nexus of emotions that led Hemingway to point the gun in the wrong direction, wing shooting the frightened old bird that had become his brain. We can't become inconsolable just because life is incomprehensible. Nature, art, food, and sex stand tethered like a hobbyhorse to a stair railing, waiting to carry us away, no matter that ten thousand "political trollops" continue to pee on the grave of the future. This kind of solid thinking and ten bucks will get you a cup of coffee in New York.

It used to be that birthdays meant something. In my family a birthday meant you got what you wanted for dinner, which for me meant pickled herring—usually homemade from a keg of salt herring—and beefsteak, both foods sonorous with fiber and eager to help build the man I would become. Frankly, I have always found the song "Happy Birthday" to be odious, right up there with "Achy Breaky Heart" and "Happy Days Are Here Again," and have never allowed it in my presence.

My wife and I had fled Michigan like orphans in a storm, not quite outrunning the three blizzards that tracked us for more than two thousand miles. Quite by accident, these blizzards also inconvenienced other travelers. My 4WD utility vehicle, a Toyota Land Cruiser, was in the hands of a hired driver taking another route, and we were in my wife's Saab, a car she has favored for years despite the fact that, out in the Big Country, Saab drivers make moues and wave at one another, which embarrasses her, as it should.

Anyway, we reached Amarillo in a state of trembling exacerbation, avoiding the Big Texan and its scrumptious five-pound sirloins and wandering minstrels because I wanted something a little more refined. We checked into a Best Western near a hospital, always a comforting sight should an asteroid strike nearby. There have been a lot of scare stories about incipient asteroid attacks of late, and they have replaced black holes in space at the top of my fear list.

Now, Best Western had always been my favorite motel chain, but when I trotted up front to check the restaurant menu I discovered this one was dry. You heard me, *dry*. Was that not impossible in this day and age? I queried the desk clerk, my body all aquiver. The reason turned out to be the proximity of the hospital. I questioned the causal relationship between the two, but all for naught. I went outside and watched the dense sleet fall, making a drive to another restaurant impossible. I had a notion to call Stanley Marsh III and yell into the phone, but I didn't know him and he was doubtless unlisted. Marsh is the reason I take the Amarillo route. I never fail to be thrilled by his splendid sculpture of the upside-down Cadillacs stuck halfway in the dirt of an immense pasture near the freeway. Along with works by Robert Graham, Robert White, and Jack Zajac it is one of my favorite pieces of outdoor art. What I was going to ask Stanley Marsh III is, Why not embed giant, upside-down, empty liquor bottles outside of dry establishments in the area, thus creating art that would also be a boon and a warning to the weary traveler?

Lucky for me I remembered that the two pairs of Paul Bond boots in my truck contained, for protection, a few Grand Crus, including a Ducru-Beaucaillou '75 and a Calon Segur of the same year. It seemed a shame to use such fabled (also jostled) bottles on a room-service meal that included a confused-looking stir fry, a rib steak, and a chicken-fried steak with cream gravy, which I turned pinkish with my Tabasco travel miniatures, but where was I to turn? We became merry indeed, so the waitress was also happy and did not comment when my bird dog Tess thrust her nose far up under her skirt when she bent over. Dogs are gender neutral when it comes to their nose interests.

Things picked up the next day, even though we were trapped in Lordsburg, New Mexico, by another storm. It occurred to me to adopt my son-in-law's custom of a birth week rather than limit myself to the arbitrary day. A sound decision that defied the frenetic pace of our culture, I thought, while packing the car and noting that the dog had eaten most of a fine slab of bacon we had bought at Robertson's Hams in Seminole, Oklahoma. This explained why she kept getting off my bed during the night for water. We joined each other in a trot along the snow-laden railroad tracks, bent on purging ourselves of the trip's gross fodder.

Counting my cabin, I live three-quarters of the year near the Canadian or Mexican border. Due to lack of ambient light and air pollution, the nights remind you of your youth, the peerless air of the northern forest night. The stars were much closer then and you could see the cinders in their bright smiles and the Milky Way was a dense ermine floss, a cumulus of stars. One aches for this cosmological intimacy. On the borders you see again in the clarity of the air these presumably same stars of your youth. They soothe you and make you a member of the universe; the ironies dissipate, and you shiver with the marvelous recognition of mortality that is a primary gift of the natural world.

On arrival my birth week continued on in my favorite area restaurants, Er Pastaro, Mr. C's, and Las Vigas, where in turn I ate my beloved *puttanesca* and mussels *posillipo*, *cabrilla* with garlic sauce, and *machaca*, which is what cattle aspire to taste like when questioned on the matter. Equally delicious in the area is the foreignness of the biotic community: the unthinkable shapes of ocotillo, agave, cholla; the sheer uniqueness of javelina, coatimundi, and roadrunner. One day while quail hunting alone in a remote spot, a pair of golden eagles followed me for a while, their position as a possible omen quickly

evaporating in the grandeur of their "selves" going about their business. I could see myself clearly from their point of view when I skid-
ded down a long creek embankment on my muddy ass.

Then one morning it began to rain, and the phone ended up
being out of order for a couple of weeks. Important phone-company
executives never allow themselves this pleasure. It continued rain-
ing for nearly a week, and we feared Sonoita Creek would flood, a
bit of a problem since it's fifty feet down the bank from our front door.
Then the rain let up for a few days, and we were relieved when the
waters subsided a foot or two on a mark we imagined on a fallen cottonwood across the creek. I was about ready for a night of untroubled
sleep and stoked the fire, looking around with pleasure at the absence
of a television set, when the skies fairly opened and stayed open all
night. This is not supposed to happen in the high mountainous desert,
where the water can drain only downhill toward our casita. I dozed
alertly, getting up now and then to shine a flashlight out on the
chocolate-colored torrent. At first light I heard a *whoosh* of sorts but
could only dimly make out the water. A huge cottonwood shot by
like an arrow and great balls of flushed tarantulas and dormant rattlesnakes raced past, though they might have been tumbleweed and
sticks. *Feets get me out of here*, I thought, and we packed a few essen-
tials, which in my case meant my favorite shotgun and what I call
my "art"—a sheaf of poems and a half-written novella. We fled, as it
were, and the sight of the flood in full daylight gave us tremors. A
fifteen-foot-wide creek was now a quarter of a mile across.

We were without food an entire hour before moving in with
friends. Second thoughts began to arise by midmorning, as our friends'
refrigerator was barren of interesting items. I recalled I had stowed a
selection of Italian wines in a closet, including a Lungarotti Rubesco,
an Isole e Olena, and a Salice Salentino, all purchased from the
Rumrunner, a splendid wine-and-food shop in Tucson, right down
the street from one of the best grocery stores between the coasts,
Reay's. The leaden, weepy skies cried out for these health potions, as
well as some breathtaking steaks sent from Boyle's in Kansas City.
Luckily I had a cudgel in the car that could double as a wading staff,

the kind you use while trout-fishing difficult rivers. We fought our way through the mud, debris, and current to get the wine and meat, my heart racing at the peril.

A few days later, in the aftermath, I searched the arroyos for bodies and the gold nuggets the sluicing water might have revealed. I was told to do so by someone in a local bar called the Big Steer, certainly a reliable source. I found neither.

An obviously simpleminded correspondent has reminded me that I had promised some "words to live by" every month. Here's something we can all do when we become quarrelsome with wives, husbands, room-mates. An argument had started over how long to sauté a turkey liver for the cats, and I had reminded the little woman that she had blown the lasagna back in July of 1966 by using insufficient sauce. Tempers flared around the home, so early next morning we took a dozen eggs out the back door and hurled them against an immense rock forma-tion. How wonderful the crisp crack and splatter against the morning song of the canyon wren. If you live in the city, there are plenty of rock-solid buildings that will work as well, since eggs at a buck a dozen beat out some fungoid marriage counselor mouthing inanities about *bond-ing,* a word with all the resonance of *pedophile.*

Another word to the faux-liberal press, who are already jump-ing on Clinton with their tiny, pink, clawed cat feet, suppurating condescension for all things "southern," most of all white male southerners, presumably because these press members saw *In the Heat of the Night* in college. You are the shitsuckers that sank Jimmy Carter's noble ship and slick-slimed the skidding way for Reagan's greed-androids, from whom we will not recover in our children's lifetimes. Read Willie Morris or dozens of others on the subject. See if you can write a piece without mentioning BBQ, dogs, the local sheriff, chew-ing tobacco, bubbas, pop coolers, and pickups. It is important not to miss the world that is actually there.

1993

VERSIONS OF REALITY

There is always the possibility of developing a new sport, or at least a parlor game, though the moment of creation tends to rely on isolation from the suffocating aspects of culture. A phenomenal percentage of discoveries on the theoretical level occur to scientists at the moment of waking, when the most abstruse of concepts gather functional dream images around themselves.

Down in Patagonia we live in a canyon without the possibility of television reception, and a radio that attracts only a few Mexican stations. I don't see the newspaper until noon, which is too late for it to have any real part in forming the day's thought patterns, and magazines are forwarded once a week with the mail. If you are a lifelong news junkie this vacuum can become vertiginous. None of this was planned, mind you. Thoreau wasn't looming in the ideological background, nor were the Zen hermits I revere before flicking on the late news.

The game I have devised to counter or encompass this reality came to me while I was sleeping at the foot of a desert canyon. There was a layer of frost on the sleeping bag and all night long the stars kept on moving, as they will. Here comes Scorpio, and only the week before Venus had nested in the cusp of the new moon! Sleep was erratic due to owl calls, coyotes, snuffling javelinas, and the fact that my pockets were full—including a monocular, pliers (for pulling out cacti thorns), car keys, and talismans; and all this useful junk had lumpishly embedded itself in my flesh. It didn't occur to me to correct the discomfort by depositing the stuff in my nearby boots because I was in the midst of a Cosmic Wine Trance. Assuming you're interested in the prescription, drink a bottle or two of good Tuscan wine, eat quite a bit—in this case rib eye steaks broiled over mesquite coals folded in a tortilla with red onion, tomatoes, and salsa—then chase the wine and food with a little Herradura tequila. The upshot is that you'll fall asleep at nine and wake up at 3:00 A.M. with mild indigestion, frost on your face, and the soul of a nineteen-year-old poet stuffed to the gills with incomprehension. Before you drifted off and the moon waned, you could see a thousand-year-old petroglyph of a half-man, half-lizard above you on the canyon wall. Now the only information that will console you is in the stars above your head. Lucky I got only one eye or I'd be keeping track of twice as many.

The idiot game you begin to play is one your mind frequently plays without you as a conscious participant. You simply count and condense the versions of reality offered to you by magazines, television, newspapers, movies, art, books, music. The middle of the night out in the open is not the time or place to become enraged so you have to keep your critical faculties bathed in acceptance. After running through a hundred or so versions, the seams have totally burst and you are a harmless nutcase transfixed by the cosmos, having left the earth behind.

Try it sometime, but leave out people for the mind, in case you didn't know, can be gratuitously cruel. Say you start with *The New Yorker* (arch, rich time stuffer) or *Penthouse* (condemned seafood restaurant), *Dances with Wolves* (one man is our friend), *Northern Exposure* (pert friendly folk), *Gourmet* (mango salad, Debbie Schwartz), *Reader's Digest* (rungless ladder), CBS news (quiet resentment), and so on. About halfway to the hundred count you will feel macerated by banality and note how, almost invariably, fame outpaces talent, and that ninety-nine percent of everything is a wet cold basement indeed, that in fact you are floating off to the final Bethlehem on a sea of bilge.

Sometimes in the process you trip and shatter. The other night in my desert canyon it was *Natural History* that throttled me. I had hastily (aversion) read a piece about the recent extinction of the dusky seaside sparrow as a result of the arrogance of NASA on Cape Canaveral and the neglect of the U.S. Fish and Wildlife Service. I can recall an Aldo Leopold quote in the piece: "For one species to mourn the death of another is a new thing under the sun."

This information "bite" levitated me with anger, breaking all the rules of the game. I actually saw the hole torn in creation that Peter Matthiessen described as the natural result of the extinction of a species. It was an unpleasant hole. Fuck the space program! If these guys are so smart let's see them create for us a new dusky seaside sparrow. I envisioned a funeral for the sparrow attended by all the bird species on earth, and, after the funeral, I put the matter to rest by seguing into *Terminator 2*, which I regard as the most contemptible movie ever made.

After another fifty or so versions of reality were allowed to drift off, I ended the game contemplating a dozen or so irreducible man-made realities out of Mozart, El Greco, Dostoyevsky, Melville, Joyce, Shakespeare, Beethoven, Bach, Stravinsky, Yeats, Turner, Rembrandt. Certain of the galaxies began to acquire color and whirl. You imagine your state of mind before you were born. There's only you and the night. Then just the night.

Perhaps my game isn't all that much fun though I've been playing it for a month or so now. When I awoke that particular morning I bowed to the millennium-old rock-faced lizard king, an irreducible reality in itself. The great thought of the day was daylight. What need is there for chemicals when you can get there by yourself?

My daughters, son-in-law, and grandson were visiting and it was fascinating to watch a three-year-old eat spaghetti with his hands, a method also recommended by the food mage John Thorne. We had been cooking family dinners—with occasional breaks at restaurants—that had included green chile *posole* with epazote, Italian pork chops Modena style (Marcella Hazan), chicken with comte cheese (James Villas), fireplace fajitas, grilled rabbit and sausage with semolina gnocchi, Paula Wolfert's herbed pork ribs, and a splendid Brazilian *cozido* (ham hocks, brisket, garlic sausage, oxtails, and a half dozen vegetables) out of Felipe Rojas-Lombardi's *The Art of South Ameri-*

can Cooking. This was all relatively simple cooking that left a lot of time for naps and hundred-yard walks with no sudden turns.

There was a real challenge when Charles Morgan way down in Destin, Florida, FedExed us an eighty-pound cooler of seafood, including shrimp, oysters, crabmeat, scallops, scaup, and red snapper. We invited a bunch of people and, even so, it lasted only two days. The freshest of seafood doesn't require backspin and irony; you must simply allow it to taste like itself. Crab cakes with no filler are a luxury, as is Caribbean crabmeat salad with the simplest vinaigrette. We made a scallop seviche, an oyster pan roast (for breakfast), and stuffed the whole red snapper with lime slices and cilantro, roasting it with a baste of dry vermouth, butter, and lemon. The next evening I turned with relief on my tingling goutish toe to spaghetti and meatballs.

I keep getting asked by letter and on the street by Jane and John Does dressed in spandex how they can prepare simple "gourmet" dinners in ten minutes so as to prolong, presumably, their cross-training and spritzer-drinking binges, massage and colonic appointments, drumming and marriage-counseling sessions, and tarot-card swap clubs. An easy answer here. Scoop ample quantities of Skippy on two paper plates. Handcuff each other and then slam your faces down into the plates with gusto. Good for the gluteus maximus. And it will bring you together at the sink, plus you won't have to violate your space by answering the phone.

Back to the game. Doubtless we humans need, or are sold, all these versions of reality to locate ourselves. Raymond Chandler can still be quite a help in L.A.; the same with James Lee Burke in Louisiana. I assume a lot of folks have headed for Alaska hoping to find the witty paradise of *Northern Exposure*, which has struck me as often brilliantly written. I have to admit that many, many years ago I liked Warhol's prolonged film about the Empire State Building, which was made simply by training a movie camera on the Empire State Building. There is also the question that perhaps I've spent too much of my life refusing to locate myself by anyone else's version of reality, offering up hearty handclaps to the void. Maybe I made up all these fibs because no one asked me to be headmaster of a home for dysfunctional cheerleaders.

The lizard man up on the rock face changes moment by moment until my mind stops itself, at which point he becomes fully disinterred from the past. We can be reasonably assured that he did not have to deal with countless varieties of consensual reality but, at the most, two: his own sign as a local shaman and the reality represented by an immense boulder at the foot of another canyon a mile south. On the surface of this boulder are five *metate* holes about a foot deep where various wild seeds and nuts were long ago ground into flour for food. Around the holes the granitic rock is smooth where Hohokam bottoms had sat at their work. The lizard man helped interpret reality for the workers, who doubtless wondered on occasion if the guy knew what it was like to have a real job.

1993, previously unpublished

ADVENTURES OF A ROVING GOURMAND

THIRTY-THREE ANGLES ON EATING FRENCH

Maybe it's a sin to think about food so much, especially about French food, which is so decidedly foreign to us in nature. We have to write from our own point of view, and mine is Calvinist–Swedish Lutheran, at least in my childhood and up until I left home. The great Austrian poet Rainer Maria Rilke, who was thrilled when he discovered Quaker Oats early in this century, wrote, "What is fate but the density of childhood?" Part of childhood is to "eat what is set before you." Part of jumping off the porch and leaving home is to look for new things to put on the plate. I fled to New York City and discovered garlic at age nineteen. More than forty years later and sitting before the fire in my cabin in Michigan's Upper Peninsula, I just checked my garlic supply. Seven heads, enough for another few days at best.

When the renowned French gourmand and writer Gérard Oberlé was at my home last October, I served him an ample bowl of oatmeal, partly in jest. His very large face pinkened as he shoved it away. "Gérard does not eat cow food," he said with the giggle of an immense girl. He watched me eat my oatmeal with sympathy and curiosity. "Why do you begin the day with punishment?" he asked.

I wanted to say, "To live to eat another day," but all the evidence isn't in yet on this subject. Besides, Americans talk a big game, with their countless self-improvement projects, but it is in France that I see people eating dozens of different vegetables, fruits, and grains. They don't have to talk about it because they do it. Balance is a matter of culinary tradition, not something that is prated about endlessly in magazines and the "modern living" pages of newspapers.

This is a cultural inclination rather than a rule among the French. I am drawn to French food out of curiosity and pleasure rather than for health reasons. I am not a Francophile, a term that raises as many parodic images as Anglophile. Many of us have had professors who, after three months in France or England, would smoke a cigarette like Jean Gabin or wear a thirty-buck tweed coat and affect an Oxonian accent. True Francophiles also have invariably collected dozens of places that are forever unavailable to whomever they are speaking. "But of course, you fool, one only goes to Luberon in the last week of April. And I said lunch, not dinner. Lucette and Jacques are always out of sorts by dinner. Lucette's mother is a virago with goiter. Don't tell me you didn't meet her." That sort of thing.

I find Paris a great deal friendlier than New York or Los Angeles. Of course, there are irritations. There are even irritations in your own home, where you are presumably in control. The idea that a croissant or baguette with coffee is enough for breakfast strikes me as idiotic and certainly accounts for all the flaring tempers in France in the hour before lunch, by which time people are dazed by low blood sugar and howling with hunger pangs. Just the other day at my cabin, I took a two-hour stroll at dawn, then fished for twenty minutes or so, and then had the classic breakfast of beans, bacon, and trout. Of course, I'm not shuffling important papers on a desk but the baguette and coffee must presume absolute nonmovement. I've been advised so often in France to save myself for lunch, but what good is that if you have to sink your teeth into your arm for a pick-me-up?

Yet after more than a dozen trips to France and despite making a largish collection of French cookbooks and wine, I'm still not sure I've done any truly deep thinking on the subject of French food. This morning, in the spirit of privation caused by high blood pressure, high blood sugar, and mild gout—none of these, of course, triggered by a recent three-week trip to France—I began to wonder if eating in France doesn't adapt many of the attitudes the human race usually reserves for sport, albeit more sedentary sports, or games like bridge, pool, chess, and poker. And I've often wondered if the legion of thin Parisians doesn't maintain the relentless habit of walking in order to get ready to eat. Sport, of course, requires mental dexterity, a trained body, and acuity for what's coming next, even if it's food. While cooking or waiting for a meal in a restaurant, many of the French have the hard-edged concentration of Tiger Woods approaching a tee shot.

Historically speaking, great cuisines—like Chinese and French—tend to emerge from economies of scarcity. "We use the whole animal" has always been the motto of the innovative cook. As for myself, I have not shrunk from grilled pigs' ears, though I prefer the tails. And two years ago in Burgundy, when Oberlé made me a *tourte* of pigs' noses, I was thrilled indeed. It is labor-intensive to prepare four dozen swine noses for the table. That leaves most of us out, including restaurants.

Our food writers tell us that we and the English are beginning to achieve a level of restaurant parity with France. This is not quite laughable and xenophobic if you consider that the food writers are talking about, at most, two dozen of our restaurants, in which, given a fat wallet, you can eat very well indeed. The claim also assumes ready access to New York, Los Angeles, San Francisco, or Chicago, or to stellar culinary outposts like the Lark in Detroit or the Mansion in Dallas.

The trouble is that there's no real fallback among our ten thousand other restaurants. Certainly, you can occasionally manage an appreciable meal, but I keep thinking of a *routier*, a French truck stop, where I had a wonderfully sautéed duck leg and thigh with potatoes nicely browned in goose fat with garlic. In the center of the room was a serve-yourself counter heaped with an assortment of vegetable preparations, fresh lettuces, and a variety of shellfish on ice. A muscular woman emerged from the kitchen still whipping a very large bowl of fresh mayonnaise. The truckers sat at long tables in the back, while we tourists were in front with a splendid view of their big trucks.

This experience made me a little melancholy. How wonderful it would be to have this simple lunch on one of my aimless seven-thousand-mile car trips in the United States, or even in Los Angeles during a screenplay-money trek. I don't want a "skinless, boneless chicken breast" served with a raspberry-kiwi salsa devised by Chef

Ralph. If you lacked a meat mallet, you could use the bottom of a laptop computer and make a reasonable paillard out of this skinless, boneless chicken breast, and, with a classic sauce, serve it to your pooch—say my English setter Rose, who helps me gather true fowl: quail of four kinds, woodcock, and ruffed, sharptail, and Hungarian grouse.

So if you can accept that we have a couple of dozen good restaurants in America, and you preferably live on one of our two dream coasts, and assuming you make several hundred thousand bucks a year, you can eat quite well beyond the confines of your own kitchen. And in big cities you even have a fallback position in the ethnic restaurants where a tradition is being carried on, but in the country as a whole you need an as yet uninvented food compass. Available food guidebooks have a woefully low batting average. We're not necessarily talking about the fate of nations but in a profligately fertile nation my common experiences after thousands of restaurants is one of regret. You see fellow diners gagging with melancholy.

Much has been made in recent years of the specific benefits of drinking red wine with rich meals and how the French beat heart disease with this pleasant method. Forgotten in the marvelous equation is the fact that the French appear much less stressed by the daily impedimenta that haunt us all because they presume they're always right. I've never been sure how sincere and deep this conviction is, but it is certainly an operative grace note. Doubt in itself ruins digestion. Blatant confidence is a wonderful lubricant for questionable behavior, not to speak of an ideal way to reduce stress until it's an infinitesimal brain wart.

My wife, Linda, and I were staying with Oberlé and his partner, Gilles Brézol, in Burgundy—not the fashionable wine-producing part of Burgundy but to the west, in what must be called the cattle country, near the Morvan. It is a strain to think of all that Oberlé represents beyond being a writer and dealer in rare books. Rather than using a prettier, literary metaphor, I would say that he is the Michael Jordan of French cuisine, while Brézol is a deft point guard. In France, there is a good deal of resonance to the word *gourmand*, none of it pejorative except in the minds of the emotionally dysfunctional.

Back to the notion of the confidence of being right. Oberlé thought we might break up the routine of eating at his *manoir* (an overwhelming routine) and travel to Vézelay, where his friend Marc Meneau is chef at his three-star L'Espérance. To make it a well-rounded experience, we visited the marvelous and unique Basilica Sainte-Madeleine for at least fifteen minutes before starting lunch with four smaller courses in the garden of L'Espérance preceding going indoors for the larger items. We began with what looked like cubes of fried croutons, which you pop in your mouth and slowly break with your tongue, loosening the foie gras and truffles with which they're mysteriously stuffed. Next came a small packet that resembled something *en croûte*, but the enclosure was actually very thin roasted piglet skin wrapped around morsels of meat from the pig's tail and the tiniest fresh fava beans from the garden just over the wall near our table. Next we had a simple hollowed-out potato containing a ragout of squab hearts and decorated with a sautéed rooster cockle stuck in the top. We cleansed our palates, as it were, with a bowl of chilled gazpacho, in the middle of which was a dollop of mustard sorbet— odd-sounding but it worked fine.

On our way inside, my wife implied that we had already had more than enough. In a technical sense, she was right, but then again we were having a luncheon feast, celebrating something or other, perhaps Life herself, a real big mama who always urges us on to clean our plates.

Inside the lovely main room, we were served an entire poached foie gras accompanied by some beans and small pork bits that had been cooked overnight in a champagne bottle in the embers of a fireplace. Foie gras has always been tough on what's left of my system, but after ample amounts of Meursault, Nuits-Saint-Georges, and Vosne-Romanée, I felt appropriately that I was representing American honor and was in no mood to shirk, though the next course, a *hochepot* of sausage, filet, oxtails, and marrow, very nearly finished me, even before my favorite French dish of all, the legendary *pou-*

larde demi-deuil. Translated freely, this means "chicken in half-mourning," because black-truffle slices are stuffed up under the whole chicken's skin to give it a funereal look, not because it's dead but because it's enshrouded with this rapturous fungus.

Now I was quite full and barely managed my rhubarb torte. We also shamefully skipped the cheese course, using as an excuse that the day was overwarm, not certainly that we had had too much to eat. In the spirit of "being right," it is quite inevitable that you have eaten the appropriate amount. After this five-hour lunch, we mutually agreed that we should skip supper when we got home, though Oberlé was a little dubious about this heresy.

Let's step back more than a little, though our range is less than infinite since it is impossible, despite the hyperbole of professional food writers, to speak of food in a cosmic context. Perhaps it is even inappropriate to use the same adjectives with food that we do for Mozart and Gauguin. If the veal chop is "marvelous," what do we have left for van Gogh? Quite a puzzle, and it bespeaks again our limitations with language rather than the limits of language itself. When we read a newspaper every day, not to speak of magazines, we see that common print usage is a blunt tool indeed. Yet who cares if language is a big net between us and food; it certainly is a smaller net than the one between us and God, women, and nature. There is also the palliative that if language rouses our appetite, we can always trot off to the kitchen and make something to eat. Right now, at my cabin, I'm bathing a half-chicken in a full head of chopped garlic, lemon juice, olive oil, and hot peppers. Utterly ordinary in my scheme of things. Immutable nature is right outside the window, not to speak of inside my skin, but at the moment God and women are somewhere out there, beyond viable usage. Food, quite wonderfully, is in your face.

A very young child can be quite violent and captious about food, forcing parents to become Calvinist bullies. Such "clean your plate" fascism is apparently contributing to our country's large proportion of real fatties. Rather than the tack of "you must grow and get big" the French tend to coax their children by convincing them that the food tastes good. In my own case, I suppose I am truly my rural-born father's son, as he favored fish and game, homemade sausage, and the freshest vegetables (he was an ardent gardener). Other than dried salt cod and herring the only fish readily available in our area were those we caught ourselves. I still eye and sniff cynically the product in fish markets, having so often eaten my own fresh fish, often within hours, if not minutes, of making the catch.

There has been a recent, though perhaps waning, craze in our urban centers for certain ordinary food items, such as meat loaf and mashed potatoes. These items are spoken of condescendingly as "comfort food," as if the resident chefs transcended these plebeian items on a regular basis. Only they don't. Try finding in our restaurants a good roasted or pan-fried chicken, a simple piece of peerlessly fresh sautéed fish—items that are ubiquitous in France. I managed to have a fine roasted *poussin* at Lutèce years ago, when the chef was the grand André Soltner, who said in reference to the current, often silly, innovations of younger chefs, "I myself have never devised a recipe. I simply cook French food."

Well, yes and no. Obviously, some innovation is critical or a tradition atrophies, withers, and is of interest primarily to food antiquarians. Chefs such as Alain Ducasse and Marc Meneau have gone their own way, much in the way of an experimental novelist who, after all, is still writing novels. I feel more comfortable and curious at Meneau's L'Espérence than I do at such a temple of gastronomy as Taillevent. In the latter, seven of us managed a tab of $2,800, mostly because we became ditzy with the wine list. You don't go to Taillevent because you are hungry but because you wish to be teased back into comprehending a classic tradition: you are eating Stendhal, as it were. At L'Espérance, you are eating a French version of Gabriel García Márquez where the clarification of the French tradition is radical indeed. The taste for one of these restaurants over the other is mostly a matter of temperament. Great restaurants are not in a sack race except in the minds of food ninnies.

*   *   *

It's mid-August and the weather is cool and rainy after a dismally hot, humid summer. I have put away my rather shabby fishing gear. Part of geezerdom is to not throw away one's favorite old equipment and clothes, though you would certainly throw away letters and photos of old girlfriends because you are finally worth divorcing.

This week, along with writing, an evil profession, I'm working my English setter bitch, Rose, twice a day for a total of at least three hours. Much of the Upper Peninsula is rather rough, summoning up a sturdier appetite than, say, a day of meetings in L.A. or New York, where babbling lips burn few calories. This morning at seven, I put my *estouffade de boeuf*, a somewhat generic beef stew from the Camargue region of southern France, in the oven. I say *generic*, because a half-dozen recipes I have for this dish vary the ingredients a bit though they usually include lesser cuts of beef, much garlic, a few tomatoes, red wine, a few anchovies, herbs, and Provençal olives. You cook it for hours and hours at low heat.

After literally hundreds of attempts, I have accepted the fact that I'm not a very good French cook. This realization was slow in coming. I'm a bit better when I'm not writing because the parallel universe of fiction is not conducive to the attentiveness required for even average French cooking. It's a little like a surgeon trying to handle his investments without advice. The illusion that because you're good at one thing you're inevitably good at others is relentlessly comic. Jordan played baseball like Leonard Nimoy sings ballads.

It's now five o'clock and I'm on my second glass (a twelve-ouncer) of Gigondas, a Côtes-du-Rhône I favor. I just tested my *estouffade*— really quite good, though it occurred to me that I had forgotten to blanch the salt pork (an uncalled-for ingredient) that I'd used to brown the beef, so it's a tad salty. I yelled "Motherfucker!" rather than "*Sacré bleu!*" French recipes lack the forgiving nature of BBQ. When my French friends arrive, I barbecue with my special sauce of lust and violence. The dish makes them loudmouthed and dumb, the way it makes us. It once cost me six hundred bucks to get a Weber grill to Oberlé in Burgundy, which was a lesson in "free trade."

The dinner is very good, accompanied by some fresh green beans from my wife's garden. I used to say "our garden" but I mostly look over the fence. While eating, I think of other food and become melancholy about the best first course of my life. It took place at the Passadat, a restaurant in the hotel Le Petit Nice in Marseilles. It looked like a crab cake but in fact it was a lightly bound patty of the meat of fresh frogs' legs, held together by paper-thin pralines of pork and served with a tablespoon of creamy garlic sauce. American ponds are full of frogs but we don't use them in this transcendent manner. I'd be proud to be a bullfrog who bit the big one in this fashion.

A very cool dawn and there is a sense that I may have forgotten, on purpose of course, to thoroughly defat my *estouffade*. We peasants need our fat for the rigors of our labor, but then I recall I'm not quite a peasant anymore. I awoke with Rose staring me in the face, which was bathed by her unpleasant breath. A lothario I know claims that vegetarian girls smell and taste better. This is the sort of claim that cries out for government- or foundation-funded research, but I am passing the project on to younger writers who, swamped in the ironies of obtaining their MFAs, are crying out to return to earth, to sink themselves in reality pudding.

Meanwhile, as my errant mind would have it, I'm involved in the ideological struggle between process and content in American and French cuisines. The profit is in a process, non–labor intensive, that makes minimal content sufficiently appealing. This is the law of fast food and there's a smidgen of it in any restaurant, and more than a smidgen in chains that pretend to be non–fast food but where there's only a few oafs in the kitchen manning the microwaves. But then we have all sensed the fraudulence in most of our restaurant food, even though we can overlook the main principle behind it, identified so gracefully by the great Tuscan writer Umberto Eco: Americans are spectacular at imitating the genuine, and in this case it is more profitable to imitate genuine food than produce it.

These thoughts are pushing me back toward my bed but the NPR news is discussing a Turkish earthquake "catastrophe" and I wonder again why I bother accessing, moment by moment, all the bad news in the world. My oatmeal looms, a viable penance to begin the day, followed by two more "C" memories. First, a *raie au beurre noir* I had at L'Acajou, a French bistro in New York City. This is a well-browned chunk of skate or ray wing full of the tender little intriguing cartilages that enable this creature to move along like an enormous underwater bird. This is followed by memories of Carcassonne, both William Faulkner's marvelous story and the city itself, sitting nobly on its ancient battlements, where I managed one of the most monstrous cases of indigestion in my life after eating an entire *cochon du lait*—a whole tiny piglet cooked five different ways and arranged artfully on the platter at a fine restaurant called Barbacone. Much of the impulse behind my eating is aesthetic, but then occasionally a sort of overdrive kicks in and there's Mom and Grandma standing behind me howling for me to clean my plate. It's clearly their fault but also my own if I cannot liberate myself from their dire influence.

Moving west and south of Carcassonne in my mind's eye I ponder Basque cuisine. That's it! For dinner I'll make a simple *poulet Basquaise*, the chicken parts (the sacred thighs) nestled in their comforting bed of eggplant, mushrooms, red and green peppers, a head of garlic, and so on, a perfect marriage of process and content. If you don't have an hour to cook your dinner quit your job. I recently read in the *New York Times* about some young brokers who don't have time to buy toilet paper so they go without.

There are culinary traps in Paris that must be avoided. I've learned that you really can't manage two large meals a day without imperiling your well-being. Have some not so simple fish for lunch, say at Le Récamier or at Maison Prunier, or the best sole I've ever had, which was at that temple of conspicuous consumption the Ritz, or a simple lunch at Benoît's. Above all else, you must walk two or three hours a day in this, the finest walking city on earth. Of course, sometimes nothing helps. You struggle along the sidewalk watching French-women *click-clicking* past you, their high, gorgeous bottoms rubbing cheeklettes together in those soft, thin wool skirts. Your roiling tummy can't keep up with them. There ought to be a speed limit for these walkers.

Once, I was strolling off lunch along Rue St. Jacques after closely examining a number of meat and fish markets along Rue Buci. Just because you are full doesn't mean you lose immediate interest in food. Perhaps trenchermen, gourmands, are teethed before they are born, or at least gum their way into the world, and for them only *more* approaches enough. Anyway, I glanced into a nondescript café and there was Francis Ford Coppola working on a dreaded laptop. He looked up, waved, and said, "I have just the place for us to eat," rather than "Hello, how are you, isn't art wonderful?"

The next evening, a bunch of us went to L'Ami Louis, including Danny DeVito and Russell Crowe. Francis, as a very full blown food bully, did the ordering. I didn't mind because I'm a food bully and an amateur nutritionalist myself doling out advice as I smoke and drink several bottles of life-giving red wine. I had been advised that L'Ami Louis catered to Americans and wasn't what it used to be. Nothing is. Nothing ever was. Francis ordered our table of eight a gross of snails, a platter of foie gras, a leg of lamb, and "some chickens," among other goodies. The restaurant was exclusively stuffed with French. The meal went on and on. Jack Nicholson once said to me, and it bears repeating, that "only in the Midwest is overeating still considered an act of heroism." If so, Coppola would be an honorary homeboy of the heartland, and so would Orson Welles, who on a number of occasions made me feel like a gaunt Mary Poppins.

We had a dozen or so bottles of fine Bordeaux, and Coppola directed the check to DeVito, not because he had eaten the most but because one of the finer Hollywood traditions is that whoever is doing best that year picks up the tab. I was sure it exceeded the recent bill at Taillevent, but as an *invité* I wasn't concerned. A less pleasant Hollywood tradition is when the star gets fifty times what a writer does for making the whole thing up. I was secretly delighted when

an angry studio head said to me, "You're just a writer." In my experience French food in L.A. has been curiously soulless except for the
old, now defunct Ma Masion which was Orson Welles's local favorite, and a recent experience at the Little Door on Melrose was very
pleasant indeed.

Last evening, after an overample portion of my *poulet Basquaise*, I
ran Rose on grouse and woodcock for an hour. She ran too far into
a rather nasty swamp and went on an immovable point. A half
dozen grouse were roosting in trees, and Rose's stiff head drooled. I
barely made it out by dark so this morning I chose a more wide open
area called the Kingston Plains, where she managed to point a pair
of sandhill cranes, and then a single sharp tail grouse. Near a lake
we sat and watched an osprey catch a fish and eat it without salt
and pepper.

    This arduous two-hour hike gave me yet another new lease on
life, and at the grocery store I bought a bottle of salt-free ketchup as
a gesture toward bodily perfection. True, I'll never be one of those
fey, scrawny yuppies you see in male clothing ads, but surely I can
slow the natural progress of deliquescence. I have been eating so much
garlic that last night I thought my flatulence might propel me off the
bed onto the hard floor, where an injury was certainly possible.

    I have been meditating on my own mediocrity. Almost con-
sciously, I summon up a justified feeling of humility about my cooking. I have studied the work of great chefs such as Meneau, Fernand
Point, Ducasse, Joël Robuchon, and Olivier Roellinger, and read the
work of Waverly Root, Elizabeth David, Paula Wolfert, Patricia
Wells, Alice Waters, and Richard Olney, but all of it comprises
"head" knowledge. The culinary arts are no more democratic than
the others, and sincerity of intent is worth about as much as last night's
flatulence. Great and good cooks serve a very long apprenticeship.
I've been studying how to write for forty years and I'm still learning.
My cooking is similar to, but less in quality than, those hot new
American chefs who are innovative before they learn the language.

It is similar to thinking you can write French poetry after a couple of years of college French. Get down on your knees, preferably before the sacred stove rather than a dysfunctional cheerleader or your own errant cooking ego. Even your departed mother-in-law, a torturous virago, could cook better than you can.

There. This lesson may last well into the next day. A certain daffiness is in order in both work and play, cooking included. Maybe what we call dignity is only faux Republican indifference? Once, in the kitchen of a considerable château in Normandy about twenty-five years ago, I watched Christian Odasso, the brother-in-law of my friend Guy de la Valdene, prepare an asparagus soufflé buried in which were seven whole eggs that poached as the soufflé rose. Odasso made a map so that when he portioned out the soufflé, none of the eggs would be broken. This was all the more extraordinary because we were all quite stoned, marijuana being basically a nerve medicine in those days. Like mountains for climbers and rivers for kayakers, recipes have levels of difficulty, and that one remains unthinkable for me.

Eating in French homes is a radically different experience from the restaurants. In a home, you have removed the overwhelming motive of profit. Restaurants are for hopeful, carefree pleasure and convenience, also for dishes that are complicated and beyond one's range of cooking talent. For instance, I have a passion for *tête de veau* (the tongue, cheeks, brains, and neck meat of a calf), but have seen it made in a home only once, and that was at Guy de la Valdene's, when he had inherited his mother's French chef, Richard Labbe, for six months. It's not necessarily appetite-enhancing to see a Holstein calf's head lowered slowly into a bubbling pot. The final result was indeed delicious, but the process had been a little onerous.

Once when I arrived at Oberlé's in the autumn, I noted an ample bowl of black truffles. I said, "Gérard, you shouldn't have," and he replied, "But I have no heirs." This is the true spirit of generosity. I tend not to think of the best restaurants in my life but the best individual dishes, no matter where they are cooked. At Oberlé's there have been a least a dozen, from his preparations of whole foie gras to his coq au vin (you must have a rooster for this dish) to his *poulet demi-deuil* to his tiny lamb legs *en croûte*, not to speak of his colleague Brézol's vegetable dishes.

Another time, my publisher Christian Bourgois made me some wonderful Niçoise *farcie*, at his home. This is vegetables stuffed with various forcemeats, emphasizing again that the food of southern France is easier on the system. This, of course, assumes that you are willing to eschew outright gluttony. Once on a food tour of the south with my friend de la Valdene, we had strictly limited our food budget to a thousand dollars a day but went well over this limitation every day for a week. It would have been worse but Guy had been attacked by a *crustace sauvage* (bad shellfish) and was off his feed for a couple of days, during which he mostly watched me—with his large, glowering Gallic eyes—eat.

Lulu Peyraud is in her early eighties and lives at Domaine Tempier, the vineyard in Provence that she and her late husband, the fabled Lucien, founded. I've been through at least fifty cases of their Bandol, so you must trust me. Lulu is at a pinnacle of "home cooking," which means a great deal in this case. Alice Waters and Richard Olney did a cookbook revolving around Lulu's kitchen, which itself revolves around a very large wood range. Yup, wood. I recall standing there while she grilled a hundred mussels for a few minutes until they popped open, then added a touch of Les Beaux olive oil to each. I've eaten at Lulu's home on two occasions, and I'm rather haunted by this vineyard. The house and gardens still seem turn-of-the-century, the Provençal light is diffused by the granitic mountains, and the estate is so close to the Mediterranean that there is a salty tinge to the violet-blushed air. It was at Lulu's that I ate four dishes that were the best of their kind: a Provençal daube (a beef stew); a *soupe de poisson*; a seventeen-pound snapper wrapped in grape leaves, soaked in olive oil and garlic, and cooked slowly on the wood grill; and two tiny legs of lamb, about two pounds apiece (not the mutton we are sold as lamb), braised with the smallest fresh April vegetables, including artichokes. At one endless lunch with Olney and the wine importer Kermit Lynch and his wife, Gail, a photographer, I tasted a fifteen-year succession of Bandols, after which I was taken to Marseilles to chat before a thousand or so folks. This didn't exactly pan out, as they say.

"Eat or die" was the motto of a food column I used to write. Who can quarrel with the profundity of this logic? By *eating* I don't mean banal pit stops for an injection of fuel but something more appropriate to the putative human spirit, something to which you can bring your curiosity and enthusiasm. Even dogs love good food. Rub a piece of steak with garlic, fry it in butter, and give it to your pooch. The dog will say clearly, "This beats the shit out of kibble." And a nice slice of fresh foie gras (not the canned kind) will make the dog shiver in admiration for you in a way that no woman ever has, not even when you spring for a three-carat emerald. However, as I rediscovered this morning, these Frenchified treats do not ensure obedience. Rose busted a grouse covey that wouldn't hold and became something like an unguided missile. She reminded me of those wayward wives on their bowling nights in small midwestern cities. Pure naughty.

Instead of being pissed at Rose, I sat against a stump, my brow furrowing over what I might make for dinner. The day was too warm to make lamb shanks with white beans and garlic, a dish I had had in Auvergne, and the heat made it impossible to run the dog far enough to merit the meal. A cassoulet, for instance, requires three hours of walking before dinner so you can eat the dish and an hour afterward to digest it. Brandy or Calvados helps somewhat, but without the walking your dreamlife will become the tormented march of dead meat. I glanced around at the passing clouds and figured the approximate distances to some of my favorite restaurants: about four hundred miles to Gibsons in Chicago, and about twelve hundred to Gotham and Babbo, Gramercy Park, or Elaine's (for my habitual massive veal chop with spinach sautéed in oil and garlic). It was something like five thousand miles to my seventy-seven favorite places to eat in France. My agent and long-term friend, Bob Dattila, has frequently remarked that it's too bad you can't drive to France. I agree, and not because I share his Sicilian fear of flying (actually shared by all ethnic groups), but because riding in a wheelbarrow would be generally more pleasant. Occasionally, I'm able to wangle a first-class ticket on Air France, where the food and wine are more than acceptable, but as a proletarian I find the expense (to whomever) quite embarrassing, if endurable.

I ended up making a simple whitefish chowder, using an ample amount of salt pork, a staple of both sets of my grandparents, but my heart was with Olivier Roellinger at Maison de Bricourt in Concale: the spider-crab timbale, the tandoori monkfish, the huge wild oysters with fresh morels, the lobster grilled with West Indian spices, the St. Pierre with lemongrass bouillon and baby favas, the mango and passion fruit with crème anglaise. That's basically all, not counting the Lynch-Bages and the Meursault. I'd even settle for the five different kinds of headcheese we bought from the renowned butcher Fernand Dussert at his shop in Arleuf in the Morvan. Or a plate of simple charcuterie from Les Mouettes near my hotel in Paris, an ideal lunch after you get off a plane, shower, and stroll.

I think it all began with a number of mystifying experiences at the old Brittany du Soir in New York in the early 1960s. I recall, when I was a poet-lackey at the state university at Stony Brook, taking a visiting French poet, Jean Guillevic from Bretagne, to the Brittany du Soir. He demonstrated to me just how much a poet should properly eat and drink. From that point on I could never resume my career as a male model.

O God, what should we do? We're hungry at least a couple of times a day, and why should we eat like denatured cows? Throughout the world, folks are eating different things, requested by billions of different voices driven by billions of perceptibly different brains. Evan Jones, in his fine and compendious *American Food,* tells us what some of us here used to eat, but it is the French who have specific answers, followed by the Chinese and the Italians. This is the age of all sorts of odious and banal lists, but in this case I'm right, and anyone who disagrees is wrong.

* * *

On the last night of a recent trip to France, I wanted to go to L'Assiette Lulu for the great blood-sausage Parmentier, among other things, but then, because I'm a memory buff, I recalled I had been there the night before. In my room, I studied two menus of twenty-four and forty-seven courses that Oberlé had devised for friends, both meals taking place at L'Espérance. They made me feel like a melancholy little piker in the face of the glories of extreme French cuisine, beside which we are all children here in America. Of course, we're in the driver's seat, but there is no map to indicate where we're going, though it demonstrably isn't toward fine cuisine.

This last night in Paris I settled on taking Dattila and his friend Betsy to a restaurant of the *sud-ouest* (hearty food), Thoumieux, which I had been to a dozen times. It's over near the Invalides, decidedly non–haute cuisine, and is favored by writers and generals. Dattila is a heavy eater, and, besides, I was going home the next day, so I ordered some grilled fresh sardines, snails, foie gras, a roasted guinea hen, cassoulet, and a porterhouse. The waiter, who knew me, was slightly appalled, but I explained that I was returning to the Great North, far from any French food, and then he commiserated. "Poor poet," he said, patting my bony shoulder. I'm pretty sure there's bone in there.

1999

WILD CREATURES:
A CORRESPONDENCE
WITH GÉRARD OBERLÉ

November 4, 1999

My dear Jimmy,

For over a month now, stuffed in my reference library like a large truffle in a *poularde de Bresse,* I have been writing bibliographical notices for a marvelous collection of cookery books printed throughout Europe between the 16th and the 20th century. I have been marinating in this gastronomic literature to the point of engorgement in lieu of revitalizing myself with you, as we do each year in the woods and swamps of the northern Michigan peninsula, flushing the grouse and the woodcock.

And here comes the postwoman with the November issue of the *Men's Journal* in which you describe your culinary experiences in France. In the article, you celebrate my hospitality, awarding me with the epithet of "the Michael Jordan of French Cuisine." This sporting metaphor served my entourage with a good chuckle. My friends are all aware that the most exerting exercise I allow myself consists of the nightly ascent of the stairs leading to my bedroom.

I agree with Baudelaire when he dresses Brillat-Savarin with vinaigrette and baptizes him "a man of great renown who was at the same time a great fool, two things that go very well together." But amongst all the foolishly pedantic maxims found in *The Physiology of Taste,* Savarin's bogus masterpiece which entirely finesses the subject of wine, I nevertheless retain the following: "He who entertains friends without devoting special attention to the meal prepared for them, is not worthy of having friends." In the logwood cabin at Grand Marais, where you simmer your poultry with a pound of garlic and just as many spices, you reflect with nostalgia upon my pork-snout pies, my truffled chickens *demi-deuil* and my tender legs of lamb *en croûte.* A worn-out proverb—

stupid as are all proverbs, since what is defined as "popular wisdom" is simply the scum of nations—professes that "small gifts sustain friendships." The sweet lie! Gifts, like cigars and orgasms, must be grand! It is the exceptional dishes that maintain friendships not the skimpy leftovers. A friendship cannot be purchased with a tip. And to return your tribute of "sated gratification" with one of "touched appreciation," know that I too owe you some magical moments. Last year, quite precisely on the 3rd of October, we had been roaming for hours the wild grasslands surrounding the delta of the Sucker River, without having driven out the least woodcock, when you sat down in the middle of a vast prairie and began once again to sing "Moon River." For that matter, you never sing more that the first two words of "Moon River," which you modulate into a sort of thanksgiving to the beauty of creation, in the manner of the *Hamdouli-llah* of fervent Muslims. From there, you revealed a secret to me: this scenery is that of the enchanted flower garden, the vast glade filled with amelanchiers, dogwoods and blackthorns in which unfolds the scene from *The Road Home* where the young painter, abandoned by his mare, must return by foot to Grand Marais by the light of a full moon. I experienced this moment as a privilege. And I would not have been more moved had Monsieur de Ronsard himself guided me into the forest of Gâtine. At times, when my dog Elliott leads me to the clearing at the far edge of my land, I am apt to sit on an old tree trunk and sing "Moon River."

We are, you and I, children of the woods. I was born under the guardian shade of the oaks and beech trees of the Col de Saverne and I spent my childhood trekking through the Fossé de Pandours and other Gallo-Roman vestiges that sleep under the Vosgian forests. I endured my Parisian years as an exile and only recaptured peace of the senses and the soul, here, near the Morvan, an ancient mountain rich in legends, a natural sanctuary, my own "magic mountain." It has been many years since I have picked up a gun but I have never abandoned the taste for wild birds. Ground game is not my cup of tea and were an Animal Court to exist as in the German romantic tales, I for one would not be accused of Bambi's orphanage. I leave to others the heady venison, the hares *à la Royale*, the boar's heads *à la Saint Hubert*, the

saddles of deer and the sauces *Grand Veneur*. But in my great Book of
Friendship, I dedicate Chapter One to all those buddies—hunters and
cooks—who have delighted me with partridges, prairie chicken, wild
ducks, woodcocks and quails, with ortolans, pheasants, and wood
pigeons, with rock partridges and waxwings.

It is to you that I owe my most lavish "volucrovoristic" agapes.
These wildfowl feasts, so often shared in north Michigan, are prepared
and consumed ritually, and when the roasted woodcock appears on its
toasts, it is the final act of a ceremony that has lasted several days.

Do you perchance recall October 16, 1998? I shall refresh your
memory but first allow me some digressions. An obscure author by the
name of Horace Raisson—a friend of Balzac but completely forgotten
today—who turned out a few unimportant books around 1840, wrote as
an epigraph to his *Code Gourmand* the following blasphemous maxim,
blasphemous only to nibbling mice: "Great thoughts are begotten in the
stomach." I cannot imagine the writers whom I admire shunning the art
of the table. Intuitively, I suspect that the verses of an anorexic poet,
unless he were truly ill, are sickly and undernourished themselves. A
Muse adept of Cuisine Minceur can go get screwed by the fashionable
poets, the obsequious parasites who reside in the salons where the
society birds swoon at the murmur "Kindly dim the lights a trifle."

The great bards, the epic geniuses as well as the suave elegiac
poets, do not disdain terrestrial foods. I except from this Epicurean
company the cricket-eating mystics of the desert, tormented by purely
spiritual hungers; the stylites quartered and parched on their pillars,
who masticating exclusively on dry grass produce only orations and goat
droppings. Though I may admire them as builders of sand castles of the
soul, nevertheless I think that these great desert fanatics are, above all,
most seriously deranged.

But let's return to October 16th. The marvelous fraternity of
authors that you had invited that evening at Lake Leelanau laid claim
to no such religion. Your friends Guy de la Valdene, Jim Fergus, and
your neighbor Nick are musketeers as deft with the fork as they are with
the musket. Each member of this improbable "Wild-Birds-Boys-Band"

had brought the spoils of his hunt. My skills at handling a pan, at whipping up a *Beurre Blanc* or at stuffing a pigeon, undoubtedly contributed in great part to my admission into the bosom of this intimate and fun-loving circle. From the refrigerator of his superb polished-metal trailer dating back to the '60s, Jimmy Fergus turned out a handful of Sharptail Grouse (*Tympanuchus phasianellus, Gélinotte à queue fine*) which he had shot in South Dakota, a Sage Grouse (*Centrocercus urophasianus, Tétra des armoises*) and a Blue Grouse (*Dendragapus obscurus, Tétra sombre*) shot in Colorado, along with a Nebraska Grouse that you call Prairie Chicken (*Tymphanuchus cupido*) and a few Ptarmigan Grouse (*Lagopus mutus, Lagopède alpin*), rare birds that are only found above 10,000 feet on the peaks of Colorado. You and Nick lined up a dozen woodcocks and Ruffed Grouse (*Bonasa umbellus, Gélinotte huppée*), the grouse indigenous to Michigan whose white meat can only be compared to the delicate flavor of a suckling veal or that of a Bresse spring chicken.

When one is past fifty and certain senses (I am mainly referring to those that offer so much delight in breaking God's Sixth Commandment) have begun to quiet, can there exist on earth a greater pleasure than sharing a sumptuous dinner amongst true friends? Yes, perhaps there is: that of preparing the meal with these same friends, together plucking and cooking the birds while downing a few bottles of old French wine. That evening, each of us cooked the birds in his own style. Guy served us the fillets of the Sage Grouse, scalloped and presented on canapés of Portobello mushroom caps. I prepared the Blue Grouse in a casserole, browned and flambéed in Calvados, then simmered slowly with raisins, Juniper berries and small pieces of larding bacon, deglazed with cider and garnished with cabbage that had cooked in a stock of grouse and woodcock giblets and livers. Nick took care of the woodcock barbecue. As for you, my dear old Coyote, you treated us to a novel and magical recipe to which no cookbook holds the secret. When I asked where you had discovered it, you answered that you had not invented it but had dreamt it. It was called "Grouse Surprise." In this ambiguous specialty, the grouse pretends to be sweetbread and vice versa. In your next letter, please send me the exact recipe. You see, I too have not forgotten any of the culinary splendors proffered by the primitive peoples of Northern America.

In conclusion, I shall entertain you with a strange anecdote. I was recently rereading *The Greek Summer* written by my Burgundian neighbor, the traveler and author Jacques Lacarrière. This narrative contains a passage that would knock out the eyeteeth of the most seasoned "ornithophagus." Lacarrière relates how in his youth during a trip to Crete, he had dined on an eagle. From the Papago territory to the Chiracahua Mountains, from Lake Patagonia to Madera Canyon, have you ever heard of so sacrilegious a snack?

I'd like you to recount this story to the old Indian chiefs that you will cross on your walks when you return to your winter quarters on the uncertain border between Arizona and Mexico. For my part, I am not certain that I have the nerve to invite to my table a pilgrim who has ingested an eagle. How about you?

I shall end upon this thorny dilemma. May the Great Universal Pork Butcher who presides over all destinies keep your good old brown dog head intact and may He continue to use those of pigs to make his headcheese.

Pax tecum,
Gérard

November 8, 1999

Dear Gérard,

I very much enjoyed your letter. I missed your presence this fall and I'm sure Rose, the English setter bitch, did too, the way you held her on your lap every morning and tried to teach her French. The two of you often competed to find the downed woodcock and without you she often ignored her duties and ran off to look for more. As the dog of a writer Rose is properly neurotic and is interested in the next woodcock poem rather than the one already on paper. After the bird is downed she does enjoy a little of its sauce on toast. Last year, however, on those very cold mornings when you were wearing the large green coat, she may have presumed you had become an immense green dog when you trotted toward a thicket to find a bird, and thus she felt like competing.

But then much was different this year. When Guy de la Valdene arrived he brought a cooler stuffed with his splendid farm-raised chickens, and also a wild pig. His hired hand, Bill, traps these pigs when they are young, say fifteen to twenty-five pounds, then feeds them for a couple of weeks to fatten them up. Before they are trapped they forage in the dense swamps and forests on Guy's property, and I've even watched a small female, perhaps named Diana, shake a large rattlesnake into pieces and eat it. Naturally the widely varied diet of these pigs makes them especially delicious, almost painfully so compared to commercial pork which has been tortured to virtual death by the boredom of pure corn.

But when Guy arrived and I carried in the cooler containing 60 kilos of wild pig and chickens I stepped on the edge of the sidewalk and badly twisted my ankle. I howled like a truly pissed-off wolf. My ankle turned a pale purple on the very eve of my month-long hunt. I questioned the existence of God who told me merely to hobble, stumble, and crawl like a modern man. And so I did for the first few weeks with my ankle tightly wrapped in my French Chameau boots, one of my proudest possessions and a gift from Guy. I mostly mention them because my mental survival depends on certain objects. I thought my old Fox-Sterling-Worth was one of these objects but Linda gave me a new 20-gauge Arrieta for our anniversary and I shot much better with it than ever before. One day I shot my three woodcock, the limit, in fifteen minutes and then went back to the cabin, read Spanish poetry, and prepared dinner for Guy, who was hunting with our friend Nick.

That grouse "surprise" recipe you mentioned is simplicity itself, almost naïve but the sum is much greater than the parts. You simply marinate pieces of a couple of grouse, and a pound of pieces of fine veal sweetbreads in, of all things, buttermilk and several tablespoons of Tabasco for several hours. You then dredge the pieces of grouse and sweetbreads in flour and sauté them until done (not long). For the sauce you reduce a cup of the marinade and a cup of good stock you have

made from the carcasses of leftover grouse and woodcock. Often we
have extra birds that have been shot up hard and they enrich the stock.
It is especially nice as a first course. One of my favorites is the classic
salmis de bécasse but then so often the plump females are best simply
grilled until their breasts are a dark pink and not a second longer. We
know that their plumpish legs are the equal of the finest female thighs
in the world!

I think I told you that I finished my novella *The Beast God Forgot
to Invent.* Anyway, I've begun another that deals with the captious and
banal aspects of success called *I Forgot to Go to Spain.* In there my hero
questions if food and cooking are not one of the last vestiges of true
freedom for modern man? À la Foucault, nearly all of us eat zoo food in
the zoo we are confined in by society and culture. In modern America
we are pigs eating a confined diet determined by the economic powers
of our society. True varieties of food become more limited because they
are not as profitable for the grocery industry, what you yourself refer to
as "industrial" food, whereas the true food is what we bought at the
market in Moulin. Fast food is zoo food.

Hunting and fishing take it a step further in terms of food. Since I
was a boy up in the woods I've loved eating the fish and birds I've
managed to gather. I also like to pick berries and morel mushrooms.
Woodcock and grouse are food that emerges naturally from the totality
of the life I live as do trout and bass. And in hunting I have this glorious relationship with my dog and our elaborate unwritten language.
When I am hunting I reach the zenith of my mammalian attentiveness.
Perhaps you remember D. H. Lawrence said, "The only aristocracy is
that of consciousness." I am most happy as a Pleistocene biped when I
am hunting and fishing and then cook what I have killed.

Tomorrow I'm thinking I'll make Linda a simple grouse pie. The
crust becomes a lid so none of the flavor can escape. I use a few peas,
carrots, and small chunks of turnip. Tonight, though, I am thinking of
that pâté we made last year with you as our noble leader chef with forty
wild quail from the Mexican border and also twenty doves. It was good,
wasn't it? Right now I'm having a glass of Domaine Tempier Bandol
and letting my imagination retaste that glorious pâté.

Don't be upset with the story of a Frenchman eating an eagle! I read a true story of two Italians that tried to cook and eat a vulture. My neighbor Nick has tried to cook both a swan and a seagull. Once at a long poker game at a hunting cabin I ate five deer hearts. No wonder I have gout. But because of my wisdom I have never eaten more than a gross of oysters a day.

> More later.
> Your Friend,
> Jim Harrison

November 22, 1999

My dear Jimmy,

I was very touched to learn that you and Rose have missed me. During our walks through the moors of Traverse and Grand Marais, I did only my duty, you know. I adore Rose but, alas, I am sad to say that she behaves like many women I have known. Rose is a tease! All she enjoys is going hunting, pointing at game, and showing off, but as soon as the shot rings out and the bird falls, she takes off. Mademoiselle Rose does not pick up her victims! As for me, since I am not of the "Pointer" breed, I try to earn my dinner by playing "Retriever." We complement each other admirably. Rose delights me! She incarnates a certain foolishness specific to setters: a touching and comical foolishness that I always find charming in certain creatures with silky hair. I do not perceive this in my dog Elliott, an intelligent German shepherd.

"She behaves like a writer's dog," you say. Don't be naïve. Rose is a silly thing like all setters. Whether they belong to a poet or to a car mechanic, setters don't stand a chance at Harvard.

Now let's talk quail. You mentioned in your letter the prodigious pâté which you made in Michigan with the rest of the quail brought back from Arizona. In February, you will see me charge into Nogales with the firm intention of savoring fresh quail. For all feast enthusiasts, quail have always symbolized abundance. Popular depictions of the land of Cockaigne in old engravings show them falling from the sky thoroughly roasted. Already in the Bible, quail tumbled down from the firmaments to feed those unfortunate Hebrews migrating from Egypt to the Promised Land. I hope that in the Arizona desert, we will not suffer the same fate as those poor people, all victims of food poisoning consequent to the famous quail rain. The same misfortune befell a Frenchman some years ago. The biblical narrator was not familiar with the origin of the intoxication but today we understand its cause. Apparently, during spring migration, quail like to peck on the seeds of hemlock, the plant that liquidated Socrates.

Hemlock does not affect quail; they gorge themselves on it like children on candy. On the other hand, consumers of quail fattened on this particular diet drop dead as socratically as Xanthippe's husband.

As a boy in Alsace, I enjoyed hiding in the June wheat to listen to the quail. An old plowman had taught me the songs of all the birds in the county. And although I could easily identify that of this mysterious and unsociable creature—three rhythmic syllables uttered in varying shades of intensity—I have seldom had the opportunity to see a quail in the wild. These small tawny bullets crouch firmly against the ground and one has to almost tread upon them before they decide to take flight.

My family never hunted nor did the villagers of my neighborhood. From the growth of my baby teeth until my departure to high school, I was raised on the pure produce of the poultry yard, the rabbit hutch, and the kitchen garden. And when, occasionally, a wild animal course—a hare or a venison haunch—showed up on our autumnal menu, it was a gift from a Vosgian gamekeeper to his mailman. My dear papa was a "man of letters," a mailman on a bicycle, a lighthearted fellow straight out of a Charles Trenet song, who delivered love letters to the young girls of the Saverne County. In the early '50s, the post office equipped him with a motorcar. Every Thursday, I would ride with him in his Deux Chevaux, sometimes to the affluent peasant villages on the plain, sometimes towards the river locks and houses of the forestry workers living in the Zorn Valley and on the mountain pass leading to Phalsbourg.

One day I shall describe to you the fabulous lunches that I shared with my father. In Alsace, in those days, people fought to have the

mailman at their table. I recall in Landersheim a benevolent priest—
more gourmet than La Reynière, Dumas, and Dodin Bouffant
combined—who was prodigal with chicken simmered in Riesling, pâtés
of foie gras, and stewed crawfish tails. This splendid old man raised
some honeybees and fattened a few pigs in the garden behind the
presbytery. He would reprimand his maid in Latin when a dish was
overcooked. Already mischievous at age seven, I will always remember
this venerable man of God's answer, when after a notably generous feast
I served him the following insolence by way of saying grace: "But
Father, I thought that gluttony was a sin." He catechized me in Alsatian: "Kind! Besser de Büsch verplatze, dass Gottes Güete verachte,"
which means "Child, it is better to burst one's own belly than to scorn
God's generosities." If the Church of Rome were represented by more
servants of this caliber, the Christian faith may not be in crisis today.

But let's return to our quail, our turtledoves, and our pretty
partridges. The French language has not always honored birds as kindly
as in the song "My Father's Garden," to which I have just alluded. In
our vernacular, *oiseau* signifies a shady person, and to call somebody by
tous les noms d'oiseaux[1] is not to pay him a compliment. In the catalogue
of ornithological metaphors, ladies can be described as chickens,
magpies, geese or turkeys or even cranes, meaning that they are kept,
garrulous, stupid, or promiscuous. Males can also be clothed in feathers,
those of canary, linnet, guinea fowl, rooster, crow, and vulture. Suffice
it that they be tall, young, and stupid, effeminate or arrogant, informer
or rapacious. In this "Aristophanic" comedy, the farce can also be
played out between pigeons and pheasants, partridges and bitterns,
woodcocks and snipes.[2] Quail are fortunate for they are seldom referred
to in a pejorative manner. One often associates them with adjectives
such as plump, round, and warm since quail symbolize a comfortable
paunch and amorous ardor. You can say "Come, my little quail" to a
chubby child as well as to a flirtatious maiden you intend to lure into a
grove. Because, my dear Jim, quail are hot!

1. Trans.: "all the names of the birds."
2. Respectively: suckers, profiteers, snitchers, louts, featherbrains, simpletons.

I have two illustrious neighbors who have written about this long before I: the great Buffon de Montbard in Burgundy who stated: "There is more heat within quail than in other birds" and the XVI-century Bourbon doctor astrologer Antoine Mizault who wrote the following curious magic recipe based on the calorific property of quails: "Husbands who want to be loved by your wives, wives who want to be loved by your husbands, extract the hearts of a pair of quails and wear them on you: the male's heart for the wife, and the female's for the husband." I only know of one belittling expression, seldom used anymore, that of *caille coiffée*, to describe a loose woman.

But enough of quail for the time being. In another letter, I will tell you about pigeons and pheasants. Does English contain ornithological nicknames as well? I remember that W. C. Fields, one of my favorite thinkers, called his fiancées "My little Rocky Mountain Canary." In your next letter, tell me if it is politically correct to say to a lady in a bar in Tucson or in Patagonia "Hi my little quail, my name is Jerry. I'm a French hunter." Considering contemporary American practice, I prefer to remain cautious: I'll never forget the day when, as I was relieving myself against a tree in a freeway rest area, you warned me quite seriously, "You could go to jail for doing that here."

"Doing what?"

"Pissing in nature—exhibitionism!"

In 1891, America was more fun. I was leafing through an amusing little book: A *Comic Cookery Book* by a certain Fred Hull Curtiss. Do you know the guy? The title of his book bears an epigraph, "While we live, let us live." I find the request admirable. It should be presented to all the psychologists, preachers, nutritionists, and other killjoys who reprove eating, drinking, cavorting, or pissing one's name in the sand, and who make our lives a misery nowadays. Mr. Curtiss opens his recipe book with a poem. I cannot resist the pleasure of sending it to you, my chubby brother, for you are the one who wrote: "you must eat or you must die." This is how your colleague Curtiss puts into rhymes the same truth:

We may live without poetry, music and art;
On yarns that appeal to the conscience or heart;

We may live if we only have cookery books
Transforming us all into practical cooks
We may live without love; 'tis a passion but fleeting,
But where is the man who can live without eating?
He may live in a palace or live in a hut,
He may live in a wigwam or restaurant, but
While he lives in this wise, there is no use declining
The fact that he cannot survive without dining.

I agree with the hero in your work in progress: *I Forgot to Go to Spain*. Today, food and cuisine remain one of the only forums of free expression for a human being, provided that he not be one of the damned of the earth, who unfortunately are more and more numerous and have no alternative but to make do with foul pittance and meager fares.

Be well. I am off this instant to beseech the goddess Artemis to transform your game bag into a cornucopia.

Semper tecum,
Gérard

November 24, 1999

Dear Gérard,

I was so worried about not hearing from you that I went without food, if only for moments. I suffered long nights of sleeping without food and never ate at all in the toilet! You could give up your monstrous labors and live comfortably if only you would sell your daughters to King Farouk but then I heard he is dead.

We are now in Patagonia. The four-and-a-half-day trip down from Michigan was a floating diorama of bad food. I was reminded with deep sadness for my country of that pleasant lunch we had at a truck stop (*routier*) in Brittany. We arrived here in a continuing November heat wave that has broken all records. I tried to hunt Rose very early in the coolness of the morning but it was too warm by 9 A.M. I shot two scaled quail one morning, one of three varieties down here including Gambel's and Mearns, then searched for them myself while Rose sat on a

mountainside with the thoughtfulness of the Sphinx herself. There has
also been no rain for two months which makes it more difficult for Rose
to scent the birds. You must remember not all that many years ago that
when you crawled in the grass of your property looking for women it
was much easier to scent them when there was moisture in the air?
Another danger of the heat is that rattlesnakes are active. A friend's
dog, a fine mongrel named Rob, was recently bitten on the nose and
nearly died, his poor head swelling up as large as a basketball. Many of
us think of rattlesnakes as the Republicans of the natural world, the way
they attack the poor and innocent for no particular reason.

Today I shot only one quail because I was too distracted to hunt
well. However, by afternoon I had calmed down and shot several doves.
Writers are generally poor hunters because they are constantly listening
to their minds instead of paying attention. How I'd love to see even a
cow without my mind announcing "cow." A large group of doves passed
overhead but I didn't shoot because they were intermixed with meadowlarks for reasons that no one in government could tell you. Unless you
have a vast number and wish to experiment doves are best cooked
simply like woodcock. I favor an oak fire on my outdoor grill which
took three men a week to build but then I have two dozen settings for
the iron grill above the fire. Too radical of a heat temperature is disas-
trous on wild birds of any sort as they are so lean. Being plumper you
and I will be roasted in hell for an indefinite period for lust and gluttony. Imagine our shock if the afterlife is as simpleminded as Dante
portrayed it.

Not oddly, your wild quail are not our quail, though the ones I see
in French markets resemble our Bobwhites (*Colinus virginianus*), but
these are doubtless raised in pens. I believe your wild quail are migra-
tory. Our wild quail have very limited ranges. The ones I hunt along
the Mexican border are the Scaled (*Callipepla squamata*), Gambel's
(*Callipepla gambelii*), and the Mearns (*Cyrtonyx montezumae*). The
Mearns is the most rotund and best eating. However, they seem less
wary and intelligent so there are fewer. In contrast to pen-raised quail
found in butcher shops wild quail eat dozens and dozens of different
insects, berries, seeds, and the Mearns even digs for the roots of specific

forbs. This varied diet makes their flesh delicious and quite indescribable. They are mountain birds and obtained with great effort.

Alas, it is more difficult for me to hunt now that I am older, but I still do so because it is a joy for my dog and my stomach. I mentioned before that what we eat can be, perhaps should be, an expression of our freedom and imagination. In many respects I have come to understand that I'm still a Pleistocene biped. I prefer wandering in remote forests and prairies, and along peopleless rivers, and eating what I hunt and fish there when possible. Of course much of the time this is impossible but then it has occurred to me that I love both wild food and sophisticated food, it's the "suburbs" in between that are boring. For instance there is a grandeur to eating grouse but the free-range capons I used to buy from a woman down the road could also be splendid. The finest chicken in the world was the *poulet au demi-deuil* I ate at your house, and also at Mark Meneau's marvelous L'Espérance. Of course there are many fine chickens on the upper slopes of the chasm but at the bottom, the pit, the nadir, you have the Kentucky Fried Chicken and other fast-food varieties.

I have been long fascinated by sobriquets drawn from the natural world. The great anthropologist Paul Shepard has an excellent essay on the use of wild creatures in our language. I remember when I was about ten years old and my older brother told me a woman's genitalia felt like a "damp sparrow." W. C. Fields called a woman his "little chicka-dee," a particularly lovable little bird. This can take odd forms, including the wide usage of "beaver." (I have discovered that it is very difficult to cook beaver well because the fat, like the fat of the bear, tastes a bit rancid.) From my experience with actresses in Hollywood you could use "my little vulture," or, in New York, "my sweet buzzard." Cruel and mean-minded grandmothers are referred to as "old crows." My own grandmother was 97 when she died but very sweet tempered. She was arthritic and I had to lift her in and out of the car at which point she always laughed. Recently when I visited my mother, who is 85 and quite large, I had to lift her into the car and she also laughed. Lucky for me that I am still strong from eating well and hunting and fishing.

Did I ever tell you that it was my peasant background that accounts for my current love for confit? Sometimes this love is uncontrollable and I have learned that it's not smart to eat a whole confit goose thigh for breakfast. Anyway, my Swedish grandparents had no refrigerator so they stored everything from fall butchering—fowl, beef, pork—in large crocks buried in their own fat, and down in the cool cellar with smoked ham, bacon, rutabagas, potatoes, cabbage, carrots, and onions. During the Great Depression these farm families ate very well. Proust had his madeleine but I have my confit. I have even killed geese and made my own but it was of very poor quality compared to the tins you got from our charming friend Lulu from L'Assiette Lulu.

The American poem at the end of your letter was hopeless doggerel but true. Tomorrow is Thanksgiving and we go through the traditional banality of turkey though I had an excellent small *dinde* prepared by Christian Bourgois in Paris. Ours are too big. The difference is the same as that between Juliette Binoche and a 500-lb. circus fat lady.

Yr. Friend,
Jim

Sare, December 6, 1999

My dear Jimmy,

I am writing to you from a country that I had never visited. The eyes of the farm girls glow with quasi-Spanish ardor and big brothers built like rugby players regale you with all kinds of delicacies brought back from their rustic hunts and bountiful fishing trips. This country is not France nor is it Spain, and if Paradise exists, I would quite like it to resemble what I have found here. My dear Jim, I am in the Basque country!

I know that you are fond of *poulet basquaise* and that you have improved your own with the help of my friend Gilles' recipe. But it is hard to comprehend the meaning of the expression "good living" before one has explored for oneself the coast, hills, and mountains of this utopian land.

Here my hosts practice hospitality in keeping with almost biblical criteria, but for the purpose of our "bills and quills" correspondence, I shall only describe the birds that I have savored here: woodcocks and wood pigeons. The Basque woodcock is of the same species as those that live in my region—the center of France—the *Scopolax rusticola;* they differ, as you know, from your native woodcock. I was served excellent ones, a pair of females (more delectable than the males), roasted and garnished with cepes and sweetbreads, and washed down with a magnificent red wine from Toledo, a *Domaine de Valdepusa, Marquis de Grignon.*

Allow me one short featherless digression: I somewhat overindulged myself in the first course, which consisted of tiny young eels, considered one of the heights of Basque gastronomy.

In Europe, when the eels, male and female, are seized with erotic frenzies, they leave the lakes and rivers and ponds to indulge in furious orgies in the faraway Sargasso Sea. From their eggs are hatched larvae which are brought back by the Gulf Stream to our estuaries as *civelles,* called *pibales* here: delicate wriggling babies, three or four centimeters long, served piping hot, in earthenware saucepans with extra-virgin olive oil, *Espelette* peppers, and garlic.

For the last few years, Nippon gourmets have decreed this marvel a delicacy for their dainty and minuscule stomachs and Japan has taken over our young eels. The ration it allots to us will soon end up reaching Beluga prices!

I have always detested what is called *menu dégustation,* a pompous euphemism to indicate that you can look forward to enjoying mere samples. I find the process as frustrating as if you were only allowed to read the table of contents of a voluptuous book. All this to tell you that I did not content myself with 50 grams of *pibales.* I won't describe the *piperade,* nor the hake served *à la Koskera,* nor the admirable *Ossau-Iraty,* a goat cheese made by shepherds in the mountains. I will tell you another day all about the *axoa,* the *chipirons,* and the exquisite hams from Monsieur Oteiza's pigs.

Today we shall celebrate the creature that coos. The one hunted here is called a *palombe,* a pseudonym for wood pigeon, in Latin: *Columba palumbus.* Already in Virgil and Pliny, one strived to "*Palumbem ad aream adducere,*" i.e., to bring the pigeon into the net. Today, the

palombes are still hunted in this manner during the fall season when
they fly over the Pyrenees passes to winter in Africa.

The Basques serve them grilled or as salmi. Some gourmets roast
them on a grill or on a spit in the chimney. They baste them with lard
which melts slowly within funnels held over the birds.

The pigeon is best cooked with a dose of fat, especially when the
bird is wild. Poor pigeon! From time immemorial, it has been destined
for sacrifice; could this be due to the fact that under the name of dove,
it is a symbol of peace and gentleness? The ancients saw in it the bird
of Venus. It adorned the goddess of Love's chariot, but the honor lasted
only as long as the journey; for as Apicius (or some other gastronome of
the epoch) used to say: "Once the chariot has reached its destination,
nothing prevents the driver from being devoured."

I have always loved pigeons. In my childhood every farm in
Alsace owned a pigeon house. In the cultivated fields surrounding the
rich villages of the plain, entire families of pigeons could be seen squab-
bling with crowds of crows over the grain left behind by the harvesters.

Pigeons were everywhere: painted on the ceiling of the church
above our altar boys' heads where they symbolized the Holy Spirit; in
the school's playgrounds where we played *pigeon vole*[1]; in our spring
plates, swaddled in bard, like an infant Jesus, set delicately on beds of
tender peas, tiny white onions, and precocious hop shoots.

I, too, cooed under windows when as a young lovebird still fledg-
ling, I believed in the "tender love" ascribed by our national fabulist to
these birds notorious for their faithfulness. But I soon understood the
expression *se faire pigeonner*[2] because in French *un pigeon* can also signify
a sucker. Do you have anything similar in English? In some gambling
dives, card players will *plumer le pigeon*[3] without a qualm.

An elegant gentleman, who graciously invited me for a meal at the
Musée de la Chasse de Paris last week, gave me a meaning for the verb
pigeonner that I had never heard before. During the Ancien Régime, the

---

1. Trans.: "Simon says."
2. To be duped.
3. Fleece the sucker.

rural gentry's wealth was measured by the size of their pigeon houses. To fool possible future son-in-laws, some squires did not hesitate to bore holes in their dovecotes and thus could "pigeon" the candidates as to the size of the dowry. This brings us to the ladies. From the verb *pigeonner*, the French language produced the adjective *pigeonnant*. It is a fairly recent word and I think is linked to an advertisement for a brassiere. Women's bosoms are sometimes called *pigeonnantes* as their softness and rounded curves bring to mind a pigeon's breast.

This appealing publicity has no doubt "pigeoned" many a lovebird. The padded Wonderbra is but the intermediary stage before a markedly less appetizing trickery made of pure silicone. However, the verb *pigeonner* has not always had a derogatory signification. In the XVI century *pigeonner* someone meant to kiss in the manner of amorous pigeons, putting one's tongue in the other's mouth. This takes us back to Madame Venus, otherwise known as the goddess Aphrodite.

My dear Jim, you must wonder where these carrier pigeon ramblings are leading. I'm getting there. From Aphrodite derives the word *aphrodisiac*. And for the Egyptian Nubians, a fairly mischievous people who have adopted me these last ten years, the pigeon is considered highly aphrodisiac. It is consumed only under special circumstances: the eve of a wedding, the rekindling of failing ardor etc. . . . In Assouan, I eat pigeon every day. You cannot imagine the jokes all about me which this diet inspires, recounted on the terraces of the cafés. Nobody dares turn his back to me and when I pass by, the fellahs all but shelter their goats, donkeys, and buffalo cows.

While traveling in Anatolia, I saw gigantic pigeon houses inhabited by thousands of birds but not a single person would cook a pigeon for me. The Turks raise these birds solely for their droppings, which they use as fertilizers.

When you come back to the Morvan, I shall cook for you stuffed pigeons fashioned in my own manner. It is an Alsatian-Egyptian compromise that I prepared for your friends La Valdene and Odasso in their Moulin in Normandy. The birds are stuffed with wheat germ or bulgur, chopped-up livers and hearts, raisins, crushed almonds, and Oriental spices. They are then barded with lard and lightly browned in a casserole

before they are roasted in the oven and regularly basted with a mélange of
pigeon broth and Muscat wine. This sauce condenses slowly, caramelizing
garlic cloves amidst the Corinthian raisins and small bacon cubes.

I am going home next Thursday after a stopover in Paris to see my
publisher. He has just brought out my second novel, a copy of which I
will send to you at Patagonia. My pseudo-detective goes off to Turkey
where he is badly "pigeonned" by a "pheasant."[4] We'll talk about
pheasants in another letter. In the meantime, keep shooting quail for
my February visit.

The species described in your letter do not exist in these parts
where we are only familiar with the *Coturnis coturnis*. Besides, the latter
is seldom found anymore in the wild. All of the quail that you have
seen on the poulterers' blocks in Paris are bred in captivity. Soon all the
wildlife in our countrysides will be killed off by the pesticides, the
insecticides, the industrial practices of our computerized farmers, the
greed of the food-processing giants, the hypocrisy of the agricultural
labor unions, and the resignation of my compatriots to eat whatever
shit is presented in the publicity ads. Over here the crusaders for
Animal Rights raise a hell of a racket over a few pigeons shot down by
hunters. Instead, one should boycott "industrial" chickens and pork
mass-produced by criminals who pollute the countryside and make fools
out of consumers. But, *Stultorum infinitus est numerus*, said the Bible,
which can be translated as "Unfortunately, fools are numerous."

May the dove of peace caress you, Linda, and silky Rose, with
gentle wings.

Your friend,
Gérard

Patagonia, Arizona
December 19, 1999

Dear Gérard,

I felt melancholy after reading your letter because I have never
been to Basque country. When I flew over it I wanted to get out of the

4. A crook.

plane which is a difficult procedure. The Basque are as inscrutable as the Etruscans, and are neither French nor Spanish, but Basque. I don't think I told you but at a Basque tapas bar in Barcelona I ate twenty-one delicious tapas in order to prolong my stay at the bar, behind which was a black-haired Basque girl who made my poor old heart beat like the kettle drum in Stravinsky's "Le Sacre du Printemps."

I should get myself to Basque country because all the evidence points to the fact that after death we won't be able to take trains. Part of my melancholy is that I just finished a novella, and it is the process that gives pleasure, not the completion. My shooting, which has been poor, will very probably improve. It's never as good when I'm writing and when I've been obligated to become hundreds of different people. A good hunter can only be one, a hunter.

Guy de la Valdene described to me the Egyptian pigeon dish you made for them at the moulin at St. George. You grilled me some pigeons simply for brunch once before I got on the train for Paris. Oddly, in America we rarely eat pigeon, though I've ordered squab, young pigeon, from the purveyor D'Artagnan and found them quite good. I've always used young pigeons to train my English setters Tess and Rose, and afterwards braised them with peas and carrots from the garden, also a few wild leeks from the woods.

I've been told that taxonomically pigeons are very close to doves, which I favor highly. The wild dove here in America, both the mourning dove and the white-winged dove, are much smaller than adult pigeons. The Mexicans call them "palomas" and I thought "palombe" were French doves. Once in New York Jeanne Moreau recited to me a French poem about doves when I brought her flowers and a bottle of Cristal champagne. The quality of voice can have a higher sexual content than breasts or oysters.

Of the many, many wild birds I've eaten, doves take second place after woodcock. They do not need our help and are best grilled over a wood fire basted with a little butter, salt, and pepper. When I was younger I could eat a dozen at a sitting but now only three, or four, or five. Maybe six. Once in London I ate a number of "wood pigeons" on successive days and their flavor was reminiscent of doves.

Sad to say much of the taste of any creature depends on what it eats, not all but much. Wild creatures taste wild. I equate wild with delicious. A veterinarian I know planted the seeds he took from the crops of a number of Mearns quail, growing sixty different plants. In the crops of the doves I've been shooting lately I've found as many as a dozen different seeds in a single crop. If you recall from Michigan certain ruffed grouse that have been eating the desiccated fruit of blueberry bushes are especially good eating. If you talked to an educated cannibal in New Guinea he would tell you that Republicans taste disgusting because they eat such boring food. Both Reagan and Nixon are said to have loved cottage cheese with catsup. The men who tear the world apart are often little boys.

I need to come to France at least twice this year to research whether or not my appetites are waning, and find out whether or not they can be revived. Driving on a tiny mountain road the other day in a state of extreme exhaustion from finishing my novella, I had the notion that I'd take my ice skates to the Petit Nice, a little hotel in Marseilles, this winter. I would skate around the frozen harbor looking at dolphins under the ice, and then return to the Passadat for an enormous lunch. What a splendid idea! When I came to senses I stopped in an immense mountain pasture, sang a love song to Rose, and shot five doves and a quail. Interestingly enough I once saw a dolphin in Marseilles harbor but no one believed me despite the fact that I have seen thousands of dolphins in the Atlantic and Pacific. I have even been underwater near Key West when they were making love with more energy than even the French. I was too timid to join them. I fear such muscular women.

Yes, "pigeon" is a term often used for a sucker, or a "mark" for a criminal. In my youth a pretty girl could be called a "cute young pigeon." Such usages are slowly passing out of our language now that the familiarity with animals is lessening. I once pointed out that most of the people now in America who eat chicken, beef, and pork have never had the pleasure of knowing an individual chicken, cow, or pig. There is a presumed virtue now in remaining distant from the sources of our food. That's why the monsters of industrial food can get away with selling their inferior products. It is imitation food. I hope that France can hold the line against hormonal beef and genetically engineered crops. There is even a rising protest in America over these matters. What have we become that we have to search for a good egg, an acceptable loaf of bread, a chicken that does not taste like Styrofoam, a steak that does not taste like a rubber ball? This is why I felt like Alice in Wonderland that day we went with you and Gilles to the market in Moulin. If France cannot hold the line against the global shit-extruders she'll no longer be France but another version of New Jersey.

Of course it goes without saying that I'm willingly a fool and it is perhaps primitive to think there is secret power in eating wild food, but then the power is in the taste that enlivens the imagination and increases reverence for life. I think I have told you that of the dozens of times I've eaten bear I have bear dreams. We must bow Buddhist style to what we properly cook and eat. It is hard to bow at McDonald's. My waking and sleeping hours are full of birds. In the Middle Ages hell was conceived as a place without birds. I actually spoke my limited French to three crows near the graves of Simone de Beauvoir and Jean-Paul Sartre in that cemetery near Montparnasse. Crows and ravens absolutely love to eat young doves and pigeons so we have something in common.

When we were returning from hunting today Nick and I were talking about you and whether you'd like the wild quail we've eaten stuffed with sliced green grapes soaked in a little Calvados. You sauté these grapes in the pan where you browned the quail, then stuff them in the bird. To extend quail into a fuller course I've often stuffed them with sweetbreads I've browned with morels and leeks. More later.

Yr. friend,
Jim

February 25, 2000

My dear Jim,

If one day, the Constitution of the French Republic were to be amended and were the legislators to ask for my advice, I would impose upon all the Presidential candidates a mandatory culinary test such as the preparation of a veal *blanquette*, an onion beef hash, a rabbit pâté, or an apple pie. I have always been apprehensive of citizens who cannot don an apron to treat their friends. A host who pampers me in his own pad with his own sauces, preparing and serving coffee and cigars in person—as required by *la belle tradition*—charms me far more than the lazy lord who invites me to an expensive restaurant boasting many stars.

Our one-man-one-vote suffrage system has the disadvantage of forcing down our throats all the poorly cured and improperly seasoned baloney which the candidates dish out in order to cajole those whose votes they covet, and since they must appeal to a wide electorate, their menu (which they call "the program") is often most indigestible. It would be more appropriate to ask them to prepare "live" (as are called the television broadcasts during which they enjoy exhibiting themselves) beef stewed with carrots or chicken *Ambrosia*. A chief of state skillful in the kitchen would no doubt govern with more sensitivity, voluptuousness, and generosity than a politician adept of Cuisine Minceur and Thalassotherapy cures.

You must be wondering where these digressions on our electoral cuisine may be leading. Here is the scene. During my recent and prolonged stay in Paris, I resided in the Marais as the guest of our dazzling Persian friend Nahal. My strolls in this gay historical district, where strut the young woodcock and the wild duckling, have often led me to the Hotel de Guénégaud, which was built by Mansard during the XVII century and houses today the Fondation de la Maison et de la Chasse. I will conduct you there during your next visit to Paris. You will feel your heart skip a beat at this marvelous temple of Nature, and I will get a kick out of introducing a rustic hunter such as yourself—an American savage escaped from his selvas—into drawing rooms steeped in the ancient and aristocratic tradition of French venery.

My first pee did not soil monogrammed swaddling clothes. Much like you, I more or less emerged from a burrow, but to be honest, I admit that it amuses me to trail my shabby cowboy boots under the gilding and wainscoting of so noble a residence. Boorish though I may be, I am greeted there with the utmost civility at each visit. It was in these settings that my musings on Power and Cuisine were born. A magnificent still life of game birds, painted in 1716 by one of our best animal painters, Alexander François Desportes, occupies the place of honor in a drawing room on the ground floor.

This painting, entitled *Venaison piquée menue pour mise en broche* (*Finely Larded Venison for Skewering*) is for me emblematic of what true voluptuousness meant during the regency of Philippe d'Orléans. In the foreground, lascivious as satiated bodies on furrowed sheets, barded pheasants and plucked ducks sprawl over each other with their rumps on exhibit. Nearby, on a silver salver, a dozen partridges form a corolla around a centerpiece consisting of a pheasant and a young rabbit. All these pieces are larded with meticulous art, the delicacy of which is more reminiscent of a fairy's nimble embroidery than the stitching of a kitchen boy. Two haunches of venison hang in the background.

Facetious Desportes! To animate his still life, he perched a gray Gabonese parrot on a copper cauldron. This fashionable chatterbox in vogue during the XVIII century, and the sole fowl in the picture to have retained its plumage, appears to thank its creator for making it so inedible. My dear Jim, I can personally testify to the gastronomical virtues of this particular breed of bird. Indeed, about twenty years ago, in St. Laurent du Maroni in Guyana, a Creole scullion once presented me with parrot stew. I had invited to this feast a young gastronome barely grown out of his knickerbockers, and for whom I felt that guilty fondness of the amateur pedagogue. My equinoctial and Socratic banter well nigh drowned in the mangrove waters thanks to the revolting and grossly tough "papegai." My Alcibiadian gourmet accepted to pursue our "philosophizing" but on the condition that the chow be of first quality. Ever since, I have refrained from further attempts at "psittophagie."

To curtail this Amazonian detour, let's return to Paris in 1716. Desportes' sumptuous painting was ordered by the Regent himself to decorate the private kitchen that he had fitted out in the Palais-Royal and in which he enjoyed preparing fine courses for his friends during his famous *Soupers*. I have always admired Philippe d'Orléans, a refined man who knew how to elevate debauchery to the heights of a Fine Art.

The son of an effeminate brother of the Sun King and of a fat German woman, the mannish Princess Palatine, the young man was perverted (or was it educated?) by a corrupt reveler, the Abbé Dubois, future Cardinal, for whom and in whom he ever maintained his friendship and his trust. Those who judge the various French political regimes by moral criteria paint the Duc d'Orléans' regency as an epoch of disintegration of mores and fearful decadence: the orgies at the Palais-Royal, the masked balls at the Opera, the corruption, gambling, profiteering and other beatitudes of a ruined and humiliated nation.

Along with other historians, it pleases me to study this era through quite a different pair of lenses. With the Regent came a new spirit, of light, gracefulness, and movement, an open spirit, human and free, which broke away from the barbarity and bigotry of the previous reign. Following the calamitous Madame de Maintenon, in great part responsible for the religious horrors and the unutterable misery of the end of the reign of Louis XIV, arrived upon the scene a voluptuous prince, friend of the Arts and of the Table: a composer of operas, amongst which a *Panthée* so licentious as to have been performed exclusively behind closed doors at the Palace; a talented sketcher who, in 1718, illustrated *Les Amours de Daphnis et Chloé*; an amateur alchemist under the guidance of Homberg; a scholar and . . . a master chef.

His famous *Soupers* took place in quasi-secret apartments at the Palais-Royal in the strictest privacy, guarded by young and vigorous lackeys. New recipes were invented and it was rumored that the Regent was remarkably talented in the preparation of *matelotes*.

In our national culinary treasure we possess a *sauce régence*. Perhaps it was concocted in Philippe d'Orléans' kitchen, under Monsieur Desportes' painting of larded venison. I include the recipe here in the event you should wish to impress an American historian: Dice 100 grams of lean lard into small squares and place them in a large pot with an onion, a shallot, and 50 grams of butter. Heat these up but do not brown, then soak with one glass of chicken broth and one glass of wine. Cook gently for half an hour, then add a quarter of a liter of this broth and half a liter of brown sauce. Reduce until the sauce coats the spoon.

This sauce, formerly used in *la grande cuisine*, accompanies the *poularde régence*. The *poularde*, larded and barded in similar fashion to the partridges in Monsieur Desportes' painting, was braised and served with *quenelles* of fowl and mushrooms dressed in the previous preparation.

But enough of French history and the Ancien Régime. Speaking of which, I warn you that mine will change beginning September 1.

I am off to Florida to stay with our friend Guy de la Valdene. I shall write my next letter from his grounds which I hope abound in game. Shortly thereafter, I shall meet you in Arizona. Prepare the quails, dear Sir, I am arriving!

Gérard

Patagonia, Arizona
March 16, 2000

Dear Gérard,

It's strange writing to you when you are so close. Three feet to be exact. At this moment I reach out and touch your bald head, so full of grief and torments, but also memories and questionable pleasures, the thousand meals and ten thousand books. I will begin writing my memoirs next year and you should also write your memoirs and call it "The Dark Orphaned Prince." We will trust God not to punish us for gluttony by saying, "O God, we were simply hungry."

So far at my house this past week we have eaten doves plainly roasted, rubbed with a little olive oil and black pepper. Wild doves need very little help from the cook. It is a sacrilege to distort the pure flavor of wild doves. You may do what you wish with pigeons. I also served you both scaled quail and Mearns quail. The Mearns have a milder flavor than the scaled who work harder for their living. We stuffed the quail with halved grapes, also raisins that we had soaked in good Courvoisier brandy, after first browning quail in a frying pan. (When I have done this dish in northern Michigan with grouse I have soaked dried fruit in the fabulous Sire de Gooberville Calvados but it is impossible to find it now in the United States.) We were lucky to have some Chave Hermitage, Échezeaux, and Nuits-Saint-Georges Les Cailles 1979 to drink with the birds. My friend Kermit Lynch sent me two cases of fine French wine. You should remember that we visited his office in Beaune several years ago after tasting many different Meursaults, which I love, perhaps the only white wine I truly love. That day we also had a three-hour lunch at Greuze in Tournus. I was still full when we returned to Pron but you insisted on making a *tagine de cervelles de agneau*. I had wonderful nightmares.

It used to be quite ordinary to eat parrots around here, especially in the Chiracahua Mountains. The miners and ranchers shot them but then one day in the late nineteenth century all the parrots were gone and never returned. We always make the mistake of thinking nature is endless. Of course there are many birds we don't eat that are quite delicious. Robins, for instance. Robins eat the same food as woodcock and snipe but it is illegal to shoot them. In the South some black people still eat starlings. I've tried them myself. In northern Michigan a local man was arrested for killing and eating a swan (*cygne*) which I understand were eaten in France in the Middle Ages by boiling them alive in oil which was intended to help their taste. I'm assuming that it is now illegal to do so in France. It is akin to eating the brains of living monkeys in the Orient.

I was intrigued by your comments about politicians and food. It is now fashionable for politicians in America to eat poorly under the guise of health. There is still much talk about the attempts to be on a "cuisine minceur" diet. Once in Chasen's Restaurant in Los Angeles I demanded Ronald Reagan's favorite meal, as he habitually ate in this restaurant. The maitre d' and waiter were amused and served me a boring "pot roast" which is braised beef and dark gravy. I was only able to eat it with a bottle of good Talbot. My wife makes this same dish beautifully and it doesn't require expensive wine to wash it down. Years ago when Mitterrand so seriously outsmarted Reagan at a conference I was forced to speculate in print that the food Mitterrand ate gave him the edge. Since he often visited that area Mitterrand had obviously stopped at our butcher friend, Fernand Dussert, in the Morvan and eaten the five different kinds of *fromage de têtes* that we bought there. Did I tell you that the most money I ever won at poker was at a hunting cabin? During the twelve-hour game I ate five roasted deer hearts. The next morning I was naturally attacked by gout but my wallet was full of money. My favorite part, however, is the liver of a young female deer which we might call "Lolita liver."

In the *New York Times* I recently read that President Clinton ate two French meals in a single evening, the first one cooked by the great Daniel Boulud. I once had a fine meal at Daniel's in New York but like the Taillevent I am uncomfortable with a dense crowd of very rich people.

Powerful Democrats like Clinton are more likely to eat well than Republicans because they are not ashamed of their biological functions, thus Clinton was able to skillfully fight off a right-wing "coup d'etat" over the revelation of his blow job. It was an enormously absurd chapter in American history. It was very embarrassing to try to explain this on my visits to France. We would be better off impeaching presidents for eating stupidly because then they will continue behaving stupidly, like licking China's boots while they continue to torture Cuba.

Tomorrow evening you will cook us some shrimps like they do in Marseilles with fennel seeds, garlic, and Ricard, and I will roast us my remaining doves. I think I have nineteen left, a lucky number. This will finish my game eating for the year though I think I might still have some elk in the freezer, and perhaps a wild duck or two, and also a wild goose that our friend Guy de la Valdene sent me. He also sent some wild-pork chops that we could eat as a first course with the wild goose, but perhaps in reverse. How can I write wildly without the help of these creatures? Right now I'm drinking an '87 Bandol Tourtine to give me courage to sign my name.

Your friend,
Jim

April 5, 2000

My dear Jim,

This is a belated answer to your March 16 letter which you scrawled on the small table at Hard Luck Ranch, while at the other end of the same table, I scribbled notes for my next *Chassignet in Arizona*. It wasn't that I dawdled on my *Road Home* but I did linger a trifle. First, in

late afternoon bars in Tucson where beautiful Mexican girls sang of love
and death with guttural and brazen voices, ogled by robust Irishmen still
hungover from their St. Patrick's Day boozing. Then in Phoenicia, in
the Catskill Mountains, where Hans Gissinger has just built his castle-
refuge with the consent of the brown bears which for centuries had
been the sole inhabitants of this impressive site.

It was springtime. A blazing March sun, convinced that it was
May, sent spirited and provocative rays to force the earth to bloom
prematurely. Frantic animation rustled under the dead leaves; ponds
rippled with tadpoles; dove couples billed and cooed, intoxicated with
love . . . but as far as the Teddy Bear department went, no such luck!

I would have loved to fraternize with one of those furry beasts,
coaxing it with a pot of honey, but none had rolled out of the sack just
yet. Bears are lazier than all the supine characters in Albert Cossery's
novels. When it's not time, it's simply not time.

I tried to console myself with a visit to Woodstock to see some
hippies, another variety of longhaired plantigrades whose mythical
performances had sparked my adolescent daydreams throughout the 60s.
Alas! There as well it was not time, or rather the time had long since
passed.

Today, Woodstock is a tidy tourist town. The kepi and the gun,
which had been outlawed within the community by municipal decree
during the gentle epoch of love and peace, are once again allowed. The
town has not yet passed into the hands of those bastard Republicans
(those diet-fascists); the majority still votes Democrat in Woodstock,
but in the bar where I lunched on a pastrami salad, I was forbidden to
smoke a cigar. Can you picture the scene? Forbidden to smoke in
Woodstock! The few old hippies I passed in the streets all bore lead in
their wings. Pathetic relics of the beat generation, sexagenarians
flowered like forsaken tombs, they barely had enough strength to raise
their index and middle fingers in a V whenever I saluted them with the
respect duly inspired by imperiled masterpieces. Depressing!

Gissinger has had a professional kitchen built such as I have never
seen before in a private home. He admitted to having been inspired by

Marc Meneau's, our Vezelay celebrity, the prince of pig-snout pies and *poularde demi-deuil*.

I had no difficulty in convincing Hans to organize, at the end of next fall, a culinary marathon for a few friends who know how to handle a pan, that is: you, La Valdene, Fergus, Chamonal, Meneau, that little *bougrelas*[1] from Strassart, the subtle Christian Odasso, and of course my little big self! Everyone will bring his science and possibly the spoils of his hunts. You could even hunt in the Catskills; apparently the area is teeming with grouse and woodcock.

Guy would prepare his boned and stuffed wild turkey, a marvel which I tasted in his "Dogwood Farm" in Florida. Christian could try his hand at a salmi of wood pigeons. Gissinger would cook a saddle of deer or a leg of venison prepared like a chamois from his native Helvetia. You could give me a new edition of your grouse and sweetbread dish. I would try to impress you with creams of boletus and hen pheasant, with feuilletés of pigeons and almonds, with pâtés of woodcock and of dove such as those I made for you at Lake Leelanau last year. If American customs' officers were as corrupt as implied in certain films, I would bring over a kilo of Monsieur Pebeyre's fresh truffles.

This attractive project will undoubtedly take place, providing we survive what soon awaits us in France: the Parisian agapes at the Musée de la Chasse, the diners chez Lulu's at the Assiette, the *Journées du livre et du vin* at Saumur, the gastronomy week in my house, the follies of the *Etonnants Voyageurs* in St. Malo, etc.

And we shall continue to mock, as you do in your letter, the dietary tastes of those who govern us. Mr. Nixon and Mr. Reagan's favorite meals are distressing.

I have never been interested in the court cuisine of contemporary France; I fear that it may have lost some of its splendor since the sophisticated era of the Regent which I evoked in my last letter. Monsieur Chirac is an avowed partisan of *tête de veau* and Mexican beer; as he strides up and down the isles of the Salon d'Agriculture, he displays

1. Name of King Ubu's son in *Ubu Roi* by Alfred Jarry.

an insatiable appetite for anything labeled *terroir*.[2] François Mitterrand had a decidedly less rustic palate. I know that he had a passion for shellfish. Under his reign appeared what has been called *la gauche caviar*, a sort of "socialist gratin" whose taste buds favor turbot in lobster sauce or Ballotine of pheasant St. Hubert more readily than herring and potatoes in oil or Saveloy vinaigrette. Since the election of Mr. Jospin and the advent of a certain "political correctness" advocating the virtues of "neither too much nor too little," the priority has been given to a pleasant mediocrity that one of my jester friends has baptized *gauche tarama*. It's pink, it's cheap, it's not fattening, it's discreet, it's simple and a tiny bit chic after all. No doubt, it wasn't convincing enough, for on the day I returned to France, in a sudden cabinet re-shuffle, Mr. Jospin added a few ladlefuls of caviar onto his morose tarama.

I don't know what Giscard d'Estaing liked to eat but his slender-ness has always seemed suspect to me. Pompidou probably remained loyal to the high-calorie dishes of his childhood in Auvergne. He had the cheerful and wily rotundity that reassures at once, the bourgeois food-lover and the crafty peasant.

You are correct in mentioning that over here we found it difficult to understand the grotesque Clinton blow-job scandal. America is the most puritan and pornographic country that I know. I wasn't surprised by all the hype. In France, country of extremes (extreme taste, extreme clamor), land of freedom but also of hypocrisy and denunciation, a few miserable ortolans—the last savored by F. Mitterrand shortly before the first measures of the Office for the Dead rang out in his honor—were stigmatized with a vehemence as pharisaic as that of the wretched prosecutor who pursues Boner Bill with bigotry and sanctimonious condemnation.

Let's leave aside governmental paunches, my dear Jim, and turn to the Sancho Panza prize that you and I shall design and award every year for the work of a poet or novelist who, besides serious literary qualities,

2. Local product.

will have to display a large stomach. He will be asked to cherish his paunch and swear that it will never be subjected to a weight-loss cure.

Thank you again, my little Jimmy, for all the generosities that you lavished upon me in your house in the valley of Sonoïta. Thanks for the oatmeal in the morning, the walks in the canyons, the quails and the pigeons, the tequilas at the Wagon Wheel Saloon, the exploration of the valley of San Rafael, the dinners in the Mexican restaurant of Nogales. Thank you for our fraternal conversations.

It is with these thanks that I end our little correspondence on hunting and cooking, as I look forward to your next visit here soon for new adventures and discoveries.

Your friend,
Gérard

AMERICAN FOOD JOURNAL

"What does it mean, anyway, to be an animal in human clothing?" asked novelist Barbara Kingsolver.

This question has been disturbing me a great deal in the past few years, especially during late nights and early mornings when the ticking of my biological clock can resemble an air hammer due to natural fatigue or questionable behavior. We're more likely to question the need for sleep or sex than we are the obvious food, shelter, and clothing, and since most folks who read this are not likely short on shelter and clothing, the question of the human animal and food presents itself in dense immensity. I'm not dismissing sex lightly, but it's after four in the afternoon and I'm feeling decidedly nonmental pangs of hunger. If you get a hard-on during dinner, you're either fourteen or feeling the wandering hand of a partner, or you're inside of one of those apocryphal stories where someone is under the table, whether it's from the *Arabian Nights*, Boulevard Montparnasse, or just off Sunset Strip.

There's an almost visible barrier to any deep thinking about food. The first indication of the whisper of the word *food* and the twelve billion neurons and thirty-two billion synapses in our brains activate. Am I hungry or not hungry? If I'm hungry, what do I want to eat? And this may or may not depend on what's available. Adding to the confusion is the idea that the five billion souls on earth have slightly or radically different tastes, just as voices, features, even brains are identifiably different. And what you wish to eat within the evolutionary curve will depend on good and bad food memories, not to speak of certain health and possibly ethical considerations. We are memorably punished by truly bad food, and we tend to learn more permanently from bad experiences than we do from the pleasure of the good.

* * *

As I sat in my small studio at the Hard Luck Ranch (actual name) in the early waning sun of a December afternoon, I was reminded of the irony that very good food can also be painful and unpleasant. The day before, my wife had laboriously made genuine *boeuf bourgignon* for a friend's birthday. Our kitchen in the casita down here on the Mexican border smelled like a bistro in Lyons. For some reason I ate far too much of this stew and also drank a great deal of red wine. I can't seem to learn from experience, other than momentarily until my "animal" appetite overwhelms my good sense, a trifling contest like a heavyweight fight that ends in seven seconds.

It was a rumbling, gaseous night. I had hurt an ankle again while quail hunting. Would my ankle be less susceptible to injury if I weighed less? Possibly. There are loud voices down at the creek crossing a hundred yards from the bedroom. Young men drinking beer, revving their battered Jeeps and Camaros, and yelling, "Fuck you, you fucker! You fucking fucker, fuck you!" With my mild success in Hollywood I could have helped this dialogue despite the drum-hard belly bloat under the sheets. I awake at dawn sadder but not conclusively wiser, only to lose my setter, Rose, on a walk. Without a shotgun I'm not, in her view, a serious person. She returns in an hour or so and despite the exercise of the search my sore tummy settles for two tortillas and some beans for lunch.

Of course this is a setup. While writing late in the afternoon I envision my simple intended pasta with garlic, olive oil, and health-giving broccoli, but when I reach home I discover that my friend Abel Murrieta has dropped off ten pounds of elk. I love elk! It's better than venison, antelope, and bear, and every bit as good as moose. What better accompaniment to pasta with broccoli than a couple of ample pieces of elk steak sautéed in butter, medium rare? I eat two pieces while my wife eats only one. She says she is no longer hungry. What an extraordinary idea. Who needs to be hungry to eat?

Now it is nearly midnight, my mind clear and my stomach relatively docile. The moon is gently waxing over America, her collective gut

packed with mostly trash, her skies electronically filled with the croak-
ing shitbirds of politics, masses of feathered, ex–fraternity boys trying to get their hands in the national till.

I am preoccupied with something far more important: my food
memories. Early in September I began a food journal that would include a driving trip to Montana to fish brown trout, the festive eating
in northern Michigan during bird-hunting season, and a twenty-five-
day book tour, when I would visit cities as varied as Vancouver, Brit-
ish Columbia, and Oxford, Mississippi. With a fresh journal at the
ready, I expected our great land to yield up nutritional secrets, though
I was probably on a second bottle of Côtes-du-Rhône when this
thought occurred.

Frankly on driving trips from the heartland west we tend to think
of anything we eat that is not outright bad as good. "At least I didn't
puke afterward" dollars up as a good review.

The first night out, in a motel in Ladysmith (lovely name), Wisconsin, I began, prematurely, to lose heart. Perhaps this was only the
honeymoon blues, but the file of American-food research spread on
my desk was discouraging. Tacked onto the knotty-pine wall there
was a print of a sad-eyed faux-Spanish donkey carrying a burden of
red flowers. This donkey seemed to speak to me in the manner of
childhood movies featuring Francis the talking mule. I swear the
donkey's pink lips were moving and the voice was that of an Irish
tenor: "You are an artist acclaimed by at least a handful of unname-
able critics. Do not waste your talent describing in detail the plates
of lukewarm dog shit that daily fuel the bodies of three hundred million of your fellow Americans. Spend your time on the pinnacles not
the suckholes. As Yeats said, 'What portion in the world can the artist have / Who has awakened from the common dream / But dissipa-
tion and despair?'"

Of course I disagreed. I'm a midwesterner who doesn't counte-
nance voices from the nether void, but then how much can you say
about the generic gravy that is trucked to thousands of restaurants in
mighty plastic barrels? I had carefully noted on trips to supermarkets
that the nearly invariable item in every cart was soda pop. Billions

are spent on flavored sugar water for a low-rent sugar rush, and what cost a nickel when I was young now costs about fifty cents. If you get them hooked you've made a fortune. Whether it's dope or sugar. It's also arguable that fast food and butter are killing as many people as cigarettes. I like to make this argument in public with great authority because I smoke, I don't like butter, and fast food repels me.

Back to the song of the road. Other than a few staples, at one time in our country to a remarkable degree we ate what was indigenously available. It was a matter of geography, of culinary regionalism, also the hunting, fishing, and gathering in an area, and how much we grew in our gardens. In the nineteenth century it was only the high-end urban restaurants that offered exotica from other regions and continents. Now the situation is reversed, with only the high-end restaurants using fresh local produce, unfrozen prime meats, and free-range fowl. In our time this emphasis was pioneered by the renowned Alice Waters at Chez Panisse in Berkeley, and is well established in many places in New York such as the Gramercy Tavern and Craft, both under chef Tom Colicchio.

On the second day out, passing through western Minnesota, I had a baked-ham luncheon special at a truck stop that perfectly illustrates the point. Like ninety-five percent of the ham we are served, this was ham in name only. Everywhere in the midwestern countryside there are pigs but, ironically, no ham remotely worthy of the name. It is simple dead pig's ass, artificially smoked, steamed, or boiled, strictly what they call "industrial food" in France, where it has also become prevalent.

It should be noted here that small pork producers are being victimized by the processors. When I'm driving Interstate 80 through Des Moines, Iowa, I avert my face in embarrassment as I pass the National Pork Producers Council building. Pork must be sold as pork, not "the other white meat." Pork fueled our westward movement! There are thousands of delicious ways to cook pork, but it is difficult now to find an acceptable piece of sausage, only tiny wafers and tubes of tasteless ground pork. You can find great sausage at the Cornhusker Hotel in Lincoln, Nebraska, or at the Carlyle in New York City, or in the specialty sausage restaurants like the Bob Evans chain in the Midwest. If you want to experience the grandeur of pork sausage, stop at the Powhatan Restaurant, just off Route 40 in Pocahontas, Illinois. If you want a first-rate pork chop, stop at Thunder Bay Grill in Davenport, Iowa, or any of the several Machine Shed restaurants owned by the same group. At the Powhatan, though, I was swept back to my childhood like Proust and his silly cookie, back to butchering time, to the making of true pork sausage and the glorious flavor of home-smoked ham. Luckily I don't live next door or I'd get "swollen up," as farm folks used to say.

Naturally after my Minnesota luncheon ham I vowed never to eat again, but by sunset in Medora, North Dakota, I had a decent rib steak at the Iron Horse Saloon. There was the additional pleasure in the alarm of a lady at the next table when my new upper partial plate came out with my fork while I was chewing a gristly piece. She really bunched her undies. The flavor of the steak was fine and my heart gladdened. Later, while I was playing blackjack, the usual ditzy movie crew entered and I had the pleasure of being condescended to after asking innocent questions and concealing my own glorious screenwriter identity.

Oddly, outside of urban centers it is difficult to find a first-rate steak in the West, except in Nebraska and Kansas. I mean the kind of prime steak you get at Gibsons in Chicago, or Smith & Wollensky or Peter Luger in New York. The best porterhouse of my life was at the Peppermill in Valentine, Nebraska. Curiously, prime steak and sausage have become anathema to the colorful spandex crowd. I managed to get my cholesterol as low as 156 a few years ago without giving up steak and sausage, but then it's an advantage to dislike fast food, snack food, butter, and desserts. I also eat a lot of fish and game, which I catch and shoot. When people criticize me for these activities I say that I'm less evolved than they are, which makes us both feel good. The great poet Gary Snyder has noted the presumed virtue of people who keep their distance from the sources of their food. How few of them have ever embraced a piglet in their arms and reflected on the ancient cycle of predator and prey.

*　*　*

Dawn in Medora was a bit crusty, as it were, though I knew a treat was in store in Miles City, Montana, a scant 116 miles away. At Club 600 fried side pork is still served in bounteous quantity, another lovely remnant of my youth. My Swedish grandparents ate it often, with Grandpa living to eighty-nine years, and Grandma ninety-seven. My favorite breakfast is side pork, herring, and heavy rye bread; sad to say, however, good pickled herring is generally unavailable. I've often made my own out of salt herring from a grocer of Swedish descent, but my only other source of superb herring is Barney Greengrass in New York, a city, like Paris, where the wildest appetite dreams can be assuaged.

Food is not a problem in Livingston, Montana, where both our daughters, Jamie and Anna, live, and where I fly-fish for trout every September. I preorder a half dozen (or more) cases of Côtes-du-Rhône from Kermit Lynch in Berkeley, and make a sizable list for Zingerman's, the ne plus ultra of delicatessens, in Ann Arbor, Michigan. Why drive this far to go fishing if you're eating bad lunches on the riverbank? Our culture wishes to make us indiscriminate gobbling machines, and to avoid this requires advance vigilance of the sort some hearty souls devote to the stock market, a matter I gave up on more than twenty years ago when my English gambling and Australian oil stocks proved worthless. If only this money had been spent on food and wine, say a few casks of Bordeaux, which I could be drinking at this moment.

Dinners at my daughter Jamie's were not diet numbers: lasagna with a Bolognese ragu of veal, pancetta, flank steak, Japanese eggplant, garlic, carrot, celery root; a 4-H brisket with tomatoes, cucumbers, Italian green beans from her garden, after an appetizer of deep-fried pumpkin blossoms, also from the garden; a chicken fricassee with caper, lemon, egg yolk, made with free-range Hutterite chicken; lobster and yellowtail with roasted vegetables and orzo, Harrington ham from Vermont and potato salad; a pasta with green tomatoes, onions, and pancetta; a party dish of roast locally raised beef and lamb, starting with some homemade ricotta. That sort of thing, day after day.

It suddenly occurred to me that the term "foodie" pisses me off. Why not eat well during a severely truncated life on earth, our short brutish passage? Not that our culture doesn't own a large number of food ninnies, especially in urban areas in the so-called haute cuisine area. Here food is often oversqueezed, as it were. I haven't lost my food adventurism, but I no longer wish to see chefs outdo one another at my expense in the name of experimentalism and that dread word *creativity*, wherein newly minted dishes lose their connection with the earth that bore their ingredients. Of course something valid occasionally emerges, but others are welcome to be on the expensive receiving end of this hundred-to-one shot. Sometimes it is only a matter of paying a few hundred bucks to read a chef's first draft, when you would willingly have walked, as I have done, eighty-five blocks for spaghetti and meatballs as penance to purge yourself from the culinary silliness of the night before.

Cooking provides a fine binder for marriage and family and friendship, but the efforts can become fatiguing. Everyone gets tired and wants to be served. There can be a friendly camaraderie in the kitchen that easily dismisses marital and family quarrels, if only because hunger and the delight in good food are far more basic than quarrel issues like murder and infidelity. Livingston, Montana, is lucky that the famed artist Russell Chatham owns and runs a fine local restaurant. Several years ago it seemed ill advised to me for Chatham to split his attention from his painting, but he had the simple motive that there was nowhere locally for him to eat. Since Chatham is one of the best amateur cooks I know, and an old friend, I had to finally trust his impulse, though I'd guess it cost him about a million bucks. Chatham comes from the Alice Waters–Colicchio–Cindy Pawlcyn school of the freshest and finest ingredients, and part of the problem in Montana is the monthly FedEx bill, what with his fish coming from Charles Morgan in Destin, Florida, and also Harry Yoshimura in Seattle, Wm. King in Naubinway, Michigan, and Browne Trading Co. in Portland, Maine. Given the dough for the freight bill, everything is available nowadays, assuming you know what you're looking for. I've eaten at Chatham's more than a dozen times without a disappointing meal, favoring the grilled *poussin* with polenta and the duckling with wild rice and glazed turnips. For such a minuscule place, Livingston has another good place to eat in the Murray Hotel, graced by chef Scott Peterson, who has had considerable training in France.

While having a good lunch in a Japanese restaurant, Tanuki, in the army-base town of Sierra Vista, Arizona, I was full of light and dark food thoughts. As with sexuality, it is difficult to make a philosophical system about food. It is a matter of random pleasures that have a logical basis. Fast food is an integral part of a culture that demands speed so people can get at important things like making money and other understandable inanities. What's the point of making money if you don't even eat well, a basic principle for a decent life? And where is the American cuisine outside a dozen or so ethnic roots? It's hard to find except in the South, which is historically not a speed-intoxicated society, except in recent decades in some southern cities. Great cuisines, with the French and Chinese apparently the highest, emerge from economics of scarcity where the short supplies guaranteed the ultimate in ingenuity. America's breadbasket is so vastly full the bottom has dropped out and we usually get a mess worthy of the floor. Not always, but very often.

I once wrote that I like recipes that are as fascinating as dirty pictures. As I get older I am finding more of these recipes, a matter of hormonal inevitability. And I have often thought my preoccupation with good food levels itself into an aesthetic matter, a more physiological response to something finely made in terms of art or craft. A great meal is similar to one of those rare paintings you'd like to live within for a while. Maybe painters and sculptors tend to eat better than writers do because their work is more visceral. Many writers are infantile and indiscriminate, and often when they cook they treat the most basic food compositions as culinary triumphs, perhaps because they're surprised it turned out to be more than modestly edible, the usual mistake of trying to be innovative with no training. For years—forty to be exact—I've been mystified why my wife is a far better cook than I am. Easy: I'm a writer.

The difference between a reasonably good amateur cook and a real chef is the difference between a Missouri tennis-club champ and Pete Sampras. If you have spent any time in a professional kitchen you are simply stunned by the deft capabilities of real chefs. Most fine home cooks would become weeping cretins by the third day within the demands of a professional kitchen, but then this also adds a disturbing dimension. There are a number of a fine cooking schools now, perhaps led by the Culinary Institute of America in Hyde Park, New York. Of late I have also noted there are more and more faux fine restaurants led by chefs who are graduates of the cooking schools. Perhaps we should feel lucky these places exist, but the problem is in the similarity to an M.F.A. in writing. Solid basics can be taught, learned, but the true step up has always been a little ineffable, unreachable by sincerity and hard work, a matter of dimension, experience, resonance, a perfect palate, which is similar to perfect pitch. I have also noted that the best of these cooking-school graduates have spent apprenticeship time in France or Italy, but that most turn out "continental" attention-getters that lack harmony as a total meal.

My bird season this year was somewhat truncated by an oncoming book tour, something that will never happen again due to a garden-variety epiphany about the shortness of life. My favorite bird-hunting species are grouse and woodcock, and this year I had only a little more than two weeks to hunt them with my English setter, Rose. A good bird season is long and noncompulsive, with little concentration on daily success. A medium competency and a good dog will bag you enough for your friends and family, but the real pleasure depends on a leisurely pace with an intermix of good and bad weather, fresh books to read, dry firewood, good wine, fascinating dog work, and visits by hunting friends.

There's not much point in talking about how to cook woodcock and ruffed grouse because they are plainly unavailable to all but a few. Truly wild game cannot be served in restaurants in America mostly because our previous era's market hunting practically despoiled our game populations. I have never eaten pen-raised game that was more than a pale shadow of the wild, with the possible exception of some New Zealand venison that might very well have been wild in its native country. Wild salmon doesn't taste to me like the same species as the production of salmon farms, any more than the tame pen-raised quail bear up in relation to the wild Mearns, Gambel's, and scaled quail I shoot in the American Southwest, which feed on hundreds of seeds and forbs.

Of course, we don't eat game birds every evening while hunting. One of my main hunting partners, Guy de la Valdene, is perhaps a more pronounced food neurotic than even I am (in a recent note he mentioned he had eaten antelope, fresh foie gras, doves, a coq au vin made with an '82 Volnay, a Sri Lankan rabbit curry, duck confit, and so on). We've cooked and hunted together for thirty years or so, though our dishes are less gargantuan since Chatham no longer joins us. This year our game dinners alternated with a roast capon, veal chops, a Catalan beef stew, and a thrice-cooked Chinese duck and pork dish. On my wife's birthday, with both daughters visiting from Montana, there was an ample supply of beluga caviar, Atlantic salmon, fresh foie gras, and exquisitely small racks of lamb from Summerfield Farm in North Carolina (the country's best purveyor of lamb and veal). We drank a few Latours and Lafites, the remains of my once noble wine cellar, from my Hollywood heydays, though I have found my descent to Côtes-du-Rhônes not precipitous or unpleasant.

The day of doom arrived and I was off to Vancouver to begin flacking two new books. During years I'm not publishing I limit myself to a single public appearance. This is a matter of claustrophobia and the fact that in literary society the carrot on the end of the stick isn't attractive enough to make you board planes, an experience that now makes my Greyhound-bus days of the remote past look golden.

There's something essentially comic about book tours. A number of writers have noted that your persona, your ostensibly true personality, changes easily during travel. It's easy to slide back and forth between Ronnie the Rodeo Clown, the Dark Orphaned Prince, and the simply Pissed-off Artist. Of course, it's not proper to whine about success, but people do. I'm totally unsympathetic to those fungoid rock songs about the arduous life of the road, but then my eyes dampen when I recall what I feel like after signing eight hundred books in five hours. It's much more pleasant to be admired at a distance: kind letters and big checks, please. It's convenient to forget early career appearances to which only a dozen readers showed up.

The real problem, too, is that you're not very hungry after these events. Despite the idea that the American motto "Clean your plate" was beaten into you, you couldn't quite do the job on two dozen pretty good restaurants. Added to the problem is that because of the food column you used to write, many chefs still think of you as a "top gun" and insist on showing you their best, and it's only barely possible to do them justice on the days you perform your song and dance and signing. Another factor, however vague, is one of etiquette—to wit, you're not supposed to eat if someone is talking to you. If I had not broken this rule I would have lost twenty-five pounds in twenty-five days, certainly an unhealthy regimen when the supposed ideal diet, my own, is losing a pound a year.

My trick this time out of the chutes was to avoid newspapers, television, and too much jangly coffee and booze, and to read lots of ancient Chinese poetry. And never play the sensitive, remote, tormented writer, which anyway is a difficult role, or you'll be looking for a plane to Paris by the end of the first event. Above all, lay the foundation of the day with pork products, giving yourself the stalwart power of the pig, which can withstand anything until butchering time.

Lucky for me and others, Vancouver is a fine walking town and they have delicious oysters, albeit large ones perfectly suited for oyster stew. Shakiness caused by violating the rule of small amounts of booze can be resolved by oyster stew at Rodney's Oyster House, on Granville Island, plus a few beers and a nap, then a glass of Gigondas when you wake up and put on your dowdy suit of lights and hear the questionable sound of your jaw flapping. "Buy this book, or how can I afford Parmigiano-Reggiano on my bird dog's food? She likes it and won't eat Alpo." This is true.

Seattle is a problem because a friend, Peter Lewis, owns Campagne, unquestionably one of the best restaurants on the West Coast. Seattle has an abundance of fine restaurants, and when we weren't at Campagne we were at the Sea Garden for exquisite Chinese seafood, or the Harvest Vine for equally exquisite tapas. A great bonus for my usual Seattle rounds is the fact that Mario Batali, of New York fame, has a father, Armandino Batali, who has opened a lunch counter, Salumi, after thirty-one years of working at Boeing. You easily see where his son got his genius. I was fortified by testing a dozen of his homemade sausages, and also delicious oxtail stew, a pork-cheek stew, and pork cutlets fried with fresh sage. Add more than a little red wine and I was well suited to partially snooze through four hours of interviews and the making of a CD of my poetry.

Naturally my digestion was decrepit by the time I reached San Francisco, where I usually eat at Alice Waters's splendid Chez Panisse in Berkeley or at Bix's downtown. Years ago I was steamed in Berkeley because I couldn't find a place to have a simple shot and beer before a reading, so this time I opted for a fine dinner at Bix's. In sophisticated California, taverns have disappeared along with cigarettes, accordions, straight razors, and living grace. By the second night we simply called in for pizzas at my favorite West Coast saloon, the Tosca.

After Denver, where I ate only a piece of fish while others gobbled splendid steaks at Morton's, I had a twenty-four-hour sleeping vacation at home in Michigan. Buddhist texts have taught me not to eat a big steak at midnight if you're getting up at 5:00 A.M. Strangely enough, at 3:00 A.M. at my fancy hotel, a man down the hall started bellowing, "Don't kill me!" over and over. I'm old enough to remember Kitty Genovese so I checked it out, but it was only a drunk quarreling with friends. The staff at the Monte Carlo apologized, but I admitted I had enjoyed the adrenaline of real-life drama compared with what I had been doing for a couple of weeks. The problem was that my left ankle was bluish from tripping on a curb while avoiding a car hurtling toward me from my blind side the night before. This blind left eye kept me out of Vietnam, which might have ruined my appetite.

Ann Arbor was pretty good because it is the home of Zingerman's, where I had a massive brisket sandwich with horseradish sauce, and dinner was at the Earle, the single American restaurant I'm aware of with a large selection of Domaine Tempier Bandol, for reasons of temperament my favorite wine. And now I was headed south, a richer pasture than the rest of the country if you except food capitals like New York, San Francisco, and Seattle.

I often think of myself as a private detective of food whirling through the American night (and day), not only looking for the criminally ill prepared, but in ceaseless search of the genuine. Under my trench coat is a bib, and instead of gun and knife, I carry toothpicks, Pepto-Bismol, and a reasonably fat wallet. For instance, in the Memphis airport waiting for my luggage and ride, I coolly noticed there were many big, fat men, or what in the South they call "a tad burly." I'm not judgmental, because I know this porcine condition must be called "Christian fat." These men are devout and don't want to become lean, hungry lotharios, so they favor virtuous overeating, a tactic practiced in many areas away from our cities, which fairly shimmer with dank lust. Sinless fat people are doubtless headed for heaven.

Oxford, Mississippi, was tough the first evening, with an elegant meal prepared by chef John Currence at the City Grocery that included a first-rate rabbit cassoulet, which didn't exactly calm my tummy because there were a half dozen other good courses, including a new kind of pork rollatini. The next day I was saved by the Ajax Diner on the square, a southern-soul-food restaurant that is always crowded, where I was soothed by five vegetable dishes: potato salad, black-eyed peas, butter beans with beef gravy, turnip greens with smoked pork, and, grudgingly, broccoli. And after my reading there was a marvelous crawfish étouffée and rice at a private home. I was almost well by Jackson, but then there was a stomach-searing anxiety attack from being admired and perhaps too many barbecued pork ribs the night before. The act of chewing rib bones is a harbinger of our Pleistocene past, a past I daily identify with in the woods, so it is easy to eat too much from what is simply an ancient pull of genes.

Whatever self-induced physical suffering I was undergoing, much of it was allayed by the nostrum of French red wine of the first order, and by my continued reading of Su Tung-p'o, a Chinese poet of the twelfth century, who had a monstrously hard life, also consoled by wine, and lived without complaint. This book was better soul food for me than Janis Joplin's "Get It While You Can," my anthem for earlier in life, which, if continued, would have brought me up well short of my recent years. But even better than Chinese literature were the facts that I had only Raleigh-Durham and New York City to go, and that I might get to pet my dog again before my system ruptured as if someone had a dropped case of dynamite down a manhole.

Raleigh-Durham passed as a dream, partly because I was staying at the guesthouse of a private home in a pleasant rural retirement colony, where I even got to pet a Galloway cow (black with a white stripe around the middle). Charles Frazier, of *Cold Mountain* fame, did the introduction for my appearance and I recalled a story Judy Hottensen, the marketing vice president of Grove/Atlantic and my frequent companion on tour, had told me about Frazier when she accompanied him on an endless trip. One pathetic, exhausted day, Frazier asked if they could eat at a restaurant where "they didn't serve portobellos." These big domestic fungi are as sure a sign of mediocrity as skinless, boneless chicken breasts.

The first evening in Raleigh-Durham, a chef named Warren Stephens at the Fearrington House Inn cooked me a fascinating bird referred to plainly (a plus) in the menu as a "marsh hen." I decided to leave the mystery intact in the manner of an evening with lovely women for whom you don't have a last name or a phone number. The next evening at the Magnolia Grill I was replenished with oys-

ters and andouille and in the morning was off to New York, troubled
by the idea that one of my dinner partners at the Magnolia, Reynolds
Price, though in a wheelchair from spinal cancer, demonstrated more
grace and joy than any American writer I had ever met.

Writers from the hinterlands usually have a problematic relationship
with New York City. They want to have either a crazed love affair
with the city or a total divorce without having been married to her.
I think of New York as female, and Chicago male. In recent years
when traveling to New York, I always remind myself of what Dōgen,
a Japanese philosopher of the thirteenth century, advised: "No changing reality to suit the self." In other words, moment by moment, accept the raw meat on the floor, and don't waste any time on fantasies,
expectations, and disappointments. The wilderness is the best God
has done, and cities like Paris, Rome, and New York are the best man
has come up with.

Besides, there's no end to what you can find to eat there. There's
a tug at my heart and stomach when I pass through the Village, where
I discovered garlic and red wine in the late '50s as an indigent explorer hitchhiking in from the northern Midwest. New York is the
last singular place in America where the dimensions of food are truly
great and the local varieties of fast food aren't an obscenity. As an
instance, both Judy Hottensen and myself were all played out at the
idea of lunch, so we met one day at the Papaya King at Eighty-sixth
Street and Third Avenue for hot dogs, and the next day ate noodle
soup with chopped duck and vegetables at the Family Noodle Restaurant in Chinatown, the kind of literary lunch I truly enjoy.

My first night in New York I habitually go to Elaine's for an
immense veal chop with garlic, and sautéed spinach with garlic, but
they were closed for an election-night party, so I opted for a palat-
able braised lamb shank at La Goulue, going to bed without unpalat-
able election television. The second night, after a Barnes & Noble
performance, we went late to one of my top-five favorites in New
York: L'Acajou, where I had rabbit stew, but by then I was truly a

frayed warbler and couldn't eat enough to produce the wonderful nightmares caused by indigestion.

The third night, at Mario Batali's Babbo, I had what was easily the best meal I have ever had in an American restaurant. Batali himself dined with us and walked me through the courses, all of which I at least sampled. *Antipasti:* spicy two-minute calamari; marinated fresh anchovies with roasted peppers and black lentils; warm lamb's-tongue vinaigrette with chanterelles, pecorino Toscano, and a three-minute egg; Babbo salumi with cipolle Modenese, celery root, and pear vinegar; testa with waxy potatoes and thyme vinaigrette; duck bresaola with Winesap marmellata. *Primi:* bucatini all'amatriciana with guanciale, hot pepper, and pecorino; goose-liver ravioli with balsamic vinegar and brown butter; beef-cheek ravioli with crushed squab liver and black truffles; spaghetti aglio e olio with red and black pepper; and tripe alla parmigiana. *Secondi:* barbecued squab with roasted-beet farrotto and porcini mustard; grilled quail with wilted chard, chanterelles, and saba; and, finally, fennel-dusted sweetbreads with sweet-and-sour onions, duck bacon, and membrillo vinegar. There were half a dozen exquisite desserts, a few double magnums of Barolo, and the obligatory grappa.

This dinner was a mystical experience, and as such, you must yourself live through it to fully understand the mysticality, which was a little less apparent when I got up early for the airport the next morning in a driving rainstorm, with the usual flooded freeways.

My first day home I had a bowl of pea soup. Period. I was lost in thought and a bit puzzled by the thousands of cookbooks I had leafed through in my life, none of them containing skin pictures. There's a splendid *Saveur* cookbook called *Authentic American,* but looking through it, it occurred to me that as a food lunatic I had cooked many of the dishes but had been served only a few of them in American homes or restaurants, as if a grand tradition had been neglected until forgotten.

Maybe we're a bit too restless to largely work for the authentic or genuine in our eating. Or too lazy, or simply not sufficiently interested. When I first envisioned this piece, I planned to spend an entire week eating fast food, but life is far too short for this degree of squalor and self-cruelty lacks attractive flavors. The French philosopher Foucault has some elaborate notions of the culture as a zoo. The dominant ethic is Calvinist. We must eat to perform for our masters. But then if you wish to slip through the bars of the zoo, all of the ingredients are here if you take the time to learn how to use them, or if you wish to look long and hard enough for someone who knows how to cook. It's not a birthright in this country, the silliest of our presumptions. It's an art, or at least a craft. And in the interest of journalistic honesty, a suspect item, two years ago this summer, on a long drive on a hot day, I ate a Whopper at Burger King, then drove on down the street in Gaylord, Michigan, for a second course of french fries at McDonald's. I didn't die.

WINE

I have seventy-seven wine stories; better yet, call them modest epiphanies. As the century wanes into the banality of a new millennium (who holds what watch?), I consider the great inventions of the past. Naturally one must include electricity and toilet paper, and exclude computers of all varieties, but near the top of the products of the human imagination, like an ancient deity that is so omnipresent it has become invisible, is the corkscrew.

Of course, we all know that some vintners are so greedy they would rather use old rags than the sacred cork tree, but then people of intelligence have had quite enough of this economic fascism, this trough of venality that is the global economy, and have resisted. The simple physical act of opening a bottle of wine has brought more happiness to the human race than all of the governments in the history of the earth. Even organized religions are mere spiritual mousetraps compared to the *pop* of the cork, the delicious squeak when you loosen it from the firm grip of the corkscrew. And then the grandeur of the burble as we fill the glass, the very same sound we hear at the source, the wombs of all the rivers on earth.

That said, we must go to the particular; it is fruitless to keep chattering about women in general when they can be comprehended only on an individual basis, and then partially at best. Whether it is women or wine our gifts of intelligence are limited, but it is this specific charm of the immutable that fuels our existence. Taste is a mystery that best finds its voice in wine.

At this very moment I'm a bit nervous because there is a gale on Lake Superior, and the wind is so severe that a large white pine has toppled in the backyard of my cabin. The marine forecast on the radio states that the waves will reach between twenty and twenty-four feet and that the gale will last another full day. Stepping outside for a moment, I can hear the roar of Lake Superior though it is three miles downriver from this cabin. What can I do about the surrounding forest that is now twisting in the wind? Why, have my first glass of wine of the day. I pull the cork of a Lirac, the gift of a friend. The cork sound counters the shuddering walls of the log cabin. As I drink the first glass rather quickly, my metal Weber grill is blown over in the yard. The Lirac is very good, if a bit midrange, but such is its power that the storm becomes acceptable. At least I'm not in a boat. Another smaller tree falls and my dog barks. I'd offer her a glass but she doesn't care for wine. I read from a volume of Chinese poetry. The bottle slowly empties itself. Now the gale is only a gale. It's outside, and I'm inside. Three blue jays at the feeder are ignoring the storm and its sixty-knot winds. If I went outside with a full glass there would be waves on the surface of my wine. Instead, I prepare some duck confit for my dinner.

Acute fear is a peculiar emotion, always a surprise in it suddenness and power. Several years ago, flying home from Montana with my wife, we boarded a small propeller plane in Minneapolis much delayed by thunderstorms. Finally, the impatient pilot took off and halfway through the flight, when we were out over Lake Michigan, we collided with the storm, which couldn't be avoided by flying north or south. The plane twirled on an invisible pivot, bucked like a rodeo horse, then stood on its tail with wings flapping like the rare anhinga bird, which resembles an airborne serpent. The passengers moaned and hooted and vomited like doomed owls. I'd like to say I was fearless but it would be a pointless lie. I'd planned on strangling the impetuous pilot, but when we reached Traverse City he emerged from the cockpit soaked with sweat and with an utterly tortured expression of apology.

We reached home after midnight and my wife went promptly to bed. I was still trembling from having kissed death's ass and fetched two wines from the cellar, a Migoua and a Tourtine Bandol from Lulu Peyraud's Domaine Tempier. I slowly drank both of these superb bottles while meditating on the essential criminality of flight and on how even birds have the wit not to fly into thunderstorms. After a short while, this blessed Bandol began to take over and I again realized that we are only flowers for the void. Finally the wine swept me back to Provence in late April, where I had eaten and drunk so happily at Lulu Peyraud's house after we'd knelt in the courtyard by the grave of her husband, Lucien, who had created this splendid wine. By the time I went to bed, the flight had become merely another tidbit of horror to file in the brain, detoxified so nobly by the wine. Despite their frequent strikes, I fly Air France to Europe because it serves interesting wines, the only pallia-tive for the blasphemy of flight.

Naturally, we save our best bottles to celebrate or commemo-rate. Some twenty years ago, by sheer luck, I was able to buy a pri-vate collection for a modest price. A man had a liver problem, but for personal reasons he did not want to sell his wines to a restaurant. I heard about it and moved quickly, and have placed the experience up near funding my remote cabin in Michigan's Upper Peninsula and our little winter casita near the Mexican border. Buying this collec-tion, now mostly dissipated, allowed me to drink some wines that writers are only rarely allowed to approach for financial reasons, and also to treat friends. Guy de la Valdene, a dear friend and the pri-mary wine guide of my life, was at my house for bird hunting on the eve of going off for very serious surgery. We sat at my kitchen counter and gently drank two bottles of 1953 Richebourg. On another occa-sion, when Guy made *salmis de bécasse*, we drank several bottles of Grands-Échezeaux, his father's favorite wine. And just a week ago, the night before Guy left following our annual grouse and woodcock hunt, we had a splendid 1967 Latour, the best Latour of my life ex-cept for the 1949 I shared with my daughter on the night before she was married, along with the 1961 Lafite-Rothschild we had had ear-lier with dinner.

Such bottles truly resonate in the memory, growing even more overwhelming as they distance themselves with the years. I close my eyes and let my taste memory become vivid, somewhat like a sex fantasy that makes your hair stand on end and goose bumps rise on your arms. Now that I no longer write screenplays, my tastes have necessarily had to become more modest, and I have to depend on the kindness of friends and strangers with bigger wallets. I have in the past few years developed a taste for about thirty different Côtes-du-Rhônes, though naturally some of the most expensive ones, like Crozes-Hermitages and Gigondas, are the tastiest. Côte Rôtie is, of course, off to the side, all by itself in lonely splendor. Last fall when my latest novel, *The Road Home*, had begun doing quite well in France, I shared several celebration bottles of old Côte Rôtie with my friend and publisher Christian Bourgois. Success in itself can be quite disturbing, hard to accommodate, and I have spent as much time as possible alone in my room, where a number of good bottles have consoled me, including two Côte Rôties sent over by Dominique Bourgois's father, and two bottles of a fine year of Château Beychevelle, which were a gift from Jeanne Moreau, whose gorgeous voice obviously has been nurtured by wine.

Sometimes a humbler wine totally fits the situation. One day last fall in Paris, when I was angry from doing so many interviews, I left the hotel lobby and walked over to the Select on Montparnasse, a café I visit every day when in the city, and had a simple but delicious bottle of Brouilly. My anger subsided when the resident cat allowed me to pat it, and by tilting my head I had a good look at a woman's legs in the corner. I shall ever after think of thighs when I drink Brouilly.

I have left out American wines because I can think of only one truly great one, the 1968 Heitz Martha's Vineyard, and I have no story attached to it. Doubtless there are some considerable American wines, but most are too thickish and oaky for my taste.

I shouldn't forget how wine can assuage grief. Once, my phenomenal bird dog, an English setter named Tess, over whom I shot more than a thousand birds, got a stick caught in her throat and began to hemorrhage. After two late-night trips to the veterinarian she was finally pronounced out of danger. I had been so shattered I hadn't been able to eat dinner, and after she finally slept I remembered that on this very day a friend had sent a fresh foie gras from D'Artagnan. It was 2:00 A.M. when I finished steaming the foie gras over Sire de Gouberville cognac. I ate it with a baguette and my best remaining bottle of Margaux. I don't recall the year of this fine wine, but I raised my glass to my sleeping dog, who had been nearly lost but was found again.

Lastly, but perhaps most important because we do not know what happens after death, I owe to wine the fact that I'm still alive. Some years ago I was in bad health and several doctors learned that I was utterly addicted to V.O., a Canadian whiskey that, though delicious, is a poor substitute for water or wine. I explained the mortal problem to my friend Michael Butler, who works for that great importer of French wines Kermit Lynch. We decided that some magnums of Châteauneuf-du-Pape Vieux Telegraphe might help me through the harrowing ordeal I was facing. One evening in our little casita, I set out a bottle of the V.O. and sat down in a rocker, staring at this dread potion for four hours, drinking nothing but the spirits of denial. If I couldn't stop whiskey I'd have to give up alcohol altogether, and what then would become of the lonely bottles in my cellar? I rocked like an autistic child. Tears formed, but I won. I dumped the bottle of whiskey in the sink, had a glass of the Vieux Telegraphe, petted my dog, and went to bed, a new man in an old bottle.

1999

MEATBALLS

What idiosyncrasies feed our private hungers, our food and sexual vices? Despite the culture's attempt to make us march in lockstep like Boy Scouts—largely for economic reasons—we are perverse dogs who own unique histories of mind. One of my old friends is phobic about rats, having eaten them frequently during his childhood in Calabria during World War II. Once, while we were sharing a couple of gallons of Cribari, a profoundly mediocre jug wine of the 1950s, this friend admitted that, cooked with sufficient garlic, rats weren't all that bad. Another friend was caught masturbating in childhood and his mother flayed his genitals bloody raw with a coat hanger; he became a princeling of the New York art world and never intentionally ate rat. Both friends, neither of whom I've seen in decades (the latter was murdered in Puerto Rico), shared with me a passion in our late teens and early twenties: spaghetti and meatballs. We three were poor and battered, having given ourselves to art, a deal that doesn't guarantee enough to eat to load an average fruit picker.

"I was starving in an attic three feet from the moon." If I recall correctly, this is how Knut Hamsun begins his novel *Hunger*. In the late fifties I lived a total of about a year in New York City and Boston, though the latter rather briefly. I worked for a period at a book discount house on Forty-second Street and took home only about thirty-five bucks a week, which had to be stretched to cover my windowless room (it had an air vent at the bottom of which rats fed), my subway fare, and food. I knew no one in New York but imagined I was leading a literary life of some sort, keeping a journal full of piths and gists. I had to try to eat on a dollar a day, which would leave me enough for three or four twenty-cent beers. Lunch was often a fifteen-cent herring sandwich on rye bought at a workingman's restaurant over near Hell's Kitchen. My favorite dining place was Romeo's Spaghetti Parlor, where a large bowl of spaghetti with marinara sauce was forty cents; fifteen cents more afforded you a meatball. At the time this meal seemed utterly delicious, but then my father used to say, "A saltine is a feast to a starving man."

At odd times I still love spaghetti and meatballs. It is soul food, a balm, a food nostrum that helps me understand the often questionable arc of my life. I have even found a place to have it in Paris where I can ignore the ironies of a couple of grand and a dozen credit cards in my wallet and simply eat spaghetti and meatballs, unmindful as a heroin addict with a dirty needle that mad cow disease might lurk in any meatball. Memories of true hunger can fuel gluttony, but then I console myself with the idea that I've been victorious over cocaine and Canadian whiskey, the love of which was a spike in my head that I pounded daily until a few years ago. If I were also to deny myself my food extravagances I would not have the heart to write, and would become yet another of the body Nazis that abound in our culture.

Sad to say my own version of spaghetti and meatballs falls well short of those of my wife and eldest daughter, Jamie. Perhaps by the time I taste the sauce (overfrequently) and eat several of the partially cooked meatballs the edge is off. It is next to impossible to find a truly good version in a restaurant because I feel that, at its best, the dish deserves a roasted-tomato sauce made with fresh herbs. This limits it to August in northern Michigan. I also tend to have a heavy hand with the garlic; on one occasion I used thirty-three cloves to commemorate our Lord, and also because it is my favorite number in roulette, and my age when I escaped the rather vivid prospect of suicide.

Certain Gucci-Pucci-Armani Italians have told me that they have never eaten spaghetti and meatballs. Tuscans look down on the Calabrese and Neapolitans in the same way that New Yorkers regard poor white southerners. These Cerruti aristocrats tell me that the dish is an American perversion of Italian cuisine, to which I always

reply, "I don't give a shit." Their tiny, pointy shoes cause them lifelong discomfort and you can't eat a largish meatball with pursed, dry
lips. I should also mention that I make *bollito misto*, and that I have
often shaved Italian white truffles onto my morning oatmeal. But then
let's not be nasty. It's better to meditate on the dark freight of power
and grace that spaghetti and meatballs can offer your life.

Sauce

Pour a liberal amount of good olive oil in the bottom of a baking pan. Halve a dozen or so tomatoes and place them in the
pan. Sprinkle them liberally with chopped garlic, fresh basil,
and thyme. Cook for about an hour at 325°F. Chop this roughly
and you have your sauce.

Meatballs
1 pound ground chuck or veal
2 beaten eggs
5 cloves garlic
¼ cup chopped parsley
3 or 4 anchovy fillets, preferably salt-packed
Ample extra-virgin olive oil
Salt and pepper to taste
½ cup to 1 cup freshly made bread crumbs

Sauté the garlic, finely chopped, in olive oil until translucent.
Add the anchovies and let melt, then add the parsley and wilt;
let cool. Mix the meat with the eggs. Add the cooled garlic, anchovies, parsley, salt and pepper, and bread crumbs. Form your
meatballs, but not too large or they'll crack. Brown in olive oil,
then cook slowly. Mix in your roasted tomato sauce.

2001

EPILOGUE:
A HUGE HUNGER IN PARIS

It is interesting to note that I have lost three pounds during a diet that began in 1970—a little over two ounces a year, and this without cheating on the scales, shedding clothes, or purposely dehydrating myself by avoiding alcohol and ignoring such salty necessities as herring, headcheese, and aged Asiago. How did I accomplish this long- term weight loss? Sheer, poochy courage of the sort that minute by minute does battle with the recidivism that mocks more than ninety percent of such diets. I also cannot ignore the thousands of hours of sometimes brutal exercise, the five figures spent on clinics and a wall of diet books, and another thousand hours in the rigors of meditation, thinking about this controlled deprivation. No kudos, plaques, or trophies need be offered. Such successes give the soul the gentlest of massages, and this is quite enough. If my life expectancy holds, I will lose another two and a half pounds before that final big diet in the sky—or, more likely, the really big diet in the earth. I only offer this in encouragement for others who may have faltered on the path.

But how much can you do with negativity and self-denial in a nation struggling for its soul life against legions of politically correct dweebs in high and low places, where the simplest notions of vigor, humor, and jubilance are scorned and proscribed? I'm not sure.

This seems much less true in France, though I have no authority to say so, and even the awesome might of the CIA is occasionally guilty of costly error with other countries. Maybe the French, like the Arabs, are largely misunderstood. If you mention to an American intellectual that your books are doing well in France, he will invariably tell you that the French love Jerry Lewis. This may be so, though in a half dozen trips I've never heard anyone mention the man. If one were a ruthless, smirking billionaire like Ross Perot, it would be fun to hire Jerry Lewis to shadow vacationing American intellectuals in Paris. Just when these smart folks were feeling they were having an authentic experience with a brioche, old Jerry could dash out of an alley and pitch a sack of dog shit on their table. That sort of thing. One could think of dozens of such pranks.

On a recent book tour of France I felt somewhat overappreciated. I normally keep myself free from such experiences by sticking to a few hideouts in our hemisphere. In fact, I can't think of a public appearance I care for except in restaurants and an amazingly small number of bars. It is pleasant to be appreciated and understood, but the experience is not up there with Mozart, sex, or fine food, catching a big fish, burning calendars, stomping on clocks, or watching a gaunt black bear feed on wild strawberries and beach pea. I like to think this is less because I am a shy midwesterner than that I am aware of the captiousness of literary history, in which the best attempts to arrange a reputation inevitably come to a ghastly end. Votes won by anything but the work itself are of short duration. The only truly viable publicity stunt for a writer is suicide, profitable for your heirs but no good at all if you're planning to open trout season next year.

Paris offers a number of humbling experiences, primary among them her beauty and food. Perhaps our folklore allows us to accept that a city must be ugly. We have some near misses in San Francisco and Seattle but nothing on the order of Paris. Architectural history is an area in which it is difficult to figure out where we went wrong, other than that a nation hell-bent on the fast buck doesn't offer itself many aesthetic considerations. Why don't you go read a book about it? If I knew everything, some crank might throw dog turds at my *rognons du veau*. (There never seemed to be any point in eating a brioche, which is the moral equivalent of a club sandwich or pasta salad.)

Back to Paris and Lyons, and the train between them that goes two hundred miles per hour, a speed that alternately enthralls and frightens. Whether this spiffy bugger could successfully knife through a herd of Holsteins or Charolais seems to be an appropriate question.

At Lyons I had dinner at La Mère Brazier, which included a couple of *crêpe aux truffes* and a *volaille de Bresse demi-deuil* with slices of truffle stuffed up under the thigh skin, cheeses, fruit, and lots of Côte de Beaune. Now, this was not an elaborate meal, but it left all but a few others in my life filtering down further toward the bottom. Frankly it was a mystery why it was so superb. Another of the top meals of my life was homemade but Lyonnaise in origin—a *salmis de bécasse*, an elaborate woodcock preparation from a Bocuse cookbook. I was also relieved to not see a jogger in the area.

In Paris a half dozen meals were remarkable, and two, at Le Récamier, and Aux Fins Gourmets, were well up the ladder toward La Mère Brazier. At Le Récamier I got a clue to an irritating mystery. My publisher's son could moo like a cow. This was not a childish imitation but a moo of grandeur, and since I come from a farm family I know whereof I speak. This moo was soulfully elegant, and I tingled with hot envy thinking of the uses it could be put to at Columbia studios or in the Guggenheim Museum, for instance. The moo, I sensed, was above my abilities, and without starting over at sixteen, when I began to write, French cooking of the highest order would be forever beyond my reach. Such cooking is notably undemocratic and anti-American, in fact, and few of our citizens—André Soltner and Alice Waters, to name two—have passed the equivalency test.

As I write this, I'm having a simple bunch of leftovers, a pasta made of Swiss chard, fresh tomatoes, and copious garlic, and a duck leg and thigh, somewhat more complicated in origin from Madeleine Kamman, if I recall correctly. You trim your duck legs and thighs of excess fat, slather them with Dijon, press them into homemade bread crumbs, roast them slowly at low heat, make a sauce of the pan-browned bits with cider and duck stock. Anyone can do this, and it's a type of French cooking that is satisfying but somewhat less than heroic, as are several dozen other French recipes stowed in my head and hands. After a dozen tries over the years, I can cook a Muscovy duck eighty-five percent as well as Soltner, but all the art is in the last fifteen percent and is the reason to go to Lutèce.

The other day I came across an extraordinary new cookbook with the unlikely name *Dad's Own Cookbook*, by Bob Sloan. At first it struck me as mostly a primer, but on further study I ordered a several copies for gifts. The book assumes that you know nothing when you approach the stove, and this might wound some vanities but needn't. We all know any number of men who can cook a virtuoso (to them) dish or two, but outside of this they are strictly road kills in the kitchen. "Wait until you taste Fred's barbecued ribs. He's got a secret ingredient." You know, where the secret ingredient might well be coal tar or ketchup or puréed maraschino cherries. Fred beams, the big ol' boy, because he's made something to eat beyond the can or sandwich.

It's not entirely Fred's fault. Beginner cookbooks are rare beyond the bridal variety, which contain nothing you might want to eat, while grown-up cookbooks frequently appear coy and presumptuous to the neophyte or to one who may have a heartier appetite. Sloan covers all the basics and, beyond a few quibbles, the goods are delivered in the form of admirable recipes, so your lessons are not only edible they are a pleasure to eat, from the Hunan orange-ginger roast pork to the chicken with tomato and sausage.

I suspect that the reason I was taken by the book comes from the same, not totally lighted part of my brain as do my darker thoughts about French cooking. If I had fully understood the book's contents twenty years ago, I could have saved myself a river of frustration in the kitchen, not the less poignant now that it has dwindled into a trickle of occasional anger.

Men are often clowns at the stove for the ordinary reason that they are militaristic when they attack a recipe. It is something to be overcome and defeated, preferably in a straight line. It reminds one of Caesar's legions marching across Greenland's ice only to find there was no enemy. Better by far to read a recipe at bedtime while listening to Mozart (the bark of a newscaster will lead you astray) and mull over its contents during the usual nasty day of work.

Ultimately, stereotypes are murderous, and the newest versions in the arena of the politically correct are especially so. Certain scorned stereotypes are the oldest hat in the closet, but they are still largely observed. Mom cooks, even if she works. Dad reads the paper and eats because he makes more money or is simply a garden-variety asshole who doesn't want to learn anything new. If he can't be the best he'd rather watch Barry Bonds. He doesn't yet know that he's among the ten percent of imminent divorces that extrude directly from bad food and unshared labor, a hundred billion bucks down the drain because this nitwit won't go into the kitchen.

The most frequent political question I got in France was, Why is Clinton flinching when he has three more years? This is the time for strength, for *puissance,* just short of arrogance. The Republicans need voice coaches. As far as I know, no one but Nixon and Checkers ever whined their way back into power. When someone throws a shadow punch, you don't flinch. There is the hideous suspicion that Clinton might be on some sort of crypto-jogger diet. In their own equally dark times, Jefferson and Teddy Roosevelt would revive themselves with a gross of oysters, a haunch of venison, a casserole of garlic, and a magnum or two of Bordeaux. Put on your bib, Bill, and stop flinching.

1993